Praise for *VENL*

"Michael Fox, Carlos Martinez, and JoJo Farrell cut through the mist that usually surrounds discussions of Venezuela to enter a world of impressive political and cultural diversity. *Venezuela Speaks!* is a geography of struggle, a sociology of passion, and an ethnography of hope, of the unrelenting insistence that people have a right to control their own lives, and that in doing so, a better world will be made."

— Greg Grandin, author of *Empire's Workshop: Latin America, the United States, and the Rise of the New Imperialism.*

"*Venezuela Speaks!* provides a platform for Venezuelan revolutionaries to speak for themselves, to tell their own stories, to use their own words to explain the Bolivarian Revolution. Unadulterated, captivating, and a must read for anyone who wishes to truly understand today's Venezuela and its historic political process."

— Chesa Boudin, author of *Gringo: A Coming of Age in Latin America* and *The Venezuelan Revolution: 100 Questions - 100 Answers.*

"The authors of this book are not starry-eyed ideologues; they are experienced activists who have traveled the world observing diverse efforts at ending poverty and injustice. They portray a Venezuela in struggle that we can all learn lessons from in our efforts to save humanity from itself."

— Dr. Kevin Danaher, Co-Founder, Global Exchange and Green Festivals.

"I once asked a woman in Caracas if she was a follower of President Chávez. She replied, "No. He is following my ideas." *Venezuela Speaks!: Voices from the Grassroots* gives the English reader an opportunity to hear some of these ideas directly from the mouths of those whom Chávez is trying to follow."

— Charlie Hardy, author of *Cowboy in Caracas: A North American's Memoir of Venezuela's Democratic Revolution.*

"This collection of brilliantly organized interviews embraces the complexity of Venezuela's hopeful revolution without simplifying or understating the country's grassroots fervor. It brings the voices of those who share the burdens and benefits of transforming Venezuela directly to the reader, straight from the hearts and streets of a nation going through historic changes."

— Benjamin Dangl, author of *Dancing with Dynamite: Social Movements and States in Latin America* and editor of the Latin American news website *Upside Down World.*

"*Venezuela Speaks!* is… a kind of radical hearing aid - appearing at a time when North Americans especially would benefit from doing a lot of listening."

— Max Elbaum, author of *Revolution in the Air*, and editor of the *War Times/Tiempo de Guerras*.

"This book is a must-read for those who have gone through the secondary books on the Chávez phenomenon and have gotten a fair share of analysis and theory. *Venezuela Speaks!* represents a necessary balance to these works by providing extremely interesting insights from the "people" in their own words."

— Steve Ellner has been a professor at the Universidad de Oriente in Puerto La Cruz, Venezuela since 1977. His most recent book is *Rethinking Venezuelan Politics: Class, Conflict and the Chávez Phenomenon*.

"This book is a must read for all who are interested in the critical dynamic between grassroots social movements and sympathetic governments. It is clearly not enough to elect somebody different, though that helps; movements must stay mobilized and must still struggle in contested terrain for every real gain. *Venezuela Speaks!* shows us how."

— Peter Rosset, author of *Promised Land: Competing Visions of Agrarian Reform* and *Food is Different*.

"The revolution within the revolution are the many, powerful voices of the everyday people of Venezuela. They have suffered and survived the era of the oligarchy; they rose up in El Caracazo (1989), dreaming of another world; they voted in numbers and often for the Bolivarian regime, and they came out on the streets to defend their government in 2002. These are the people. They have words. *Venezuela Speaks!* gives us a taste of them."

— Vijay Prashad, author of *The Darker Nations: A People's History of the Third World*.

"When we hear about Venezuela, we often hear about the Chávez administration, or the opposition. But we hear very little about the ordinary people who are running the literacy programs, staffing the missions, and creating a radio collective or a worker cooperative. This book gives us some of those voices, which are essential to broadening the debate about contemporary Venezuela."

— Sujatha Fernandes, author of *Who can Stop the Drums? Urban Social Movements in Chávez's Venezuela*.

VENEZUELA SPEAKS!

VENEZUELA SPEAKS!

Voices From The Grassroots

Carlos Martinez, Michael Fox
and JoJo Farrell

PM PRESS
2010

Venezuela Speaks!: Voices from the Grassroots

Editors/Authors: Carlos Martinez, Michael Fox, JoJo Farrell
Translators: Carlos Martinez, Michael Fox
Photographers: Sílvia Leindecker, Carlos Martinez, Michael Fox,
Lainie Cassel
Photograph Editor: Sílvia Leindecker

All interviews conducted October 2007- November 2009

ISBN: 978-1-60486-108-2
Library of Congress Control Number: 2009901390

PM Press
PO Box 23912
Oakland, CA 94623
www.pmpress.org

Cover Design by John Yates/Stealworks.com
Layout by Josh MacPhee/Justseeds.org

Printed in the USA on recycled paper.

CONTENTS

PART VI: THE STUDENT MOVEMENT

PART VII: COMMUNITY ORGANIZING

Venezuela – 2008 Population, roughly 28 Million People.

ACKNOWLEDGEMENTS

ew places are easily understood from the outside, but following the 2006 Venezuela Presidential elections, it became clear that the international media was increasingly losing its touch on Venezuelan reality. The idea for this book took shape during this period, with innumerable support from countless individuals.

First and foremost, we are grateful to the countless Venezuelans who took the time to sit down with us for many hours and share their experiences and histories. Many appear in this book. Many do not. If not for their support, advice, suggestions and contacts, *Venezuela Speaks!* would never have made it past the idea stage.

Our transcribers were integral in putting these people's words on to the page. Among them, many thanks to Angela Pinto, Leonela Delgado, Cesar David Escalona Diaz, and Erwin Cox.

We are grateful to the advice and support provided by Chesa Boudin, Eva Golinger, Greg Wilpert, Kirsten Moller, and Kevin Danaher, who helped to get this project off the ground. Thank you also to Juan Carlos Rodríguez; Roberto Rodríguez; the Casa Azul; ANMCLA; Antonio Frausto; Alvaro Cabrera; Alvaro Morillo; Lisette Torrealba; Marcela Fica and Roberto Fogolin; Julia Pereira and the *Centro Internacional Miranda*; Maria de Los Angeles Peña and Fundayacucho; and Micaela Ovelar and Patrick Leet at the Bolivarian University. Edward Ellis, Jennifer Martinez, Megan Hise, Karin Orr, Jill Replogle, Zachary Hurwitz, Marc Becker, John Gibler, Yeiber Cano, Jordan Klein, and Maryann Fox all took a look at early sections of the manuscript, and helped with countless suggestions, revisions, and edits. Marybeth Stocking supported us as an intern in the early stages of the manuscript with transcribing, translating, and editing. Greg Wilpert revised sections of the manuscript and we are honored to have him write the prologue to the book. Leo

Lameda, Skipper Bailey, and Dario Azzellini's guidance and advice were also significant for the development of the book.

James Suggett could almost be considered a co-editor, providing us with contacts, conducting and transcribing the interview with Cesar Carrero, adding his suggestions and comments to numerous chapters, and acquiring last-minute pictures of María Vicenta. Michael Fox's loving wife, Sílvia Leindecker, deserves extra special recognition for her constant support and understanding through the many late nights. Sílvia is the photographer behind many of the pictures in the book, and spent many long hours over the last year editing and preparing all of the photographs for publication. Lainie Cassel, Michael Fox, Carlos Martinez and Edward Ellis also contributed photographs.

Kate Mcmahon, JoJo Farrell's beautiful fiancé, sacrificed much for this book. She edited and re-edited, and remains his inspiration.

Many thanks to Ramsey Kanaan and the rest of PM Press for running with the project. Countless gratitude to both Ramsey and our editor, Romy Ruukel, for their professional and timely work.

The contact we made with the various people presented in this book would have been impossible without the foundation provided by the work of organizations such as Global Exchange and Venezuelanalysis. The Venezuelanalysis crew deserves special thanks for continuing to produce some of the most in-depth on-the-ground investigative English news on Venezuela despite economic hard times. Perhaps most importantly, this book would not be a reality without the constant support and encouragement from Kirsten Moller and Global Exchange. We are indebted for their excitement and support.

And, of course, many thanks to our parents, who gave us the wings to embark on this type of project; families; friends; anyone we may have forgotten to mention here; and countless others who played a pivotal role in helping bring this book to fruition. We are grateful, and hope that the words on these pages will bring the international community that much closer to the Venezuelan reality within the Bolivarian Process.

PROLOGUE

Greg Wilpert

It would be easy to believe that what has been happening in Venezuela since 1998 is solely the result of the election of Hugo Chávez as president. As the present book shows, however, Chávez's election fits into a much broader context of the development of social movements in Venezuela. Chávez would be unthinkable without the movements that support and animate the Bolivarian Revolution. Similarly, Chávez and Venezuela's social movements have emerged within a much broader context of recent changes in Latin America, which have to do with social, economic, and political changes that took place in the continent during the second half of the 20th century.

Following World War II, approximately from the 1940s to the 1970s, the nations of Latin America and of most of the rest of the Third World pursued policies that came to be known as "import substituting industrialization," in which countries tried to industrialize and develop economically by restricting imports and replacing these with domestically produced equivalents. It was a time in which national governments and national capitalists generally cooperated in the belief that only such cooperation would advance their countries economically.

However, in the course of the 1970s, a worldwide recession led to a gradual replacement of state-interventionist economic policies with free-market "laissez-faire" doctrine eventually known as "neoliberalism." The causes for this transition were both economic and political-ideological. On the economic side was the collapse of the Bretton Woods financial system, which had regulated the world's exchange rates between 1945 and 1973. The fixed exchange rate system gave national governments a certain degree of control over their national economies and over capital inflows and outflows. However, when the Nixon administration decided to pay for the Vietnam War by printing dollars, and when OPEC's oil embargo caused financial instability, such enormous pressure was put on the fixed exchange rate system, that it had to be completely abandoned by 1973. This, combined with the development of new communication technologies that further aided the flexibility of capital, meant that capital could now flow around the globe with far fewer restrictions, creating a dynamic that could threaten governments with disinvestment or an investment strike if governments did not create more favorable investment conditions in the different countries. Of course, more favorable investment conditions generally meant elimination of trade barriers, deregulation of workplace and environmental protection, and lower taxes for corporations and the wealthy.[1]

On the political-ideological side, the transition towards neoliberalism was aided by Pinochet's coup in Chile (1973) and later by the electoral successes of Margaret Thatcher in Britain (1979) and Ronald Reagan in the U.S. (1980). In one country after another, politicians that represented the interests of transnational capital attained political power. Bretton Woods institutions, the World Bank and IMF, and later the World Trade Organization (previously the General Agreement on Tariffs and Trade), all controlled by First World countries, also began re-tasking themselves in order to push neoliberalism in their development programs. Though some governments, such as that of Chile, participated willingly, many Third World countries were often forced via the threat of withholding credit to open their economies to the neoliberal principles of transnational capital.[2] As a result, the neoliberal ideology of the economist Milton Friedman replaced that of John Maynard Keynes as the world's dominant economic practice.

As more wealth was redistributed towards the rich and transnational capital (or finance capital) acquired unprecedented power, neoliberalism was an unmitigated success from the perspective of the world's upper class. According to its advocates, however, neoliberalism was also supposed to bring about stability, and steady and continuous economic growth. In the time that it was the world's reigning economic doctrine, however, it proved to be a failure on both these accounts. Despite providing some relief from inflation, neoliberalism usually meant increased hardship for the poor. According to the World Bank, the ratio between the average income of the world's poorest twenty countries and of the world's twenty richest countries increased from a ratio of 18 to 1 in 1960 to 37 to 1 in 1995.[3] Measured in terms of growth of per capita GDP, the neoliberal era also did not do as well as the previous era of state-driven development. Between 1980 and 1999, when neoliberalism reigned, per capita economic growth in Latin America was a mere 11 percent, compared to the 80 percent growth in the previous twenty-year period, between 1960 and 1979, when state-driven developmentalism reigned.[4] In regard to stability, neoliberalism contributed to many economic calamities in Latin America, such as Mexico's financial implosion in 1994, Argentina's in 2001, and the worldwide financial crisis of 2008-9.

In Latin America, the economic failures of neoliberalism combined with the political failure of representative democracy and thus contributed significantly to the rise of the New Left. Throughout the continent, politicians would promise pro-poor policies only to reverse themselves upon taking office. Perhaps the most extreme instance of such a reversal happened in Venezuela, when former president Carlos Andrés Pérez ran for a second non-consecutive term in 1988 on an anti-neoliberal platform. A few weeks after taking office in February 1989, however, he implemented a harsh neoliberal IMF-imposed "structural adjustment," which led to country-wide riots and then to police repression that killed anywhere between 400 and over 1,000 Venezuelans. Populist neoliberals, such as Alberto Fujimori of Peru and Carlos Menem of Argentina, were also among the most notorious representatives of this type of politics.

That is, the failure of neoliberalism to deliver on its economic promises to the general population also meant the rise of resistance to this economic doctrine throughout the continent. In Brazil, the landless peasants movement organized massive land occupations that directly confronted the power of the country's landed elite. In Ecuador and Bolivia, indigenous movements mobilized against their respective governments' environmental policies and the usage of natural resources such as water, gas, and oil. In Mexico, the Zapatistas emerged to stage more violent forms of resistance in Chiapas. And in Venezuela, as a consequence of the aforementioned IMF riots of 1989, new urban community associations and political parties emerged that provided an important impetus for the emergence of Hugo Chávez in 1998.[5] After Chávez, one country after another elected leftist leaders; in South America, only Colombia and Peru seem to have escaped the trend so far.

The degree of leftism in the governments of Brazil, Argentina, Chile, Bolivia, Uruguay, Ecuador, Paraguay, and Venezuela, of course, varies greatly from one country to the next. Spanning the left-of-center political spectrum in terms of willingness to challenge the old neoliberal hegemony and to introduce more radical policies of redistribution and democratization, they range from the more moderate left governments in Brazil, Chile, and Uruguay, to more leftist in Argentina, Ecuador, and Paraguay, and yet further left in Bolivia. In this context, Venezuela is the most radical of them all.

Since his election, Chávez has not only become an unapologetic spokesperson for the necessity to overcome capitalism as an economic system, the need to defeat U.S. dominance in the world, and the drive to replace or at least complement representative democracy with participatory democracy; he has actually delivered on many of these promises. Venezuela has probably gone further than any other country in reversing the neoliberal policies of the past through nationalizing key industries, reintroducing extensive social programs, promoting social ownership via cooperatives, and through re-regulating capital. Chávez has been one of the main promoters of regional Latin American integration by forming Bolivarian Alliance for our America (ALBA), supporting the development of the Union of South American Nations (Unasur), and promoting energy integration via PetroCaribe and PetroSur. In terms of going beyond representative democracy, Venezuela continues to actively give its citizens the opportunity to participate in all levels of politics, especially locally, via the direct democratic communal councils.

This is not to say that Venezuela has always been successful in moving towards what Chávez calls "21st century socialism." As readers of this book will see, even Chávez supporters complain about the government's many broken promises, inefficiency, and unfulfilled projects. Perhaps one of the greatest shortcomings of the government is its inability to overcome legacies of the old regime, such as of clientelism-patronage, of corruption, and of "personalism."[6] But, as the organizers and activists represented here will be quick to point out, this does not mean that the project of creating a better society in Venezuela can be achieved by rejecting the Chávez government. Rather, most would say that the Chávez government still represents the best hope for a better society, despite its many shortcomings. To learn about these sentiments and about the movements that stand behind the Chávez phenomenon is thus as important as learning about the Chávez government itself. One cannot truly make sense of one without the other. And making sense of and defending what is happening in Venezuela is perhaps one of the most important tasks for progressives around the world today, since Venezuela is at the forefront in the effort to find a real progressive alternative to capitalism, to representative democracy, and to U.S. imperialism.

INTRODUCTION

"The people understand that the process is not of one person but of every-one, and we have seen that there are not one or two people who are talking, but the people. The people who will not stay quiet." Iraida Morocoima

While President Hugo Chávez captures headlines throughout the world, a much larger story of Venezuela, involving a wider cast of characters continues to be largely ignored by mainstream media. From reading mainstream coverage of Venezuela, one is often left with the impression that President Chávez is the sole mastermind behind all that is taking place in the country, with or without the support of the Venezuelan people. Chávez has certainly brought the charismatic leadership necessary to unite many previ-ously divided grassroots sectors, and he has provided a framework and name to Venezuela's current political process, the *Bolivarian Revolution*. But a rigorous look at Venezuela's political situation and the various on-the-ground experiences reveals that, to a great de-gree, this is a process being constructed from below. Without the active participation of large and diverse sectors of society, Chávez's moment on the scene would not have lasted much longer than the short-lived 2002 coup, which took him from office for a brief forty-seven hours.

In order to truly understand the radical vision of society be-ing constructed in Venezuela, we need to broaden our own vision. Only by listening to the voices of those many individuals actively participating and building this movement can we begin to uncover the dynamic roots of this revolution. Greg Wilpert's book, *Changing Venezuela By Taking Power* has been significant in illustrating the Chávez government's efforts in transforming Venezuela by explor-ing its social, economic, foreign, and governance policies in great detail. Through this collection of interviews, we now seek to provide an intimate portrait of the flip side of the Bolivarian Revolution, Venezuela's various grassroots social movements, in the voice of their own members. In doing so, we hope to expand on both the understanding of social change in Venezuela, as well as the important role of social movements in a country where progressive forces have democratically taken power.

Taking Power and Building Popular Power

Winds of change have swept through Latin American over the previous decade, bringing into power a variety of progressive and center-left governments winning on anti-neoliberal political platforms. Venezuela, among other countries in Latin America, has renewed the belief that a government with a social justice agenda can promote political alternatives to the dominant model of neoliberal capitalism. This is no small achievement in an era of global disillusion following the fall of various state-led revolutions and national liberation movements at the end of the twentieth century. The idea of making change by "taking power" has regained currency amongst many observers of Latin America's new political processes.

However, the attempts by some to showcase Venezuela as a model of state-led political transformation has unfortunately led to an oversimplified understanding of the way in which the Bolivarian Revolution is actually playing out. In its most simplistic form, some have falsely juxtaposed Venezuela's political process — characterized as "top-down" — against Latin America's "bottom-up" political processes, like those of the Zapatistas in Mexico or the occupied factories movement of Argentina. Chávez's own larger-than-life personality and political presence have only reinforced this analysis. Meanwhile, international private media have transformed Venezuela into a dictatorship in the minds of many observers, to the point of influencing the progressive media's reporting on the country.

Undeniably, President Chávez continues to be the defining political factor in Venezuela, as is revealed by the typical political labels that continue to divide many Venezuelans between *Chavistas* and *anti-Chavistas*. Nor can the government's incredible efforts at transforming Venezuela through its myriad projects and social programs be understated. But by failing to see beyond Chávez and the government's anti-neoliberal policies, one of the most significant political dynamics in Venezuela has gone ignored and underappreciated

— the dynamic between a government that has committed itself to a discourse of grassroots political participation, and the response of ordinary Venezuelans to this call, often in ways that go beyond the expectations of the government, occasionally even challenging it.

It might not seem newsworthy that people who have benefited from this democratization process have turned to challenge the same government that provided them with the opportunity. But it does point to the reality that there is a greater degree of political consciousness and activity amongst those participating in the Bolivarian Revolution than the simple *Chavista* label would indicate. The claim that Venezuela lacks democracy, or a civil society independent from the state, inherently presumes that the country lacks autonomous organizations that have the ability to act on their own, much less pressure the government. Yet it is precisely in the relationship and tension between the Venezuelan government and the social movements that the process of building a participatory democracy comes alive most vividly.

The idea of participatory democracy, as opposed to representative democracy, has been a pillar of Chávez's political movement since his successful run for office in 1998. This concept offered the promise that citizens would be able to play a greater political role in the direction of their country, rather than being limited to mere voters during election time. As the Bolivarian Revolution has progressed, the concept of "popular power" has become the defining slogan of the political process, bringing with it a series of innovative policies and initiatives. The creation of the communal councils is the most often cited example in discussing the development of popular power in Venezuela. The communal councils have provided Venezuelans with a legal mechanism to locally organize themselves into democratic structures of between 200-400 families, with the greater goal of determining the way that government funds get used for development and infrastructure projects in their communities. However, the communal councils are only the tip of the iceberg of the construction of popular power in Venezuela.

Over the course of the Bolivarian Revolution, Venezuelans have created cooperatives; taken over factories; occupied urban and rural lands; launched community radio and television stations; built centers for culture and popular education; participated in creating national legislation and found numerous other means of bringing the government's discourse of popular power into reality. Many of

these actions have been motivated by the words of President Chávez
or have been facilitated by government initiatives. Meanwhile, many
people behind these actions continue to pressure the government in
order to survive or succeed.

Venezuela is undoubtedly a country in motion. While the
"taking" of political power from above has acted as a powerful
catalyst in stimulating all of this activity, by observing Venezuela's
social movements we can see that the practice of building popular power inevitably reaches far beyond the domain of government
influence. As various activists interviewed in this book point out,
organized communities and social movements have not only played
an indispensable role in the implementation of the current process
of change, but many were a force in Venezuelan politics long before
Chávez, and have simply seen their opportunity to continue to pur-
sue their respective agendas.

The Refounding of a Republic

A year before winning the landslide elections that brought
him into power, Hugo Chávez and his allies formed a new political
party called the *Movimiento Quinta República* (MVR- Movement for
the Fifth Republic). The central plank of the MVR was to refound
the Venezuelan republic based on a new constitution that would be
drafted with extensive public participation. Through transforming
the constitution, this movement would have the opportunity to take a
fundamentally different trajectory from the entrenched political system that had come to dominate the country for the last half-century.
The process of creating the Bolivarian Constitution was historic in
and of itself, as was the final product approved in a popular referendum in December 1999. The most obvious change resulting from
the new constitution was the official name of the country from the
Republic of Venezuela to the *Bolivarian* Republic of Venezuela. But
more significantly, the development of the new constitution altered
the way Venezuelan people thought about politics and government.
Suddenly, everything was open for debate as ordinary citizens had a
stake in determining the direction of their country. The Bolivarian
Constitution has become a symbol of this spirit. Waving the constitution in the air at a rally, for example, has come to mean more than
simply supporting Chávez's political project: it signifies people's
hopes that they are undertaking a historic endeavor at creating a
new country.

In this spirit, the Bolivarian Constitution continues to be a primary tool for those seeking to make its contents a reality. Like any written law, of course, it is only a piece of paper. But bringing the constitution to life may well describe the role of those social movements that have gathered force from its words, such as the indigenous Wayúu community, which has evoked the constitution in their struggle to protect their native land, and the women's movement, which has developed a government program based on the constitutional recognition of the contribution made by housewives to the economy.

By adopting the language of the constitution in their battles, these social movements are testing the validity of the constitution's content as it is being applied in the real world. The content of the constitution is one thing. Whether it is enforced is another. This, however, will only be determined through the demands invoked on its behalf, and this is the challenge of bringing social justice on paper into a lived reality. Though some constitutional articles commit the government to respect indigenous lands, the Wayúu, for example, have found that other mining-related articles may actually trump their demands by allowing companies to operate on their territory regardless of their disapproval. The organizers in the New Generation of Workers Union charge that while Article 77 of the Organic Labor Law places strict limits on the use of subcontracted labor, many private companies such as Mitsubishi, and even the government itself, continue to extensively use contracted workers.

The communities and movements presented in this book are doing the actual work of bringing the Chávez movement's promise of a new republic into fruition. Essentially, they are defining the structures of inclusion whose contours are sketched out in the constitution and the laws that are based upon it. In other words, the fifth republic was not founded on December 15, 1999 when the constitution was approved: rather, the process of creating it was simply initiated on that date.

Social Movements & The State: The Revolution within the Revolution

Political change is complex and almost always involves conflict. Venezuela is no exception. While motivated by Chávez and the hopes the constitution has inspired, the social movements presented in this book are not waiting for permission from the government to get organized. In the process of working to bring the spirit of the new constitution to life, however, organized communities have often found adversaries within their own government. While much of the blame has been attributed to corrupt or right-wing elements still functioning within the government's bureaucracy, many social movements also argue that an overly "institutionalized" approach to revolutionary change has not taken their independent initiatives sufficiently into account.

Consider these examples:

★ Inspired by Chávez' statements, the workers in the Industrial Slaughterhouse of Ospino decided to occupy and take over the operations of their factory. Three years later, however, they are still waiting to receive recognition from their municipal government as a legal cooperative managing the slaughterhouse that they struggle to maintain afloat. They mostly blame the corruption of their local mayor for this situation, but also believe that many within the government want to maintain bureaucratic control over factories, rather than allow workers to manage them.

★ Energized by the language in the constitution which states that indigenous peoples have the right to develop their own education, four indigenous communities came together to build the Indigenous University of Venezuela in the heart of the country. After ten years in existence, and numerous attempts to meet with government officials, they are still waiting to be recognized as an official university by the Ministry of Superior Education. They directly condemn the unresponsiveness of the Minister of Popular Power for Indigenous Peoples, noting that rather than support their initiative she has tried to impose herself on it by asking them to change the name of the university to the *Bolivarian* Indigenous University of Venezuela.

★ Empowered by the 2001 Land Laws, thousands of *campesinos* are occupying unused lands and putting them to productive use. But in the last decade, over 200 *campesinos* leaders have been assassinated, and as of 2009 only one landowner has been held responsible for this slow massacre. While the government has pledged support for the *campesinos*, impunity for those behind the murders has continued. Some in the *campesino* movement speculate whether sectors within the government may be afraid of charging landowners with criminal charges for fear of being attacked in the media as a repressive government.

These are just a few difficult stories at the heart of the Bolivarian Revolution that have made many social movements recognize the reality that although government leadership may have changed, radical transformation will often still demand confrontation with those in political power. While the political sector opposed to Chávez and the Bolivarian Revolution (referred to simply as the "opposition" in Venezuela) remains a fundamental challenge for these social movements, the threat posed to them by a corrupt and disempowering bureaucracy is often just as menacing.

"The revolution within the revolution" is a common phrase used to describe situations where pro-Chávez activists pressure government institutions to work for their communities. The tightrope act that these organized communities must walk — by defending their government against the opposition while simultaneously challenging it — is a defining feature of the Bolivarian Revolution. This political situation is being mirrored throughout the hemisphere where social movements are involved in what Iraida Morocoima, one of the activists interviewed in this book, refers to as the "dual fight."

It has become clear to these activists that the political sector within *Chavismo* opposed or indifferent to their demands will not simply disappear as a natural part of this process. It must be pressured and held accountable not only by President Chávez and those sympathetic to greater change within the government, but also by the demands placed upon it from below. Simply put, the new republic will not simply be decreed from above, but involves struggle, organization, and people's ability to act independently when necessary.

Venezuela at a Crossroads

To say that Venezuela is currently at a crossroads is a severe understatement. It would be more accurate to say that Venezuela has been at a crossroads since Hugo Chávez took power in 1999. After a decade of rule, the Chávez government has brought unprecedented change to the country and the global political scene. Venezuela has seen a definitive shift that perhaps may be more obvious when we observe the political platforms and proposals provided by those opposed to Chávez. For all their virulent rhetoric against Chávez, and their claims that he is little more than an authoritarian populist, the opposition is unable to discard the popularity of social programs such as the *Barrio Adentro* Mission, which provides free health care in poor communities across country. The opposition recognizes that attempting to do away with such programs would be political suicide. Instead, they argue that they are more capable of managing these social programs more efficiently and with greater accountability. If anything, the Bolivarian Revolution has simply raised the Venezuelan people's expectations of the state and what it provides. Any attempt to return to past neoliberal policies of privatization and stringent cuts on social spending would likely be met with the kind of resistance that was witnessed in the turbulent decade preceding Chávez's presidency.

Meanwhile, Chávez's discourse and the Bolivarian Revolution seem to be consistently evolving. Both the vision of another society and the path to getting there are constantly redefined. Yet the barriers to more radical change are also becoming clearer and the obstacles seem as great as ever. Social movements and organized communities are no longer content with resting on the laurels of the government's popular social programs. They recognize that a significant political space has been opened, and they are asking themselves how to achieve the change that they believe is necessary to build the society of which they dream.

A significant question remains: to what extent will these movements be able to consolidate their power, chart their own course, and actually lead the direction of the Bolivarian Process, rather than be appendages to the government and to President Chávez? The fate of Venezuela's revolutionary process will depend just as greatly on the actions of those working in the grassroots as on Chávez's own deeds. Likewise, its success will depend largely on the way the government responds to, and takes into account, the proposals put forth by these social movements. The future of the Bolivarian Revolution does not just depend on whether it can continue to overcome the destabilization and fear campaigns of the opposition. It also depends on how well the government is able to listen to the voices demanding even deeper changes.

As the political theorist Marta Harnecker has affirmed, "Left or progressive Latin American leaders need to understand — as I think the presidents of Venezuela and Bolivia have understood very well — that they need an organised, politicised people who apply pressure in order to make the process advance and are capable of fighting the errors and deviations that keep on arising along the way. They have to understand that our people must be front line actors, and not limited to the second line."[1]

Beyond the social programs, economic projects, and anti-neoliberal policies promoted by the national government, truly profound change will only come from the active debate and dialogue between organized peoples and the government. It is this debate and dialogue that has set Venezuela apart from many national liberation struggles of the past, and if Venezuela is to succeed where others have failed, then it must continue to strengthen this relationship. As Vijay Prashad argues in his broad overview of the development of twentieth century national liberation movements in his book *The Darker Nations*, "The great flaws in the national liberation project came from the assumption that political power could be centralized in the state, that the national liberation party should dominate the state, and that the people could be demobilized after their contribution to the liberation struggle."[2] In other words, the "taking" of political power is only one step in the national liberation movement in which the consistent support for active and autonomous expressions of popular power must be considered an equally high priority.

Venezuela Speaks!: Voices from the Grassroots is not the definitive book on Venezuelan grassroots social movements and organizations, but a cross-section of them. The people interviewed here could not cover the enormous breadth of opinions and beliefs that are shared across the diverse grassroots sectors at the heart of the Bolivarian process, nor could they speak to the all of the views within each of their unique movements. They speak for themselves. Many of those interviewed are spokespersons for their organization or movement; many are not. All were chosen after extensive research and deliberation to present the broadest possible perspective of the countless ways that Venezuelans are mobilizing to put popular power into practice.

While many of the testimonies provided in these interviews are filled with conflict and frustration, they offer us a vision of the many political actors finding ways to continue to mobilize and strengthen the Bolivarian Revolution. Rather than let their criticisms of Venezuela's political process fill us with disillusionment, these testimonies should provide us with inspiration in knowing that so many people are actively engaged in constructing their new society, regardless of setbacks. This desire to continue struggling amidst a world of challenges is generally shared by those individuals participating in these movements, and it should be understood by those working for the same goal of a world based on inclusion and justice.

INTRODUCTORY HISTORY

enezuela has always been a land of seemingly infinite possibilities and endless contradictions.[1] A place where anything is possible, but everything is different than what most people would expect. A country "on the road to socialism," where the malls are packed with shoppers. A land where opposition student movements "defend" private property by destroying it. A place where activists in support of the government shut down the streets to pressure the government to fulfill its promises. A country where it is common — although not legal — to drive against the traffic on a one-way street.

"*O inventamos o erramos*" ("Either we invent or we err"), said Simón "Robinson" Rodríguez, one of Venezuela's forefathers, who is said to have been highly influential in the beliefs of his close friend and protégé, Simón Bolívar. Bolívar, of course, would become "the Liberator" of South America, and the namesake of President Hugo Chávez's Bolivarian Revolution.

Rodríguez's motto is as alive today as it was then. Venezuela continues to be a land of possibilities and struggle.

Early Republic

Nearly three centuries before Bolívar was born, Christopher Columbus landed near the present-day Venezuelan costal town of Cumaná in his third voyage to the Americas.[2] The year was 1498 and it was Columbus' first landing on the continent. A half-century later, the Spanish pillage of South America had already begun, and was being expedited by the discovery of gold not far from the Caribbean coast. The indigenous Caracas chief, Guaicaipuro, united tribes around the present-day city of Caracas, and valiantly resisted the Spanish inroads until he was killed in a surprise attack by Spanish soldiers in 1567.

The same fate befell many of Venezuela's native peoples, dwindling the country's indigenous population.[3] Before the arrival of the Spanish, countless Ye'kuana communities lived up the mighty Orinoco River in the present-day Southern Venezuelan states of Bolívar and Amazonas. "The Spanish came to recruit our men and women in order to enslave them, so our people fled. Those captured were tied up and forced to work on the Balatá tree plantations. When they got sick, they were left to die like animals. Many Ye'kuana were killed," says Wadajaniju, Rector of Venezuela's Indigenous University of Venezuela (Chapter 12). But the pillage didn't stop there. "With the extermination of a significant population of indigenous peoples in the 16th century... the Europeans were obliged to bring a workforce of enslaved Africans," says Luis Perdomo of the Network of Afro-Venezuelan Organizations (Chapter 14).

The African slaves were brought by the hundreds and thousands to work the coffee and cacao plantations along the Venezuelan coast, and the copper mines further inland. As a result of the inhumane conditions, there were numerous uprisings throughout the long history of Spanish colonialism. Some of the runaway slaves formed *cumbes* in the areas of Barlovento and Yaracuy, much like Brazil's *quilombos*.[4] One of the latest uprisings took place in the hills of Falcon in 1795.

At the time, Simón Bolívar was only thirteen. Both of his parents were dead, and he soon left to study in Spain where he met his wife, María Teresa Rodríguez del Toro y Alaysa. Within a year of their marriage, however, she had succumbed to yellow fever. When France invaded and occupied Spain in 1808, Bolívar — already back in Venezuela — was among those who joined the fight for the country's independence from the country's European colonizers.

Bolívar ascended among the ranks of Venezuela's freedom fighters. A congress of Venezuelan provinces declared the country independent on July 5, 1811, but Venezuela was back in Spanish hands within a year. Bolívar fled into present day Colombia, and acquired a military post under the command of the Congress of United Provinces of New Granada, which had also been formed to free the region from Spanish control. With his new army, Bolívar re-entered Venezuela in May 1813, and in an impressive four months, liberated Venezuela and retook Caracas from the Spanish, in what became know as the "Admirable Campaign."[5] By 1821, Bolívar and his army had shrugged the Spanish out of *Gran Colombia* (most of present-day Venezuela, Colombia, Panama, and Ecuador) and were embarking to rid them from Bolivia and Peru, with a dream of one great, united South American nation.

By the end of the decade, however, due to regional uprisings, internal divisions and infighting, this dream was in tatters. In 1830, Bolívar died of tuberculosis, a broken man. Venezuela fell into the hands of the oligarchy, led by Bolívar's nemesis, José Antonio Páez, and fifteen years passed before Ezequiel Zamora led thousands of men in the Campesino Insurrection of 1846. More than a decade later, Zamora fought with the Federalists in the Federal War, defeating a powerful Conservative enemy in the historic battle of Santa Inés.

In 2001, one of Venezuela's most radical *campesino* movements took the name of Ezequiel Zamora in homage of Zamora's struggle alongside the Venezuelan *campesino*. As Ramón Virigay of the *Frente Nacional Campesino Ezequiel Zamora* (FNCEZ - Ezequiel Zamora National Campesino Front) explains, "He was really near here in Santa Inés, his battles, his guerrilla war, his war of resistance, with a clear vision to continue what Bolívar had begun" (Chapter 2).

Twentieth Century

Despite this tumultuous and revolutionary past, for certain international business interests, Venezuela's history began only in 1914 — the year that oil was discovered near Venezuela's lake Maracaibo, in Zulia state, near the border with Colombia. With this discovery, the fabric of Venezuelan society was altered forever, as the slightly backwaters, agricultural Caribbean country was suddenly thrust on to the international map.

As petroleum companies such as Standard Oil of New Jersey jumped on the scene, ties between the United States and Venezuela grew, and local elites beckoned the growing interest from the North. Venezuela's petrol boom had begun: by 1920, Venezuela was the world's largest oil exporting country; by 1935, oil exports counted for 91.2 percent of Venezuela's total exports.[6]

Relations went far beyond petroleum, as Venezuelan elites benefiting from the oil boom embraced US dollars, dress, and culture.[7] As some Venezuelans say, these strong ties to the United States helped to spur the highly developed individualistic consumer society that exists in the country to this day, challenging the Bolivarian process.

As most countries in Latin America, Venezuela spent the early 20th century bouncing from one coup d'etat to the next.[8] Marcos Pérez Jiménez,Venezuela's last dictator, came to power as a leading member of the military junta that toppled a short-lived democratic government in 1948, and quickly cracked down on the opposition, outlawing the Communist party, the fledgling *Confederación de Trabajadores de Venezuela* (CTV - Confederation of Venezuelan Workers), and the Venezuelan Campesino Federation. Pérez Jiménez took the full reigns of the country in 1952 and set about to modernize the nation, embarking on major infra-structure projects including bridges and roads that still cover the Venezuelan countryside.

With the intense dependency on oil, Venezuelan agricultural production suffered, dropping from a third of total exports in 1920, to 10 percent in the 1950s, and only 6 percent in 1998.[9] As Pérez Jiménez industrialized the countryside, land was consolidated into even fewer hands, sending *campesinos* to the largest cities in search of employment, and transforming Venezuela into one of the most urbanized nations in Latin America. With extensive migration into the cities, poverty began its slow but constant rise, as Venezuela's poor *barrios* multiplied in the hills surrounding the largest cities.

Meanwhile, repression throughout the country was fierce. By 1957, the movement for democracy in Venezuela had had enough. Exiled leaders, Rómulo Betancourt (*Acción Democrática* - AD), Jóvito Villalba (*Unión Republicana Democrática* - URD), and Rafael Caldera (*Comité de Organización Política Electoral Independiente* - COPEI) met in New York, where Venezuela's major political parties decided to join forces with the Communists in the *Junta Patriótica* against the dictatorship. With weakening support from the Catholic Church, the business community, and the US government, Pérez Jiménez was losing his grip over the country. Faced with a general strike and increasing civilian-military pressure, he abandoned the presidency and fled the country on January 23, 1958.

The Punto Fijo Pact

On the day of Pérez Jiménez's overthrow, thousands of poor families in Caracas quickly occupied the block apartments that had recently been built for military housing on the hills just southwest of Venezuela's presidential palace, Miraflores. They renamed the community *23 de Enero* (January 23rd), to commemorate the uprising.

Thus was born one of the radical cores of community organizing in Caracas and Venezuela at large.

Political exiles, such as Rómulo Betancourt, returned and preparations were made for the restoration of democracy. Excitement was in the air. As Negro Miguel, co-founder of Caracas' San Carlos Free Barracks, explains, "We had just come from a fierce ten-year dictatorship under Marcos Pérez Jiménez. And then came the incorrectly called, 'democracy.' And in the beginning, we saw a change in things, and everything was very hopeful, but it's like a party and the day after you have all of the trash." (Chapter 9)

The major political parties — Acción Democrática, COPEI, and the UDR — sidelined the Communists. On Halloween 1958, their leaders met in a Caracas residency named Punto Fijo to sign a power-sharing pact that would last for the next forty years, a time commonly referred to as the "Fourth Republic."[10]

Under the new government, some freedoms returned but the radical changes fought for by many never materialized. Poverty continued to increase, and the repressive police forces from the dictatorship remained in power. According to the former guerrilla fighters, José Ñañez and Negro Miguel, repression under the new "pseudo-democracy" was just as bad as it had been during the dictatorship (Chapter 9).

In 1959, the triumphant Cuban Revolution inspired radical movements in Venezuela. In April 1960, a leftist youth wing split from *Acción Democrática* to form the *Movimiento de Izquierda Revolucionaria* (MIR - Leftist Revolutionary Movement), and guerrilla groups began to organize with the goal of overthrowing the increasingly repressive regime. In March 1961, the third congress of the Venezuelan Communist party officially supported the armed struggle. A series of civilian military uprisings were attempted, but defeated, between 1961 and 1962.

In May 1962, as a result of the *Carupanazo* uprising, the AD government of Rómulo Betancourt outlawed the Communist party and the MIR. Within a half a year, both groups had taken up arms. Members from the Communist party formed the *Fuerzas Armadas de Liberación Nacional* (FALN - Armed Forces of National Liberation) which coordinated fronts in various regions of Venezuela, including Caracas, the Falcon Mountains, and in the hills of Lara and Trujillo under the leadership of the senator turned guerilla-fighter, Fabricio Ojeda. Meanwhile, Communist party cells organized in the urban centers, and students marched in the streets. Venezuelan security cracked down ruthlessly on the dissidence. During the 1960s and 1970s, when Venezuela appeared to the rest of the world as one of the most stable democracies in the region, thousands of people were tortured, disappeared, and assassinated by the Venezuelan security forces. Venezuelans say that Ojeda was one of those killed during interrogation by the *Servicio de Inteligencia de las Fuerzas Armadas* (SIFA - Venezuelan Armed Forces Intelligence Service) in 1966, although the official government story was suicide.

In the early 1960s, with positive relations between the Venezuelan government and the US, Venezuela was also one of the testing grounds for U.S.-taught counter-insurgency techniques involving torture and disappearance. These techniques were later used by other South America's U.S.-backed dictatorships in their violent assault against student and democratic movements. By the late 1960s, due to infighting and what some say was infiltration by the CIA and intelligence forces, Venezuela's guerrilla movements were weakening. In 1966, a sector split from the Communist Party and formed the Party of the Venezuelan Revolution (PRV). The communist-led FALN disbanded by the end of the decade (although other fronts would continue for another ten years) and the MIR split into the *Movimiento al Socialismo* (MAS - Movement for Socialism), *Bandera Roja* (BR - Red Flag), and the Socialist League, with its guerrilla wing, *Organización Revolucionaria* (OR - Revolutionary Organization).

But for the business and ruling classes, the economy was up, business was booming, and those on the inside were rolling in petrodollars with the highest per-capita GDP in all of Latin America.[11] A relatively high standard of living compared to other Latin American countries kept many Venezuelans comfortable and complacent.[12]

On January 1st, 1976, Venezuela nationalized its oil reserves in an attempt to take advantage of the tremendous profits being made during the world oil crisis. Shell, Exxon, and other foreign business were nationalized and fused in to the new state-owned oil company *Petróleos de Venezuela S.A.*, (PDVSA). Over the next two decades, PDVSA would grow to become the second largest petroleum company in the world. Profits were reinvested in the company, its subsidiaries, and its directors' pockets.

If the growing poor didn't see the money that gushed into Venezuela's petrol-class through the booming 1960s and 1970s, they sure didn't see it after the bust. As Gregory Wilpert writes in his book

Changing Venezuela by Taking Power, "The end of Venezuela's golden years began in 1979, when Venezuela entered its 20-year economic decline."[13] By 1996, poverty had increased from 17 percent to 65 percent. By 1999, per capita income had decreased by nearly 30 percent.[14]

As a result, the lower classes felt increasingly isolated from public decisions and power.

"When there were elections, they said, 'Well, I'll give you some concrete blocks. I'll give you some zinc for these shacks.' But there was no growth," says María Vicenta Dávila, a communal council member from the community of Mixteque in the Mérida countryside (Chapter 18). "The people got used to this way of life," says Alfonso Olivo of the Lara state cooperative councils (Chapter 8). "And the state gave them crumbs and kept them busy until the people realized that they were worth more than that; that the profit produced by the petroleum had to go directly to the people, who are the owners of these natural resources. That was when they revolted." Inspired by the revolutionary struggle and Uruguay's Tupamaro urban guerrilla movement, radical activists in the 23 de Enero *barrio* in Caracas formed the Tupamaro Revolutionary Movement to fight against drugs and delinquency in their community.[15] In the 1980s, the children of some former Communist Party members began to join guerrilla cells of the radical decade-old *Bandera Roja* organization and continued to organize in the exponentially growing *barrios* in an atmosphere of increasing social, economic and political instability.

In 1989, Venczuela once again led Latin America in a new direction — this time with a package of neoliberal shock policies that privatized state businesses and cut social services throughout the country. Gas prices doubled and public transportation prices rose by 30 percent. Venezuelans revolted as a spontaneous uprising descended from the poorest communities and overflowed into the streets of Caracas, rioting and sacking food stores in an uprising known as the *Caracazo* or *Sacudón.*[16] As 23 de Enero resident, Coco, describes, the response from the metropolitan police was fierce as they opened fire on the *23 de Enero* and other popular *barrios* in Caracas. Thousands were killed, and many more arrested (Chapter 17).

Inflation skyrocketed and zeros piled on to the end of the national currency, the *Bolívar.* It was clear that the establishment of neoliberal policies only aggravated the situation of the growing poor. But for the grassroots communities, the *Caracazo* was a sign that organization, rebellion, and change could come overnight, without warning. "The people awake every 100 years," says Ramón Virigay quoting Chilean poet, Pablo Neruda (Chapter 2).

The Arrival of Chávez

Three years later, on February 4th, 1992, a young lieutenant colonol by the name of Hugo Rafael Chávez Frías led a civilian-military coup d'etat against Venezuelan President Carlos Andrés Pérez. While the coup did not succeed, Chávez captured the nation's attention when he accepted sole responsibility for the attempt, and told his troops that "for now" their objectives had not been accomplished. Chávez and many of the coup participants were locked in the San Carlos Barracks Prison (Chapter 9). The fact that this young coup plotter had taken responsibility for his action, and had stressed, "for now" ("*Por ahora*"), captured the nation's attention.

A movement was organized to release him from prison, and he was pardoned two years later by incoming President Rafael Caldera who had recently split from his longtime party, COPEI, to form a coalition of leftist and center-right parties under the name of *Convergencia* (Convergence). The now free Chávez traveled across Venezuela, speaking with supporters. He visited Cuba, and was welcomed on the airline tarmac by none other than Cuban President Fidel Castro, a sign to radical organizers in Venezuela that there may be something special about this little-known military officer.

A clandestine movement called the *Movimiento Bolivariano Revolucionario 200* (MBR-200 - Revolutionary Bolivarian Movement 200) had been built for the coup attempt in 1992. Its members now turned their attention to the public political arena, creating the *Movimiento V República* (MVR - Movement for a Fifth Republic) with the hopes of electing Chávez president and calling for the rewriting of the Venezuelan Constitution.

Chávez was a long shot: to win the presidency in the 1998 elections, he had to defeat the wealthy Henrique Salas Römer and the former Miss Universe, Irene Sáez. Despite the other candidates' seeming popularity, Chávez won the election and and quickly followed through with his promise to call for a Constituent Assembly to rewrite the Venezuelan Constitution. Less than a year after Chávez was ushered in, Venezuelans overwhelming approved the new constitution in a popular referendum with more than 70 percent of the vote.

It was a major turning point. The constitution was written with the direct participation of the Venezuelan people, who not only elected their representatives to the Constituent Assembly, but could also follow all of the debates on television, and participate in public forum sessions to express their opinions. "The Constituent Assembly is something which at the time was very valuable for a country which had always done things with its back to the people," says Alvaro Cabrera, an analyst with the Venezuelan government's Public Defender's Office. "Without a doubt it was the first experience where for the first time, everyone saw the possibility to influence what was happening. It opened a door."

The new 1999 constitution was one of the most progressive on the planet. As is highlighted throughout the book, the new constitution became the launching pad on which numerous new social movements would base their struggle. As the director of the Center for Women's Studies at the Central Venezuelan University, Alba Carosio explains, the constitution was gender sensitive, and recognized the unpaid work done by housewives, and their right to social security (Chapter 3). It recognized Venezuela's large indigenous population, and granted their right to their own autonomous education, which motivated indigenous communities to form the Indigenous University of Venezuela in Bolívar state (Chapter 12).[17]

As explained by Luis Perdomo, the constitution also was the impetus for the creation of the Network of Afro-Venezuelan Organizations in 2000, though its members have still not achieved their primary demand to be included in the Venezuelan Constitution as a distinct ethnic group, similar to indigenous peoples (Chapter 14).

Beginning in late 2000, the National Assembly granted Chávez the special power to legislate by decree on a wide range of issues in order to bring national laws up to code with the new constitution.[18] Within the year, the president decreed forty-nine law-decrees on a variety of issues, including regulation of the petroleum industry, micro financing, fishing and land reform. Among these were the new cooperative law that laid the foundation for Venezuela's cooperative explosion, with nearly 300,000 coops now registered by the national government (Chapter 8), and a new Land Law that limited private land holdings, and authorized expropriations of fallow land, and its redistribution to organized *campesinos* (Chapter 2).

On February 4th, 2002, Chávez announced the Presidential Decree 1666 on urban land, opening the door to Venezuelan citizens living in the *barrios* to acquire the title to their homes. This encouraged Venezuelan communities to organize into Urban Land

Committees in order to write their community charters and fight for the official deeds to their property (Chapter 1).

But while the law-decrees were empowering some sectors, they were frightening others. Chávez had won the 1998 presidency with a large middle-class constituency, who now felt their interests threatened by the new laws and constitution. They foresaw further distribution of resources away from the traditional upper-middle classes in favor of the poor masses. The opposition began to grow and organize. Backed by the traditional oligarchy and the mainstream media, they began to march daily against the new reforms.

Chávez supporters also took to the streets, organized through community networks known as the Bolivarian Circles. Venezuela's capital, Caracas, is surrounded by poor *barrios*, which house nearly half of its population of five million in sub-adequate housing and facilities. These people were seeing, for the first time in their lives, that they actually had a political say in the direction of the country.

On April 11, 2002, after rising tensions, a group of rebelling military officers staged a coup d'etat in conjunction with opposition leaders and the mainstream media. President Chávez was jailed. Pedro Carmona, the head of Venezuela's elite business federation, FEDECAMARAS, was sworn in as de facto president, quickly abolishing the 1999 Constitution, disbanding the Congress, and installing a virtual media blackout.

But Chávez supporters didn't give in. Less than two days after President Chávez was taken from office, pro-Chávez activists descended from the poor *barrios* around Caracas and the major cities, and surrounded Miraflores demanding that their president be returned to office. A few short hours later, he was rushed back to power. Carmona and the coup plotters had underestimated the response of Chávez's supporters.[19] Venezuela's social movements are quick to acknowledge that if not for their response on April 13, Chávez may have never returned back to power.

Oil Strike and Social Missions

Less than eight months later, in December 2002, PDVSA managers and upper-level staff launched a sixty-three day oil "strike" (often referred to as an oil "lockout"), which shut down Venezuela's massive oil industry, and brought the country to a halt.[20] The Venezuelan government got the pumps running again, but only after firing the management and workers who participated in the lockout, and restructuring the state-owned oil business. With PDVSA now strictly under control of the Chávez government — rather than the oil elites who had run the business since its nationalization in the 1970s — rising oil profits could be redirected to attend to the country's social concerns. The first of Venezuela's now highly-recognized social missions were launched just a few months later with funds from the oil industry.[21]

Until then, the CTV had dominated the labor movement for nearly half a century. In 2002, however, the CTV allied itself with FEDECAMARAS in supporting first the 2002 coup attempt and the subsequent oil lockout. Pro-Chávez unions walked, and in 2003, with more than 1,200 delegates in attendance, they formed the *Union de Trabajadores de Venezuela* (UNT - National Worker's Union).

The "oil strike" had pushed the Venezuelan economy to the brink. Many business owners closed up shop, either in support of the "strike," or because of it. Motivated by the surprising growth of recuperated businesses in countries such as Argentina, the Venezuelan government began to actively encourage factory workers to take over their businesses and either form cooperatives or co-managed companies with the state. The encouragement spawned recuperated and occupied businesses such as the Industrial Slaughterhouse of Ospino in Portuguesa state, whose workers have fully managed the company since occupying the installations on May 1st, 2006. (Chapter 7).

Meanwhile, more than five years after the *Barrio Adentro* Mission was launched, Venezuelans living in the poorest neighborhoods now have free, direct access to medical care in their communities. More than 20,000 medical health professionals from neighboring Cuba have come to Venezuela to attend specifically to these needy populations. Venezuelans are now being trained to take over these positions. Barrio Adentro II and III have focused on specialty and emergency care. The Barrio Adentro Mission has carried out 300 million consultations and is estimated to have saved 120,000 lives.[22] Through the Milagro Mission, hundreds of thousands have had their eyesight cured either in Venezuela or in Cuba, including indigenous peoples such as Wadajaniyu of the Indigenous University of Venezuela (Chapter 12).

Thanks to the literacy mission, Robinson I, more than a million and a half adult Venezuelans have learned how to read and write, and Venezuela declared itself illiteracy free in 2005. As of 2007, more than 300,000 Venezuelan adults had finished their elementary education, and graduated from the Robinson II mission. Meanwhile 450,000 adult students graduated through the Ribas mission, thereby receiving their high school diploma.[23] Numerous individuals in this book are either now studying in the Robinson, Ribas, or Sucre missions, or have studied in them in the past.

As explained in Chapter 15, free higher education has been made available to populations through the Sucre mission and the Bolivarian Universities. Over the last decade, the percentage of Venezuelans with a college degree has risen by nearly a third, to more than 30 percent of the population.

Meanwhile, more than a million kids per year attend the *Simoncito* mission pre-schools. The subsidized *Mercal* food markets sell products at discounted prices to millions of Venezuelans. And the Vuelvan Caras, and now Che Guevara mission, have given hundreds of thousands of Venezuelans job training while also teaching them how to form their own cooperatives — a move which expedited the Venezuelan worker-owned cooperative boom.

Ten years after Chávez came to office, poverty has dropped from roughly half of the population in 1998 to just over 30 percent in 2007. Meanwhile, extreme poverty was cut in half. Over the last decade, Venezuela's Human Development Index rose five points to .82. The infant morality rate dropped by 40 percent to 13.7 percent in 2007, and as of May 2009 — despite the oil slump and the global financial crisis — the Venezuelan economy had grown consecutively for 22 quarters, beginning shortly after the 2003 oil lockout.[24]

After ten years in office, the Chávez government has held, convoked, or participated in thirteen nation-wide elections, verified as legitimate by international and national observers. He won the latest referendum on February 15, 2009 with the approval of 55 percent of the population, which eliminated term limits. President Chávez is up for re-election again in 2012 and many believe that he will win despite having lost some key governorships and city governments in the November 2008 regional and local elections.

But, instead of simply providing handouts on election eve like previous governments, Chávez has said, "organize," and the Venezuelan people have responded, first in their Bolivarian Circles, then in their CTU (Chapter 1), and their health committees, then their cooperatives and recuperated factories (Chapters 8 & 7), and now in the communal councils (Chapter 18), which are putting community decisions directly in the hands of the residents. There are now 30,000 communal councils across the country, which have received roughly a billion dollars a year in local funding since their inception in 2006.

But the process has its contradictions, which have only grown since the 2006 Presidential elections, when Chávez was re-elected with 63 percent of the vote. "We have received support from the government through these government bodies like CONATEL, MINCI, but unfortunately governors or people responsible in these institutions are against the process, and regardless they hold public offices." Says Raul Blanco of the community Radio Libertad (Chapter 11). This is perhaps the most prominent theme that reverberates throughout this book as grassroots organizers, adamantly committed to the process, complain about the team that surrounds Chávez in the government: they call it "the bureaucracy," "the endogenous right," "the Fourth Republic within *Chavismo*," "the Boli-bourgeoisie."[25] "The government has really good intentions in this process, at least from President Chávez… Now, where are we failing? In the team that is accompanying him. There are definitely people that are in the government, who distort things and prevent us from developing this economy," says cooperative organizer Alfonso Olivo (Chapter 8).

The contradictions intensify when faced with what many consider to be the more revolutionary policies of the Venezuelan government, such as passing power directly down to Venezuelans through the communal councils (Chapter 18), or land redistribution to the *campesinos* (Chapter 2) and the Urban Land Committees (Chapter 1). Some activists blame the loss of the 2007 Constitutional Reform Referendum on the passive resistance from the "reformist" sector of *Chavismo*.[26]

Meanwhile, the Venezuelan opposition has been gaining force. In the November 2008 local and regional elections, the opposition won the keys to the metropolitan mayor's office of Caracas as well as six crucial governorships, including Tachira and Zulia along the Colombian border. Zulia is not only a bastion of the opposition, but also the heart of Venezuela's most accessible oil fields. Located along the border, it is also a Colombian paramilitary hotspot, with destabilization threats often focused in or around the region.

In 2008, taking the momentum from Bolivia's "half-moon" region, the Zulia state legislature did a feasibility study on the possibility of Zulian autonomy from the Venezuelan government.[27] The

National Assembly responded by passing a reform on the law on decentralization that put airports, ports, and roads back in the hands of the national government.

Meanwhile, in 2009, the central government brought Manuel Rosales, the mayor of Zulia state capital, Maracaibo, up on multiple charges of corruption.[28] In response, Rosales fled to Lima, where his petition for political asylum was accepted by the Peruvian government. Amidst this regional chaos, are the indigenous Wayúu, who are fighting for their native lands against coal mining by the state coal company, Corpozulia, and attempting to navigate the complexities of allies and enemies in the Venezuelan government (Chapter 13).

On the national scene, the opposition has been stretching out into new sectors. Over the last two years, opposition students have taken the lead in protests against government proposals such as the 2007 Constitutional Reform Referendum, the non-renewal of the RCTV broadcast license, and the 2009 referendum to eliminate term limits. The international media has played them out to be "freedom fighters" and in 2008, the Cato Institute granted the opposition student leader, Yon Goicoechea, the $500,000 Milton Friedman Prize for Advancing Liberty. Nevertheless, explains University of the Andes student leader, Cesar Carrero, this movement represents but a sector of Venezuela's wealthier student population (Chapter 16). The media has largely ignored the growing new generation of working class students, now able to access levels of education that were simply off limits before the Chávez administration (Chapters 15).

Despite these contradictions, difficulties, and conflicts, the Venezuelans represented in this book are quick to acknowledge that "the people have awoken." And regardless of what the future holds, "with or without Chávez, Venezuela is no longer the same," says María Vicenta Dávila (Chapter 18).

And that's the point. This book isn't about Chávez. It's about the social movements, grassroots organizations, and individuals across this country that are backing this process, and at the same time trying to find the space for their own autonomous organization. It's about what they feel, hear, and believe. They discuss Chávez and they support him, but they are all aware — like those who descended from the hills surrounding Caracas to defend their president on April 13th — that without them, he is nothing. And he knows it.

Part I:

LAND & HOUSING REFORM

ONE

One of Caracas' many barrios.

Iraida Morocoima,
5 de Julio Pioneer Camps, Urban Land Committees

(5 de Julio barrio, Caracas)

The 5 de Julio *barrio* rests on the eastern end of Caracas.[1] Makeshift orange block-homes cover the hillsides in a maze of tin roofs and winding streets typical of the poor communities that surround Venezuela's largest cities. 5 de Julio is one of the first *barrios* you come to as you enter in to the immense Petare Parish, which rivals Rio de Janeiro's Rocinha *favela* as one of the largest poor neighborhoods in Latin America.[2]

It was here that Iraida Morocoima was born, raised, and still lives. She points out her mother's house, just over the crest of the first hill, as she stares out at the mass of homes covering the countryside.

It's late afternoon on Sunday, and the streets and corridors of the tiny 5 de Julio *barrio* are busy. On the road into the community, the men lined up outside the corner store are finishing off a day's worth of beer in the afternoon Caracas sun. A few blocks away, the community has just held elections for a communal council. Iraida knows almost everyone. Like her, many of them are members of the 5 de Julio Pioneer Camp of the *Comités de Tierra Urbana* (CTU - Urban Land Committees), a social movement organized over the last seven years to resolve the lack of housing and right to land for Venezuela's poor.

The Urban Land Committees sprang to life around the February 4th, 2002 Presidential decree 1666, which opened the doors for Venezuelan citizens living in the *barrios* to acquire titles to their homes. The concept may sound simple. It's anything but. Venezuela is one of the most urbanized countries in Latin America.[3] The process of urbanization in Venezuela surged in the middle half of the 20th century. Industrialization and a large oil boom drew people into the city with promises of jobs and improved quality of life. Meanwhile, in the countryside, rural land was consolidated in fewer hands, pushing *campesinos* off their traditional property and forcing them towards the largest cities in search of employment.

As in the rest of the Americas, the newly arrived *campesinos* set up camp along the periphery of the city, slowly consolidating their shacks into sturdier block structures. In Caracas, these communities sprouted up along the lush hillsides. Streets grew in and among the homes, which were built on top of each other, quickly outpacing the arrival of municipal water, telephone and electricity infrastructure. The *barrios* grew, and in the case of Caracas, expanded to millions of people. Meanwhile, since the original founders of the communities were essentially "illegally" squatting on the land, such areas had never been legally recognized. That is, not until the 2002 urban land decree.[4]

Residents began to organize into Urban Land Committees in order to write their "community charters" and struggle for the official title to their homes, in which they had been living for decades. In many cases, the organization was successful. More than 300,000 families throughout the country have acquired the title to their homes. Iraida says that 70 percent of the residents of the 5 de Julio *barrio* now have the legal deed to their property. But some communities haven't received a single title, and the CTU say that close to three million families still live "in precarious settlements, threatened by mudslides and inadequate services."[5]

Through this process of achieving legal recognition, many community members began to question how to struggle for the rights of those who didn't have a home, such as renters, or children of community residents who were now in the same position as their parents and grandparents before them — members of the community with little hope of ever achieving their own dignified home.

In 2004, the CTU Pioneer Camps (*Campamentos de Pioneros*) began to organize as an exciting new means for community members in need of urban housing to be able to acquire it through *Movimento Sem Terra* (MST - Landless Worker's Movement) style land occupations.[6] But after only a few years, due to inaction and a lack of response from the municipal government, many of the original three-dozen "camps" had been demobilized.

5 de Julio was one of the emblematic few that not only remained active, but inspired fellow Pioneers to "continue in the struggle." In October 2007, they attempted their second land occupation in less than a year when a group of nearly a hundred activists occupied a stretch of unused land with the goal of resisting and constructing their own "dignified" housing and community. By the evening, they had been quickly removed by hundreds of members of the Metropolitan Police Force and the DISIP (*Dirección de los Servicios de Inteligencia y Prevención*), Venezuela's domestic secret service.

Two years later, after marching through difficult times, the Pioneer Camps are optimistic. Pioneer numbers are on the rise.[7] In March 2009, in conjunction with the Mayor's office of the Libertador Municipality, the Pioneers occupied and held a sixty-hectare plot of land in El Junquito, on the outskirts of Caracas, which they are now developing with a group of 120 families.[8] The Pioneers have been actively pushing for the National Assembly to finally pass an important Reform on the Regularization of the Land Law, which they helped to draft. On October 21, 2009, President Chávez signed into effect an Urban Land Law, which could quickly open the door to new occupations.

The Pioneers are confident that through their joint struggle and creative organization, they will continue to acquire more urban land and develop communities of their own.

Iraida Morocoima

The Barrio

5 de Julio was founded fifty-eight years ago. It has the same history of many of the *barrios* of Caracas, and Petare. The founders were people who came from the towns in the countryside, and who needed to live here. The people who arrived were very good workers, and those that set up at the lower end of the *barrio* were at greater risk from being evicted by the National Guard. They were the bravest. They had to join forces, and had to build their houses close together, so they could hear each other when the National Guard arrived.

After the fall of Marcos Pérez Jiménez, the local authorities let the residents stay, so community members began to construct the plazas and the common areas.[9] My mom and dad are originally from small towns in eastern Venezuela. I'm number five of my mother's nine children, and I was born here in the *barrio*.

Roots of Activism

My father was always a member of the Communist Party. He came here because he was in the guerrilla movement many years ago, before I was born, and when things got difficult for the guerrillas in eastern Venezuela, a group of them came to organize in the cities. When I was about thirteen, I began to get involved in what was previously called a Venezuelan Communist Party (PCV) cell, to do community work. But, I was always very critical of these books that they passed out on Karl Marx and others because I always thought that they weren't practicing what they were reading.

I had a brother, who was also a PCV activist, but he was recruited into the military in 1989. Those were some of our most difficult years. Due to his military experience, he was asked to train people in weaponry to participate in the coup attempt on February 4, 1992, against Carlos Andrés Pérez. At that time, we didn't know who Chávez was, but it was a joint civilian-military effort. My brother invited me to join with Bandera Roja.[10] I participated in the uprising and was fortunate to have been trained by my brother in this movement.

Afterwards, on November 27th, 1992 we carried out another attempt. We had really expected to succeed and that Andrés Pérez would leave power. Unfortunately this failed too, and the Metropolitan Police killed my brother in the *barrio* that day.

They ambushed him and they killed him. It was around noon and I was near the Channel 8 TV studio. When my father found out that we were involved, he had friends come look for me.

My father never believed in the people of Bandera Roja, because he was with the PCV, and my brother and I always had to hide our involvement at home. We had people in the *barrio* who supported us in this attempt, but always with a lot of caution. For our father, the idea that we both could have died for Bandera Roja was terrible.

I stayed connected to the people of Bandera, and I think it was at that point that I realized that I was really a part of this revolutionary process. My house was raided several times. There was a lot of police intimidation. There were raids, above all else, early in the morning. But the community made sure that the police didn't take you away. I think this strengthened the community's commitment to the *barrio*. A commitment which had already been there, but which increasingly saw that the struggle doesn't belong to one person, but everyone together, and which had continually supported us in these difficult times.

Despite of all this, I wasn't *Chavista*, because of the chameleon skin of the *Copeyanos* with whom we fought, saying that they were "*Chavista.*"[11] They were so quick to claim to be in favor of Chávez that it made us suspicious. But then I joined the CTU, and met these people — Andrés Antillano and others — whom we looked to for support and guidance in order to continue the fight that we had been carrying out. And so the CTU became a phase to continue these struggles to create the socialism that many of us had dreamt of.

The Pioneer Camps

From the CTU, the Pioneer Camps were born. Let me explain. The Pioneer Camp is like a *barrio*, giving birth to another *barrio*. We want to bring all the good things from the neighborhood, but with better planning, and we discuss this from the family perspective. One of the things that we say is that more than an individual; you are a representative of the family. You go to the assembly and then you must open up the debate within the family regarding the decisions made.[12]

We got involved in the Pioneer Camps without a structure. We began to write the rules about how to work with this new community proposal and how to build from the neglected and the poor. A lot of people saw this as an alternative solution for their housing problem. Immediately, the people from the *barrio* began to get involved with assemblies in the communities.

The goal of the Pioneer Camp is to gain access to urban land, land that was never intended for the poor class, because this city was for the rich. So we say we want socialism, and to build a process of equality within the greater city. Well, this process comes with the urban land. We can live in the same areas that the rich live, but we don't want to be like them, because being the same as them means to enter to into this capitalist market, and that is a market of exclusion. We have the right to live in the area where they live.

The Macaracuay Land Occupation

Once we decided on our organizational statutes we began to look for land. Our technical support team showed us more or less how to do this, and when we finished our survey we had an idea of a few of the vacant properties within the municipality.[13] That's how we ended up attempting our first occupation at Macaracuay, in Caracas. It was vacant land within the city that had been there for more than fifty years. And so we put it up for discussion. But we soon realized that while the authorities don't pay any attention when people move onto land in the hills, or in areas considered at-risk, when you start talking about land within the city, the authorities stop on a dime, because they could lose profits.

So, we were enormously surprised that the situation wasn't going to be that easy, confronted by people that believed that since they lived in a privileged neighborhood they have the right to offend others. We saw this when we carried out the symbolic land occupation in Macaracuay. They started to call us names, even racist slurs, and call us black. Not because we aren't, because we are, but they used it in a disrespectful way, as if we didn't have the same rights as them. We were afraid that this would lead many folks to distance themselves from the organization. What it did was unite us even more, deepening our understanding of the struggle before us.

We sat down with the local Mayor, José Vicente Rangel Ávalos, with the Vice-President's office acting as mediator, and at one point we were told there was some land in El Dorado.[14] El Dorado is a middle to lower class area on Miranda Avenue. But when we went to see the lands, we realized that they were already being fought for by the communal council from the adjacent *barrio*. They wanted to put us in conflict with the communal council, and we said, "No, we aren't going to fall in to the trap of confrontation with the community."

The failure of negotiations with the Mayor led us to attempt our next land take. We found some land in the foothills of Mt. Avila and we began to plan using what we had learned at Macaracuay. Believing that since there was a neighboring community that was going to support us, which was more like us, it wasn't going to be that difficult.

We decided to do the occupation on Sunday, October 21, 2007. We arrived at 11 am, put up signs, started to clean up the land, and waited for the community media to arrive to begin a discussion about the rights to the city. The police arrived around 1 pm, threatening us, telling us we had to go. By 2 pm the police blocked the media from arriving, claiming they didn't have permission to enter the area. Around 3 or 4 pm, they began to tell us that we were going to leave, for better or for worse.

We were almost a hundred people. They began to bring in the police dogs as if it was a war. I didn't believe they would force us out until the final moments. There were elderly people among us. We never imagined the Mayor, the son of José Vicente Rangel, a great leftist Venezuelan journalist, could do this. We could not believe that this government, supported by the movement in the current revolutionary process, would actually come against us. But that's what they did and in the most brutal way, with dogs and tear gas.

At first, we could hold out. But when they launched more than eight tear gas canisters in a small area like this, it was difficult for us to continue. That's when we decided to leave the land. There was no other alternative. We left the land humiliated and really angry for being attacked in this way, and being made to feel less than Venezuelan. It reminded me of the repressive government of Carlos Andrés Pérez, which attacked the people.

At the first assembly after the occupation a few members said, "No, the people aren't going to continue." But it wasn't like that. We decided to continue and it was as if being pushed away, our resolve was even stronger. There was gossip spread within the movement trying to divide us. Fortunately, it didn't penetrate, because the people understand that the process is not of one person but of all of us. We will not stay quiet. They want to take our hope away. When you abandon the struggle, you are lost, and we will not abandon the struggle.

There are people who believe that if you still carry out a land occupation, you are against the Bolivarian process. That is what they are told. But I believe that we were supported in our occupation. They have called me from Coche, from Mérida, and Barquisimeto, and they say, "Look, we are going to organize. We have land." There are people in Petare that say, "We are waiting to clear the land to take it."

The El Junquito Land Occupation

Until El Junquito, that was the last major occupation. In the Municipality of Sucre, now there's an opposition mayor. If they attacked us last time when there was a pro-Chávez mayor in office, can you imagine what these right-wing opposition mayors would do? It hasn't been a lack of will on our part. I think it has been because of a lack of political will from the national government. Because there are also fights over state land and it is as difficult as if it were private land. It's complicated because there exists state capitalism. And it's as if our movement has just been getting started over these five years, compared with similar processes in Argentina and Uruguay that have been struggling for thirty to forty years.

There continue to be disorganized land occupations. Because of the lack of political understanding, the people think they don't have another option but to go occupy land individually, and build a shack on one of these hills. But we are spreading the word about the Pioneer policies, and we continue to work with the grassroots, and in six months, if the people are in the same situation, there won't be unconscious land occupations, but rather conscious land occupations. The other possibility is that the people begin to get somewhere with the government and we can begin to influence national state housing policy. It's been very concrete for us to have the land over in El Junquito, where we have seen the people maintaining the process for over six months, and you can see it develop.

We occupied the land in El Junquito in March, 2009 together with the Libertador Mayor's office, and we set up numerous commissions on the right to the land and the study of the land. We know where we can build and where we can't. We have 120 organized families with us now who are going through a training process every Saturday. Some Saturdays there is a general assembly, others there is volunteer work. We are going to begin to work on production and study how we can become an *Empresa de Produción Social* (EPS - Social Production Enterprise) so we can construct our own homes.[15]

New Urban Land Laws

The Reform on Land Regularization would give those *barrios* that are built on private land the ability to acquire their land titles. That would be the most fundamental point.[16] We also spoke about the legal creation of *Bancos de Tierra* (Land Banks), which we are already creating in the Libertador Municipality.[17]

The Reform of the Law of Regularization of Urban Land is in the second round of debates in the National Assembly and we have a commission of five *compañeros* fighting there with the representatives. But while it is being discussed, we are getting the people out in the streets to demand that it be approved, and that has helped to push along the process. What's important is that the law has been constructed from the grassroots, and that it hasn't come out of the National Assembly or because the president said so.

But in the meantime, the Housing Minister Diosdado Cabello, at the request of President Chávez, came out with an Urban Land Law, which was signed by President Chávez on September 21st 2009. This law deals, more than anything else, with the recovery of urban land. It allows people to acquire urban land if it has been unused, and creates the means for the state to appropriate this land.

For us, as Pioneers, this is fundamental. For the CTU, as a movement, this is beneficial in some areas, but the Reform of the Law of Regularization of Urban Land also needs to be passed.

In the Municipality of Libertador, there is a Decree of Urban Soil, which was created by the community and approved by the mayor, and it's even more complete than the Urban Land Law approved by Chávez in September.[18] The new national Urban Land Law says that land can be bought. If land continues to be purchased, you just continue putting the land on the market. So it doesn't put a stop to the speculation.

The Pioneers are trying to promote our policy through the Libertador Municipality's mayor's office. We are organizing people in these new socialist communities.[19] The Pioneer camps are meeting on Saturdays and Sundays. We've been really busy. I think that's what's enabled us to see the steps we've taken. The movement is doing forums across the country on the discussion about the law, so that everyone understands it, because it benefits everyone. We are holding forums on the right to the city and Libertador urban land decree. These discussions are happening amongst the people. When you can hear your *compañeros* talking about the progress in the law, you can really say, "we have advanced". What we need, as Pioneers, is something more concrete.

Pioneers Policy versus State Housing Policy

We know that the housing policy of the Ministry of Housing is bad, because their proposal is to build "Socialist Cities" in the peripheries, outside of the cities.[20] And who is to build this great city? Financial capital and the large construction companies, and the people aren't participating in the decision-making. What's going to happen when the people move there? They aren't going to feel like a part of it, and there is no education, which is different than what we, the Pioneers propose. We educate ourselves, and struggle for housing, and we don't ask for it. We believe in collective property, social property. Give us the land and we will construct according to our Housing Policy law.

Our Housing Policy Law is where we lay out our policy of collective property and access to urban soil without so many hassles; where we explain how you are allowed to construct housing, and how to do it the cheapest. These are our policies that we have been constructing according to our experiences and needs. We are fighting for these to be adopted as state policies. Only one local mayor's office has put these into effect but they are not national policies yet.[21] National housing policies have remained welfare policies. We are the only alternative. More than acquiring your small home, we have a policy, the Pioneer's policy. If our policies were adopted by the state, they would allow you to build, not just a house, but a new community where housing would be constructed cheaper than it currently is, and it would resolve the problem of the *barrios* which continue to be illegally built. We propose a housing policy where people can live dignified and where housing has to be used exclusively for families to live in, not to put on the market.

We believe in collective social property, because it guarantees our permanence on the land. With private property, the market enters into the home. There is a housing market, and so we would be practicing the same as in neoliberalism. In capitalism, they build a house, they sell it and they move some place else. We are proposing to build homes to live in, where the property belongs to the collective and where it is discussed in assembly. If perhaps someone has to move, we say, "OK, you move and we will pay you the real value of your home, the cost that you invested." Not some capitalist crap. If we propose individually owned homes, we run the risk that the market will sneak in, and little by little people will leave this community that we had envisioned as being socialist.

Living in the Barrio

Unfortunately, there is also a process of inequality in the *barrios*, where there are people who have large homes and live off the rent and even exploit their renters.

In my case, I have been renting for seventeen years. Although I was born here in the *barrio*, I can't stay in my mother's home, because my two sisters and the husband of one of them live there. I've lived in four different areas of the *barrio*. I was kicked out of my last home because I supported Chávez.

My example is the norm, and the majority are many times worse off than myself. There are some that have rented for more than thirty years. Others have had to leave the *barrio* because they couldn't pay the rent. They were forced to live in a *barrio* where they don't know anyone. In our Camp, there are a lot of women, older women, too. There is a percentage of older women who after twenty years find it difficult to imagine that now they are going to win their own small home. But they understand that together we can achieve it. Not just the housing, but also the right to be together.

Analyzing the roll that we, women, play, I wonder why they ask so much why we carry the baton? It's a question of heroism, because women's children are killed, our partners are killed, they abandon us, and so we learn within our solitude to work and fight. Because it is us, women, whom they rape, whom they humiliate, who are the single mothers. We have nowhere else to turn. It is like when you leave a child crawling, and she has nowhere else to turn but to begin to walk and find a way to survive. That is us, women, a child who has been left behind.[22]

Building Unity

I think that one of our greatest strengths as Pioneers is our understanding that we can't do it alone. Alone we are weak. United, we can achieve our goals. We are all united here, but of course we are learning, getting rid of our bad habits, the individualism, learning to be useful in the best way possible. Everyone dividing up the work, that's how we operate. This is why the Pioneers are involved in the communal council. The people in the *barrio* understand that our struggle is part of their own struggle.

Through the CTU, we've had an exchange on the national and international level, and it has been a great sense of inspiration to us to see the movements in other countries, and realize that their struggle for soil is the same as ours. We have realized that you can't classify the struggles. Sometimes people try to classify them and say, "This is the CTU's fight, that is the Health Committee's fight." No, the struggles are everyone's. We are Pioneers, and we fight for soil, for land. We can't stop fighting for the road up the hill that has a bunch of potholes and is falling apart. Some have said that it's easier now because we are in a process towards socialism. We've learned that it's even more difficult. But it must be done.

Revolution within the Revolution

We are carrying out a revolution within a revolution. Not everyone who supports Chávez wants to make socialism a reality. In the barrios, this process towards socialism is very common, because it is a process of equality. No one is better than the other. Yes, it's true that the mainstream media has often attempted to individualize us, but we continue to say that we are all the same.

It is important for people to understand that we are fighting on two fronts: the struggle against the opposition so that they don't alter our goals, and the struggle against the government bureaucrats that support large financial capital who continue to give these lands to the large construction companies. That's why we say this is a process of revolution within the revolution.

We are all members of the new United Socialist Party of Venezuela (PSUV).[23] I am a spokesperson for my battalion. There are other *compañeros* that were elected to the founding congress, but the great majority are activists, and debate within the PSUV Socialist Battalions.[24] Unfortunately, even as of 2007, we were already seeing this type of dual fight within the PSUV. This struggle that we have had within the Pioneers continues within the new party.

Changing History

What is the difference now? The previous governments were populist. They gave you this or that, or you would plead with the *Junta* for improvements and then with the neighborhood associations, and successively it all came from the government that was in power.[25] So this meant that there was never an answer for the improvement of the *barrio*. Today, everyone is more informed and most everyone is in a better position to participate. In this community, there were people who had never participated, and they are joining us in finding solutions to their problems. But within the municipal government, they continue working with the clientelistic mindset like pickpockets.

Capitalism left us with so many vices that I think our greatest struggle is against these bad habits that have oppressed us. And now it's even more difficult because you have a government that speaks about socialism, but with capitalist practices. In earlier governments, for example, with Carlos Andrés Pérez, you didn't know if he was a *bicho* or *nefasto*, or whatever you want to call him, but you could go all out against him.[26] At this moment, it's more difficult, because by opposing the government you may be helping the opposition and those same business interests. But fortunately the people have been waking up, and they are more conscious. As a lot of us say, "I am with Chávez. I'm with Chávez as a tool. The guy is giving us a tool and we have to construct socialism." But I am not with these *carajos*, guys who are in favor of neoliberalism, in favor of a certain class, and many times are in the government.[27]

Chávez is a Door

Why is everyone so worried about, Chávez? What about the people? Worry about the people. The people aren't going to disappear if Chávez goes away. Chávez is like a guide. Chávez is a door — the door for the struggles that we want to carry out. But on the other side of the door are the people. I can't tell you right now if everyone understands this process. What I can tell you is that the people are learning, and it is very difficult to manipulate an educated people, because today the people have values, because the people are debating. Sometimes we are seen as if we were crazy fans running after Chávez. But it is not fanaticism. It is the same struggling people, fighting as always. The same people who were capable of forcing out Pérez Jiménez, the same people can build this socialism.

I believe that Chávez has a large fence around him preventing the information from getting to him. He has to take this fence down. Because we have tried to send little messages in every way, and it is he that has to break down this fence — this fence that has a housing policy that doesn't help anyone, a fence that has political barriers acting as ministers who are against the revolution. If you are against the revolution, you are against Chávez. So it is urgent that Chávez take this fence down, because we are going to jump over the fence that oppresses us.

On the Road to 21st Century Socialism

I believe that the road ahead for the organized community is not easy. I believe that at its base, it would be difficult for those from the Fourth Republic to trick us again. It would be difficult to have someone else come along and paint this picture and tell you, "Look, I'm going to give you this."

I believe that at this moment there are a lot of people studying, living this process, and wanting to create something else, and this "something else" is socialism. Sometimes we want to make change but we still don't know what we are building. Some say, "We are fighting for socialism, for our children. Our children are going to see it." We say, "No." You build socialism by practicing it. We have to practice it ourselves because unless you have tried it yourself, you will never understand how to do it. It's not going to be learned in books; it is through practice and constant struggle.

When we speak of a socialist society, that doesn't mean that you have to stop believing in what you have always believed, or you have to be the same as us. I think one of the errors of the majority of the socialist revolutionaries is that they have tried to create a fixed model for everyone to follow. In order to realize socialism, we must understand that we are equal, while at the same time we are different, but with the same rights. We see this in our meetings, when a Christian says, "I can't come to the meeting next week because my daughter is having her first communion." This isn't questioned, because we can't change a person's beliefs. We respect who we are, and who the people want to be, above all else, with respect to our beliefs.

These are people of the CTU and the pioneer camps, trying to exercise our rights; here, in Venezuela, we have a dual fight. But, yes, we are fighting. We are a people with values. We are a people who have been educating and learning about ourselves, demanding this access to urban land, which we know should not only be for this great monster, this octopus, that in Latin America and in the world, is trying to cheat us — the renters. Powerful people don't decree ALBA, we do.[28] Before it was very difficult to connect with people from elsewhere, but now we know what their struggles are, through the exchanges, not just for Venezuela, but also in Latin America, and in the world. Through the exchange of our struggles, we will succeed.

TWO

FNCEZ – The Ezequiel Zamora National Campesino Front.

**Ramón Virigay & Adriana Ribas,
Jacoa Cooperative, Ezequiel Zamora National Campesino Front**

(Jacoa, Barinas)

Virginia Tapia is in the large chicken coop tending to 500 hens, like she does every day. Her young children are on the other side of the pen where they are raising some 200 head of cattle for milk and meat. The cows graze lazily in the green pasture underneath the afternoon sun. Across a tiny dirt road are acres of yucca, peppers, papaya, and passion fruit. A mass of corn cobs is drying in the sun, recently harvested from more than one hundred acres in production.

Ramón Virigay is with a few coop members who are weighing out the *Cachama* that a group of locals have just fished out of an artificial pond they put in two years ago.[1] The locals gladly pay them half they would pay on the market.[2] Ramón doesn't have change, so he hands them back one of their bills and tells they can make up the difference the next time they stop by.

Ramón smiles and walks slowly back to the tiny community of three dozen recently constructed homes, which is the heart of the cooperative. They are painted red and yellow for the colors of the organization, the *Frente Nacional Campesino Ezequiel Zamora* (FNCEZ - Ezequiel Zamora National Campesino Front), one of Venezuela's most active social movements. Twenty-six families live here on the 3,000 hectare cooperative.[3] They make their decisions in assembly and collectively farm, fish, and sell their products.

This is the Jacoa cooperative in the state of Barinas, the heartland of Venezuela.

The mighty Andean mountains fold into the *llanos* which stretch over miles of rich farmland. The land is fertile, and the rivers are bountiful.[4] In the evenings, the passionate voices and quick-stepped rhythms of the regional Joropo music roll from the car stereos parked along the sidestreets of the state capital of Barinas.[5]

This is the land of folk stories and legends. Of *el silbón*, *la llorona*, and *Florentino y el diablo*. Natives from the llanos speak proudly of how their "shirtless" ancestors fought valiantly beside South America's Liberator, Simón Bolívar, and with the Venezuelan revolutionary, Ezequiel Zamora, in the 1846 Campesino Insurrection. In late 1859, only forty kilometers from present-day Jacoa, Zamora's rebelling Federalist forces defeated the Centralist government army in what is considered one of Venezuela's most historic military victories, the battle of Santa Inés.

Venezuelan President Hugo Chávez would breathe life into these legends once again as he nicknamed his 2006 Reelection campaign, "the battle of Santa Ines" and invoked the legend of "Florentine and the Devil" in his campaign against the 2004 Presidential Revocatory Referendum. He would know. This is also Chávez country.

Chávez is from the nearby Barinas town of Sabaneta, and just about anywhere one looks, the Chávez family isn't politically far away. President Chávez's brother Adán was elected Barinas state governor in November 2008, taking over for their father, Hugo de los Reyes Chávez, who had governed the state since 1998.

Barinas is also the heart of the Ezequiel Zamora National Campesino Front, or *Frente* (the Front), as the members call it. The FNCEZ was officially founded in 2004, with the union of the four-year-old Simón Bolívar Revolutionary Campesino Front (FCRSB) and the three-year-old Ezequiel Zamora Revolutionary Campesino Front (FCREZ).[6] *Frente* is now composed of approximately 15,000 *campesino* families across the country, living in dozens of cooperatives (or settlements, as they are called in the neighboring state of Apure).

The Jacoa cooperative is one of *Frente*'s oldest and most emblematic in the region. It may now be a peaceful well-organized sustainable community, but when it was formed on February 6th, 2003 (then under the FCREZ), it was at the heart of the land conflicts exploding across Venezuela. Just over a year earlier, Chávez had passed the 2001 Land Law, which limited the amount of private land a person could own, and authorized expropriations of fallow land.[7]

A violent backlash responded to the new land law, as it became a major impetus for opposition protests which culminated in the 2002 coup d'etat against the Chávez government. In the countryside, there was also violent opposition, not just from large landowners, but from local authorities, who tried to fight possible land redistributions in the local courts.

Perhaps as a result, little land was distributed in 2002, but the Venezuelan government passed out a total of over 1.5 million hectares of land in 2003 to roughly 130,000 families, including hundreds of families organized in Jacoa and other Barinas cooperatives.[8] Despite support from the national government, in order to acquire its land, the Jacoa cooperative would have to struggle for months in defiant resistance against eviction orders and hundreds of police.

Notwithstanding the open conflict, the land law had opened the door to reverse the process of Venezuelan land consolidation that had been growing throughout most of the 20th century.

When President Chávez came in to office, 70 percent of arable Venezuelan land was in the hands of 3 percent of the population.[9] Over the 20th century, Venezuelan agricultural production dropped to only 6 percent of the country's GDP as the country increased dependency on its oil industry and food imports.[10] Despite an aborted first attempt at agrarian reform in 1960, over the century, *campesinos* in search of new opportunities were forced to migrate in waves to the largest cities, converting Venezuela into one of the most urbanized countries in Latin America.

The Chávez government has increased agricultural production, called for a repopulation of the countryside, and declared food sovereignty a top priority. While the FNCEZ has been fighting for the expropriation (or as they call it, "recovery") of fallow land held by wealthy landowners, over 200 *campesino* leaders have recently been assassinated by hired gunmen.[11] In response, *campesinos* have begun to form local *campesino* militias with the help of the Venezuelan armed forces in order to protect their communities.

The FNCEZ has strong relations with Brazil's *Movimento dos Trabalhadores Rurais Sem Terra* (MST - Landless Worker's Movement) whose members have been supporting its struggle for many years. In 2005, with the support of the Venezuelan government, the groups formed the *Instituto Agroecológico Latinoamericano, "Paulo Freire"* (IALA - The Paulo Freire Latin American Agroecology Institute), where more than five dozen students from seven Latin American countries are now studying sustainable agriculture.[12]

Like the MST, FNCEZ has over the last year realized the importance of linking their agrarian struggle to urban activism. In 2007, they formed the *Frente Nacional Comunal Simón Bolívar* (FNCSB - The Simón Bolívar National Commune Front) which is now organizing communities in the Barinas state capital to form a communal city, modeled after the country's first communal city, the Simón Bolívar Communal City, recently created in the neighboring state of Apure.[13]

Meanwhile, the FNCEZ has been growing and consolidating into one of the most radical *campesino* movements in Venezuela. Young media activist, Adriana Ribas has been working with the organization in Caracas, since 2002. She has also been an active member of the FNCEZ's Commission on Gender which has been working to promoting gender equality within the organization across Venezuela. The FNCEZ now has a strong pressence in eight Venezulean states, and over the last two years has begun to work throughout the country.

The FNCEZ is, however, far from the only *campesino* organization in Venezuela. At the time President Chávez was elected to office in 1998, the Venezuelan Campesino Federation (F.C.V.) was aging. After failed attempts to revamp the Federation with the new goals of the Bolivarian movement, the Federation splintered and *campesinos* formed more than a half-dozen new organizations throughout the country — among them, the Ezequiel Zamora Front and the Simón Bolívar Front.

The *Coordinadora Agraria Nacional Ezequiel Zamora* (CANEZ - Ezequiel Zamora National Agrarian Coordinator) was created by Chávez and supporters in 2003 to unite the various organizations.[14] The FNCEZ stayed autonomous and believes that CANEZ is too connected to the Venezuelan government, while CANEZ believes that the FNCEZ's forced land occupations are unnecessarily radical and out of place with a revolutionary government in power, such as the Chávez administration.

Ramón and Adriana are members of the FNCEZ. Ramón has played a key role in the organization since its founding as a member of the Jacoa coopcrative, one of *Frente*'s oldest cooperatives.[15]

Ramón Virigay & Adriana Ribas

Personal Histories

Ramón: My name is Ramón Virigay. I was born here in Barinas, in Ezequiel Zamora, and my parents are from Táchira, San Cristóbal. They've been living here in Barinas for some time. I'm part of our organization, Ezequiel Zamora National Campesino Front: an organization of battles, of struggle, of strengths, and of tools for the war against the *latifundio*.[16] We began to participate in the organization, because as *campesinos* it was nccessary to belong to a revolutionary organization rooted in the ideals of the Bolivarian and Zamoran projects in order to achieve our fundamental objectives, among them to demand our *campesino* rights. And we are working here, and are involved in this struggle all over the place. Wherever you look, you'll find us, in each municipality where we are developing a front, we're going to spread our message of strength.

I met my wife Luz Marina Tapia in 1981; we worked as *campesinos*, working the land until we fell into our organization. We've had our sacrifices, with sweat and tears, but we've been pressing forward, and you have to humbly be sincere as a revolutionary. Most of the revolutionary men here are humble people. As a result of the capitalist system that indoctrinated us, it is necessary to apply justice in the countryside, and we need to continue pushing this and waking up, so that tomorrow or the day after, in the short or medium term, we, men and women, can carry out justice in the *campesino* sector. That's our idea. These are our ideals. That's what we are fighting for — for each of us to become an instrument in this political struggle.

Adriana: My name is Adriana Ribas. I am from the Capital District of Caracas and I am thirty-four years old. I met the *Frente Nacional Campesino Ezequiel Zamora* in 2002. Since I already had a relationship with community media in Caracas, I offered support with the knowledge that I had in the area of communication. I began participating in some of their activities, but only in a support role. Little by little, I became more active. When they were going to hold their first national training school, I told them that I wanted to participate in it as a student. It seemed to me that this was the beginning of the strengthening of the organization, and I wanted to be a part of that. That was in 2005.

The National Training Schools

Adriana: The school for political and ideological training came out of an agreement between the MST and *Frente*, when they met each other at the World Social Forum here in Caracas. The MST had a lot to do with organizing that first school; they were a great support thanks to all their experience. Some important intellectuals from the MST, participated as facilitators. About sixty-five to seventy students from all over Venezuela participated in the first school. The rest of the students were all *Frente* activists, strong organizers within the organization. These are people that continue to be there and form part of the national coordination, and the regional directorates.

The national training schools touched upon many subjects: agrarian legislation, cooperativism, popular power, class struggle, historical materialism — lets say it has all the philosophical and ideological components of any revolutionary process. It also has the technical components that one needs in order to do agricultural work, since most of the students are *campesinos* who are working the land.

Coming out of that training school, I had the objective of constructing a radio station in the Andrés Eloy Blanco municipality of Barinas. I went directly from that training school to Barinas to develop the project over a period of approximately six months, living there in Andrés Eloy Blanco. We organized various workshops with the community. Everyone there was really great. I still feel like I belong to that community.

Barinas

Ramón: Barinas is a *llanero* state, or rather, 80 percent *llanero* and 20 percent *Andina*.[17] Its strongest characteristic is its cattle ranching. It is a state with 80 percent of the best land available in Venezuela. Its rivers provide it with a fountain of natural resources. Pedraza Municipality is the capital of the rivers. Some of the rivers emerge from natural springs.

Politics here are very intense because it's the land of the *comandante* [President Chávez]. The eyes of the world, the eyes of Latin America, are on Barinas. And Chávez put his heart into the state and its large agricultural production principally in sorghum, rice, and corn. In the Andean region, the focus is on café and cacao. And in the *llanos*, you have large cattle ranches with their meat and milk production.

The Beginning of the FNCEZ

Ramón: It began here, in the state of Apure, with an organization called the Simón Bolívar Campesino Front, named after our founding "Liberator", and we formed a similar front here in Barinas called the Ezequiel Zamora Campesino Front.

And we began the fight here in Jacoa, Curito Mapurital, where in 2001 we were able to take the first steps after the new Land Law. The President of the Republic had promoted this law, and we entered into a new land recovery phase with 161,000 hectares of land in the state of Barinas. It was a beautiful battle because that's where our organization came together, or was born, with this action and this revolutionary fervor. We succeeded here, and on top of that,

Hugo Rafael Chávez Frías came here personally to hand over the 161,000 hectares to different cooperatives.[18]

Unfortunately today, because of the lack of understanding or education about the collective, some people left, but others have stayed. And those who stayed are here today standing up for this struggle, with its social project, with the production of food, with democratic decision-making, and with autonomy based on the ideals and direction of our leader, Hugo Rafael Chávez Frías.

We believed in this, and it is happening. Little by little, it is materializing. This was our idea, using the mechanisms of these land recoveries based on the law and the new constitution that came about at that time. Afterwards, it was necessary to clarify the next steps within the heart of the *campesino* movement in Barinas and Apure. There had been two fronts, but we decided to join into one organization. We held a citizen's assembly and voted on which name we would use, and the majority voted to use the name the Ezequiel Zamora National Campesino Front to drive this revolution, because Zamora passed through here.

Zamora was really close to here, in Santa Inés, with his battles, his guerrilla war, his war of resistance. He had a clear vision to continue what Bolívar had begun. Bolívar died, but his beliefs lived on. And Zamora, with his vision, tried to channel this revolutionary energy that had remained due to the injustices. And Zamora was able to see this energy, and carry it forth, but well, all of the processes have their traitors, right? Zamora died. Zamora was betrayed by the oligarchy and was killed in San Carlos de Cojedes as a result of a mysterious bullet from the oligarchy. They killed him, and that's where it ended.

So 130 years passed for this to begin again. As Neruda said, "The people awake every one hundred years."[19] And they woke up with the new leader, Hugo Rafael Chávez Frías, and here we are building this.

I believe that that's why we chose the name of the FNCEZ. It is for a man who fought with the *campesinos*, who in Santa Inés was able to defeat the enemy with their machetes and lances, on horseback and by foot. They fought from behind the mills, behind the trenches, behind the river, behind the mountain with their shirtless men, as the legend says. And as history tells us, they were able to attack the enemy. They were victorious and this energy continues to grow.

I believe that our principles are based on helping this history continue to take shape, so that our people are guided by the revolutionary energy that exists.

These are our principles. They are based on the idea that we need to continue to pass on these tools. We need to continue to strengthen our movement. Our social support is in our cooperatives, and in the communal councils, in the communes, the communal cities, in the small and medium-sized producers. And wherever there's a problem with the *campesino* sector, we'll be there, helping to ensure that this project continues, because this is a growing river, and some will carry on, and others will stay behind, but the river must continue. It has to continue its course and this is the revolutionary current, little by little pressing forward to achieve this fundamental objective.

The Jacoa Cooperative

Ramón: In the beginning, 300 families participated in this cooperative, and there were 500 families in the cooperatives that formed around the Curito-Mapurital land recoveries. It was euphoric. It was a beginning; each cooperative had its own president, with a leader, helping to take the first steps towards the consolidation of this process.

And like every process, there were mistakes and weaknesses. We have learned from these mistakes and these weaknesses, and right now we are correcting them, because if you ask us today what happened to Jacoa's hundreds of families, due to the lack of leadership or understanding, and the devil of individualism which still remains, there were people who left the cooperative.

I think that right now our motto is "organize, educate, and mobilize." Organize: that is, organize the masses. Educate: that is, we need to educate ourselves in order to begin to produce the land, to exchange, to sell. We need to educate ourselves for everything, and we are doing that. And very intelligently, Chávez set up a number of missions to educate us.

Jacoa Before the Cooperative

Ramón: Under Carlos Andrés Pérez, we're talking about thirty or thirty-five years ago, Jacoa was one of those areas where the elites divided up the booty in the mayors and the governor's offices.[20] They said, "Well, as I have the most resources, I need 1,500 hectares in Jacoa," and so they came here and they measured everything immediately.

This was idle and unworked land. There was nothing on 99.99 percent of it, just *monte y culebra.*[21] Instead, today, with the capacity of our organization and with the friendly hand of the state — despite old government structures that still exist — we have achieved some things. And we've carried out some actions, because there's a tiny refrain that says that this revolution is apathetic, and you have to give it a kick so it reacts. If you don't give it a good kick-start, the people aren't going to think, because we are still immersed in this capitalist system.

The Jacoa Occupation

Ramón: The occupation here was hard. Really hard. We had confrontations with the state because of a lack of understanding or the fact that at the time there were certain embedded groups in the government bodies — in the mayor's and even the governor's office — that largely supported the large landowners. Even with Chávez in power, there were decisions beneath him where 100-120 police were sent to scare the mothers and fathers that wanted to enter the land. So there were no options. The *mano peluda* still existed, it still does.[22] Now it's just more hidden, because the resources are distributed, and things are happening. But they camouflage themselves and dress in red, but they stay the same.

The fight was hard. People were wounded. An encampment kept watch for more than four months to protect our *campesino* brothers and sisters. It was there to protect and keep watch because the fight was intense. And when the courts ordered the land evictions, we had to get support *en mass*, with 100-200 people.

The arbitrary tribunal — a tribunal that ordered the land eviction — immediately rounded up 100-200 police who came to attack us. And we dug in, and immediately called for our cooperatives from here and there, and brought everyone together. There was no turning back. Armed, we defended our land with hammers, machetes, and pothooks. And that's as far as the police came. These were very important actions, because you could see the clarity of our cooperatives fighting for our land. What happens to one cooperative will happen to mine, so we joined together and we were ready for any attack from the courts.

It is important to realize that this bureaucratic structure has remained. And the other issue is that we need to spread the word. This cooperative is alive. We have food security here. This is one of the principles of autonomy, and the Simón Bolívar national project. Bolívar said that you had to develop projects so that they become alive, and this is alive. The children study here. We have everything we need.

FNCEZ Organization

Adriana: We have a National Coordination Team with forty people on it. All of the proposals for the year get proposed and discussed there. This is where we debate our activities, our political positions, and where we evaluate the situations in the different regions. Every year we hold a National Assembly, which is our highest decision-making body and where all the activists within *Frente* discuss the proposals from the National Coordination Team.

Ramón: We are working hard in seven states. In the other eighteen states, we've just been working for two years. We have our state committees. In Barinas state, for example, we have a committee of nine *compañeros*. We sit down and debate policies about how to proceed with our struggle. We debate this in the region, in a citizen's assembly. We go to the region, distribute information to the cooperatives so that the cooperative delegates in each region and parish can exchange and debate a plan of action to bring everyone into agreement.

This is a transitory process. It's not a straight jacket. We've always said that this is in exchange for nothing. We always tell our *Frente* delegates that this is work and more work without pay. Only the people can save the people. Only the capacity of organization of each sector, each community, which is able to share with each other a can of sardines, a kilo of rice, a kilo of pasta. That's how we take steps forward.

The information has to be collectivized. The collective has to be in control of the decisions, and then we evaluate them because you have to evaluate, to be self-critical in order to assess how we are doing. In order to advance, you have to evaluate.

Changes Under Chávez

Ramón: Everything changed under Chávez. There's no turning back. We know that Chávez is the most important political leader. He has the vision. Chávez incarnates the project of Bolívar and Zamora. He has been developing it, and he has put his foot on the accelerator. Structural changes are beginning to be made, such as the new structure of the old SASA, which is the new INSAI.[23] Chávez is putting the pedal to the metal and these changes are happening, with the missions, with the social projects, and with all of these land recoveries. Despite all of the difficulties, he has accelerated the pace of land recoveries because this revolutionary process needs a framework, an educated framework. We need to train men and women to carry on this process.

The Land Law

Ramón: I think you can say that the Land Law changed things 100 percent. Before, we lacked something elemental. We didn't have a leader who could rescue the laws and could help us to understand who we were and where we were headed. We had fallen asleep because of the capitalist system they had imposed on us. And along came a leader who woke people up like Zamora did. Chávez comes along and now we are waking up. He dusts off many of the laws, sees them as obsolete, and sees that we need to write new laws. He writes them, but with a vision and direction rooted in history.

This old state is still there, human poverty is still there, this savage capitalism that they beat into us is still in our midst. There are men and women who won't let us wake up completely, because they know that if we wake up completely, we are going to have a power called constituted popular power, and that the people themselves are going to make the decisions under the framework of the law, which says that only the people are sovereign, and nothing else.

Violence in the Countryside

Adriana: From the first moment Chávez began to talk about land reform, the cattle ranchers began to get organized in order to attack the *campesinos*. We principally blame Omar Contreras Barboza, who was the president of the *Federación Nacional de Ganaderos de Venezuela* (FEDENAGA - National Federation of Cattle Ranchers of Venezuela) at that time, and is one of the people to initiate attacks against the *campesinos*. So when the new Land Law was passed, which gave *campesinos* the opportunity to denounce unproductive land, and moreover the ability to occupy those lands and make them productive, the landowners began to attack *campesinos* and order the assassination of *campesino* leaders — the majority of whom were leaders in the FNCEZ. Just between 2001 and 2002, within a period of seven months, there were seventy-five *campesinos* assassinated. It was intense how a month would pass and you would hear about one assassination and then fifteen days later you would hear that another person was killed.

Ramón: Since the beginning of the revolution there have been 217 *campesinos* assassinated at the hands of hired assassins and paramilitary forces. As a result of recent assassinations, we have held marches and we have done actions against paramilitarism. We organized a mobilization in Apure, Alta Apure Guasdualito, with more than 5,000 *campesinos* marching against paramilitarism. We've also demonstrated in *Sur de Lago,* where we discussed the idea that cooperatives and settlements need to organize to protect themselves and to protect food security, with the creation of the territorial guard and the Popular Bolivarian Militia.[24]

Chávez has launched a proposal for the Popular Bolivarian Militia. And under the framework of the communal councils, communes, communal cities, we are developing the project of a popular guard and popular militia. We also have to create the popular Bolivarian militia here, which is accompanied by the Venezuelan army to ensure our security. I think that if we create these mechanisms, under the framework of the military law that President Chávez has revised, we would be largely able to minimize attacks from the oligarchy and paramilitary forces.

Impunity

Adriana: Impunity continues to be a major issue. Once, the National Assembly organized a commission on the assassinations, but nothing came out of it. At that time, there were 180 cases of execution in the *campesino* sector, but the Attorney General's Office only recognized 75. But nothing was done. We have evidence of who is assassinating the *campesinos*. What more evidence do they need? I don't know if they are looking at it from a public relations point of view. Maybe they think that accusing a landowner of being the mastermind behind these executions will be seen as victimizing them, and the opposition will come out saying that they are another political prisoner. Or maybe there just isn't enough interest because they are *campesino*s. Maybe it isn't relevant from a political perspective.

But the situation of impunity is very concerning because we aren't just seeing this in the *campesino* sector. Labor activists are being assassinated also and nothing happens. I think getting into it with the landowners touches too many interests, and there is a certain complicity within some sectors of the government. There are only seven people that have been jailed for the assassinations. Only one who planned the murder, a landowner that paid for the assassination, and the others all actually performed the executions.

The State Steps In

Adriana: After the third year the Land Law was in effect, the state took over the process of expropriating the land directly, rather than the *campesinos* simply going in and working it. I don't know if this was a conscious decision by the government to solve the problem of the assassinations or because they came to an agreement with the landowners. So now the conflict is not with the landowner directly.

Now, the *campesinos* denounce unproductive lands at the *Instituto Nacional de Tierras* (INTI - The National Land Institute), and INTI does the inspection and declares the land officially unproductive. That's when negotiations begin between the state and the landowner, or the state sometimes simply expropriates the land and turns it over to the *campesinos* who made the denouncement. We still have the option of organizing monitoring camps outside of the land. So you declare the land unproductive and set up a camp with the families that are going to occupy the land and wait until INTI arrives. Once the lands are approved, the whole process of awarding the lands to the *campesinos* begins, where they are provided with the land title and loans from the government.

Ramón: The INTI is still an old structure that is still a little rough around the edges. We haven't finished filing it down. Our *comandante* has fought hard, but the elites in this country are rotten. There are threats against the directors, and they haven't been the most reliable, because it's been rough going. There are a lot of backdoor meetings, corruption, good ol' boy politics.

I think that this revolution begins with the land recoveries because it's the only way to access everything. If there's no land, there's nothing. There have been some struggles that they have joined, but for the most part we have always fought with our own strength, energy and will. And in the land recoveries, it has always been the decision of the *campesinos* to press forward, because there's always the fear that the director will back away from making a decision, because he's from the oligarchy, that's who has the resources, that's who has the money, that's who has the influence with the governors and the mayors. So there are a series of factors that compel the director to make whatever decision as a result of the fact that the oligarchy has more access to power to influence all of these things. As a result of this old system, the oligarchy was the one who most benefited from the state.

Relationship with the State

Ramón: We've been working with the State in two ways: one, to battle, fight for our rights and our demands, and the other is to converse and dialogue to achieve peace in the development of agrarian policies. We have realized that there are ministries that, as a result of the system, still function as part of the oligarchy, through the tentacles of those who are entrenched there.

We spent a year in negotiations. It was a year of work, dialogue, discussions, round tables, agreements, meetings, workshops and everything. And we have realized that some 60 percent of this was for nothing. Our organization has made a new decision to hold the government responsible, and say, "you failed us here, and we're going to strengthen ourselves here, because this isn't working."

Adriana: Our work with the government has progressed a lot, of course with contradictions and weaknesses. Every month there is a meeting with the *Ministerio del Poder Popular para la Agricultura y Tierras* (MPPAT - Ministry of Popular Power for Agriculture and Land) — not just with people from the FNCEZ, but also people from CANEZ and other campesino organizations. We evaluate the areas where we have to work, put forward project proposals; we also discuss the National Cultivation Plan, the national agricultural policies, and the resources that are going to be provided by the Ministry. If the government receives a hundred cows then we determine how those are going to be distributed and those types of things. They take into account the proposals of the organized groups more at the moment of distributing something we have won. So it's no longer just some government employee going to three or four farms to distribute these things himself, which was a demonstrated failure.

Now, any financing coming from the *Banco Agricola* (Agricultural Bank) or the *CVA* (Venezuelan Agrarian Corporation) or any other state institutions is going through the communal councils. So for example, a communal council located in the countryside holds their assembly and evaluates what their necessities are. Based on that, the Agricultural Bank, for example, will provide the resources and the communal council will be responsible for distributing this to those who ask for financing. So if I am a cooperative, I need to tell the communal council that I have an agricultural project and the assembly needs to approve it.

Many of our settlements have benefited from this. The Simón Bolívar Communal City has benefited greatly. They have had months of negotiations with the government and the state is providing a lot of support. Some communities are making progress and there are others with setbacks. But, this relationship is good because it's not the politics of the state coming to the *campesino*, it's the politics of the *campesino* going to the state.

FNCEZ & INSAI

Adriana: When INSAI was being totally restructured and was in the process of hiring new personnel, it opened the opportunity for its regional directorate positions to be occupied by members of the social organizations. So in some states we have directors inside the institution that respond to the interests of the *campesino* sector. There are fourteen people with director positions from *Frente*, and we have periodic meetings with them. INSAI is the institution that is responsible for food safety; including everything that has to do with agroecology, providing free cow vaccinations, fertilizers, all of that stuff. They have a huge job and many people from *Frente* have been trained there.

Latin American Agroecological Institute

Ramón: The IALA is a school in which *Frente* participates and shares experiences with various Latin American countries. Those at the IALA have come here to help, to work, to do semester-long internships. And, the IALA is a source of agroecological development. I mean, they will be the future men and women who are going to promote agroecology, because it isn't being practiced anywhere, and they are doing it. They grow plants and fruits without the need to apply chemicals or fertilizers.

Sustainable Agriculture

Ramón: Agroecology is important because by working more with it, we are hitting the multinational companies hard. They are the ones that want to kill us. They bring genetically modified products here, and they're taking our natural seeds. If we think about it, our parents worked with agroecology, because they never used pesticides. The best agricultural production was developed long ago. So, yes, I believe that there are sources of agroecological development here. There are tiny things that we have been working on, and there is virgin land and forests in some parts, and we can take advantage of it.

Gender Work in the FNCEZ

Adriana: *Frente* has a Commission on Gender and I am part of that commission. In the 2005 National Congress, *Frente* came to the conclusion that we needed to push forward work around gender, from the woman's perspective. We needed to redeem the role of the woman, to make her visible. Our priority is to work towards gender equality because as a *campesino* organization we have very strong *machista* and patriarchal tendencies. Even though our *compañeros* might have good political stances and do good work in the countryside, this doesn't mean that they have a gender perspective about what they are doing.

So a group of us started working along with Yolanda Saldarriaga, who you could say initiated all of this work around gender and pushed forward strongly on the issue within the organization. Honestly, I personally was very skeptical given the cultural conditions of the organization. I mean, this is a wall that we have in front of us and in order to tear that down you have to begin by reeducating the youth.

We have organized two national gatherings on gender. The second one was very well supported on both a political and logistical level, because the *compañeros* in the National Directorate recognized that this issue needed to get worked on, not only within the Directorate, but also amongst the rank-and-file. They realized that this isn't about a competition between men and women, but rather this is an issue that confronts capitalism and patriarchy. So we did the second gathering in November of 2008 and we had somewhere between 300 to 400 women attend.

After this gathering, we had regional gatherings on gender that in general were very successful. We have been able to introduce, at least in theory, gender-neutral language within our assemblies and meetings, so that our *compañeros* have to use the word *compañeras* as well. The *campesina* women learned about articles in the Land Law and the constitution that benefited them, specifically as women in the countryside. We discussed how we as women also reproduce our own roles that keep us invisible. I think that we are improving because in the beginning there were just three or four of us introducing the language of *compañeros* and *compañeras* and attacking sexist jokes and all those things that affected and bothered us.

Union in the Campesino Sector

Ramón: I think that our struggles bring us to a place of integration. We, as *campesinos*, unite our forces when we see something happening to someone in the *campesino* sector.

I think that we in *Frente*, have been pulling together and offering our grain of sand. Chávez speaks of Bolívar often, about his history. And the general of the people, Ezequiel Zamora, is the continuity of Bolívar, so this gives us a base from which to struggle as the Ezequiel Zamora Campesino Front; it is a battlefront rooted in this energy. This is something that gives us clarity. And here we are, carrying forth. Everyone gets involved to achieve the greatest amount of happiness as possible for everyone in the countryside. And if we all get involved, we can achieve anything we want.

Part II:

WOMEN & SEXUAL DIVERSITY MOVEMENTS

THREE

Alba Carosio − "Investigation, study and interpretation of the problems of Venezuelan women to achieve EQUALITY."

Alba Carosio,
Center for Women's Studies

(Caracas)

The authors on Alba Carosio's bookshelves read like a who's who of radical feminist theory: Kollontai, Millet, Firestone. Alba admits they all had a great impact on the fledgling Venezuelan feminist movement of the 1970s. But Alba is not stuck in the past.

Alba is cofounder and director of the *Centro de Estudios de la Mujer* (CEM - Center for Women's Studies), based at the *Universidad Central de Venezuela* (UCV - Central University of Venezuela). When the center was founded in 1992, it was the first such institution in Venezuela. More than simply a research center, the CEM has played a significant roll in pushing forward the agenda of the women's movement during the 1999 Constituent Assembly and throughout the Chávez administration. "We research in order to make change, and once we make change, we do further research," she says.

With proposals from the CEM, Article 88 of the 1999 Venezuelan Constitution recognizes work in the home as a contribution to the economy, making housewives eligible for social security benefits.[1] Venezuela's constitution also set a powerful precedent by using gender-neutral language, where all individuals are referred to in both the feminine and masculine form.[2] Immediately following the passage of the new constitution, President Chávez ordered the creation of the *Instituto Nacional de la Mujer* (Inamujer-National Women's Institute) in order to coordinate and execute the government's public policies aimed at improving the lives of women.

The Venczuelan government has continued to champion women's rights with an array of initiatives. The *Banco de Desarrollo de la Mujer* (Banmujer - Women's Development Bank) was created on International Women's Day in 2001 as a means to challenge the economic inequality traditionally experienced by Venezuelan women. As a social development bank, it provides low-interest micro-credit loans and training to support women in creating worker-owned cooperatives. As of 2009, Banmujer reports that it has supported over 2 million people and has provided over 100,000 loans, creating 440,619 jobs in the country.[3] Five years later, in accordance with Article 88 of the constitution, the government launched *Misión*

Madres del Barrio (Mothers of the Slums Mission) to help mothers from Venezuela's poorest communities escape from the vicious cycle of poverty.[4]

This momentum has continued with the passage of a new law on violence against women in 2007, establishing courts dedicated to defending women against violence throughout the country. In March 2008, President Chávez expanded the National Women's Institute into the Ministry of Women's Affairs, which in 2009 became the Ministry of Popular Power for Women and Gender Equality. Despite these advances, women still face discrimination on a daily basis in the home, on the street, and in the professional world.

Although Alba's offices on the UCV campus may appear to be a long way from the women living in the poor *barrios* that the government's policies are largely aimed at, she sits at a unique cross-roads between the past and the future; dictatorship and democracy; academia and activism; the roots of feminism and the present. Alba is infused with excitement when talking about the advances women are making in Venezuela, understanding the long road that the women's movement has taken to arrive to the point it is at now. Yet her excitement is tempered by the understanding that genuine political and cultural change is a slow process.

Alba Carosio

Personal History & History of the Women's Movement

My name is Alba Carosio and I have been a member of the Venezuelan feminist movement since the 1970s. I moved to Venezuela from Argentina during the era of the dictatorships permeating the Southern Cone at that time. I moved to Maracaibo and this is where I joined the feminist movement by becoming a member of an organization that existed at the University of Zulia called the Feminist League of Maracaibo, which is still alive today.[5] That was in 1975 and in 1982 I helped form the Woman's House of Maracaibo, which was the first Woman's House formed in Venezuela.[6] That, however, is no longer in existence. During the 70s throughout Latin America there was an effervescence of movements towards the political left arising from all the experiences of injustice at the time. It is well known that Latin America is the continent with the greatest inequality in the world.[7] These movements were influenced in part by the

Cuban Revolution and the liberatory thought that corresponded to those years in the 60s and 70s in Latin America, as well as throughout the world, because in the United States at this time there was also the movement against the war in Vietnam and the other movements for equality and peace. Likewise, in Latin America, we experienced this movement to the left that was suffocated.

Many of us women were activists in these leftist movements, but at this time we also began to discover that there existed a specific oppression towards women. During this era, there was a predominant belief that this oppression towards women would disappear when the revolution came about. Well, in the end, that revolution never came about but within these very revolutionary movements, many of us women felt terribly pressured. Many of the men in these movements were simply chauvinistic. For example, the responsibility of taking care of the children of the family fell completely upon women. This same thing happened throughout Latin America. So beginning around the mid-70s we began to come together in groups to reflect internally.

We began to ask ourselves what was going on with us as women: did we have to begin to organize ourselves separately from men, or was this a struggle that should be parallel? Was this a movement that had no reason for existence and should we simply add ourselves to the struggle for general liberation and forget about the struggle specific to women? Would we be considered counter-revolutionaries, as some were saying at the time? So we began to reflect on all of those things within our own lives. We were influenced at this time by various writings, like those of Alejandra Kollontai, who argued for the liberation of women within socialism as well as the writings of Flora Tristan and Kate Millett, who wrote the famous book *Sexual Politics*. Also by Shulamith Firestone, who spoke of feminism and revolution. All of this we discussed within the context of our own realities.

From this experience, we began to form a movement here in Venezuela. It was an experience that was reproduced throughout Latin America, of course with its distinctions, considering that some countries continued to suffer under terrible dictatorships. At this time, we were also influenced by the writings of other Latin Americans such as Julieta Kirkwood, the Chilean feminist. It was the Chileans who coined the phrase, "Democracy in the street, democracy in the home, democracy in bed," which means that the struggle for women's liberation must work parallel to the struggle for general liberation. In other words, our struggle cannot wait, with the expectation that with a national or even international revolution there will automatically be liberation for women as well. The movement had its strongest presence, naturally, in the universities, where many women were beginning to amass as students. The women within the parties of the left also began to share the same kind of reflections. And those women who were coming strictly from the feminist movement began to come together with those women from the left parties as well as with those women from the government-affiliated parties, in this case *Acción Democrática* and *COPEI*, the Christian Democratic Party.

Reform to the Civil Code

The first great battle that united all of us was for the reform of the Civil Code in 1982. Until that year, in Venezuela, parental guardianship was not shared between men and women. Children born out of wedlock were considered illegitimate, which of course was a truly stigmatizing thing. These illegitimate children did not have the right to take on the last name of the father, and likewise had no rights to demand any inheritance or financial support from their father. Of course, these children were not considered illegitimate on the mother's side, who could not negate that a child is hers when she gives birth, and thus all the responsibility for the child would fall exclusively on her. Conjugal rights were not shared equally between men and women before this, when women did not have equal rights with men within a marriage. What we today call a normal marriage was not a right for Venezuelan women at this time.

So not just the feminist movement, but the women's movement in general, united around this. I say this because of course at this time, during the 1970s and 1980s, many women still did not want to call themselves feminists. There was still a dominant black legend about feminists that would come from women on both the left and right-wing. Women on the left would accuse us of dividing the struggle for liberation, and the right wing would call us crazy lesbians; that our beliefs were too utopian, and that the woman's only role was with the family. So while many women wanted to struggle for women's rights, they did not want to call themselves feminists, something that still partially remains today, but at the time, was in the majority. Nonetheless, little by little, those of us that called ourselves feminists began to come together and explain ourselves to those women on the left. Of course, feminism has more in common with the left than the right-wing, by its very liberatoy nature and commitment to genuine social change and liberation. That is not to say that there are not strategic moments in which we must unite, given the fact that we all as women share in common a situation of oppression. So at this moment we could join together with women who did not talk about, or even think about, a general revolution.

In fact, the Reform to the Civil Code was brought forward by a female minister from COPEI, Mercedes Pulido de Briceño. Of course we participated because this was a just initiative. Also, because feminism carries with it some important ideas that it incorporates into social struggles, such as the belief that we don't have to wait until things are perfectly ordered; that things will go about getting fixed gradually; that social justice is something we obtain gradually. So although we were following someone from the COPEI party, how could we disagree with the disappearance of a distinction between legitimate and illegitimate children? You don't have to be a feminist to realize that there simply should not be first class children and second class children.

Beginning of the Centro de Estudios de la Mujer

During this time, all these groups continued to join together and there was the formation of various initiatives and institutions that continued to propel the women's movement. There existed, for example, something called the *Coordinadora de Organizaciones No-Gubernamentales de Mujeres (CONG* - Coordination of Women's Non-Governmental Organizations), through which many of us organized ourselves to attend the Fourth World Conference on Women in Beijing in 1995. Throughout this time, there was also the creation of various ministries committed to women's issues that would appear and disappear and with very low budgets, but that nonetheless played an important role of providing an impulse and uniting those committed to the women's struggle.

As all of this was developing, the CEM was founded in 1992 through the Central University of Venezuela in Caracas. Universities have always been places where women would enter and begin to question. First, because they have the opportunity to reflect and are in contact with ideas. Secondly, because women that study feel great discrimination. After we make an effort to study that sometimes is even stronger than men, they obtain a career, and we enter the job market and experience discrimination for being women.

So in 1992, a group of us women gathered sufficient strength to develop what was at that time the first center of academic studies focused on this subject in Venezuela. Our first director was María del Mar Álvarez de Lovera, who apart from being committed to social struggles, always studied the subject of women.[8] She is a woman definitively from the left and her moral and ethical commitment to the women's struggle was never in doubt. Around the same time, there were similar initiatives being developed in other universities, such as at the University of the Andes, the University of Zulia, the University Lisandro Alvarado of Barquisimeto, the University of Carabobo, and all of these began to build relationships with each other.

We, as a studies center, are like a reference point for the study of women and women's struggles. Here we have done the principal investigations and analysis on the situation of women in Venezuela. Outside of doing studies we give classes, we have a degree focused on women's studies, and we also do work in the communities, for example with women who are victims of violence. This has always been a studies center with a committed style of research — of research and action. That is to say, we research in order to make change, and once we make change, we do further research. There is a permanent dialogue between theory and practice.

The Constitution

Since 1999, when the constituent assembly was held for the creation of the new constitution, the proposals from the CEM have been taken highly into account. If you observe the constitution, you will see that it is the first constitution to utilize language sensitive to gender. Apart from that, sexual and reproductive rights are included in the constitution: the right to decide how many children one wants to have; equality with men; and measures for affirmative action which today we consider measures for reparations towards women who have historically suffered a series of discriminations. Affirmative actions are measures taken to repair the damage historically done to women. This includes giving social and economic value to domestic work — the work traditionally carried out by women in the home. These were proposals that were taken to the constituent assembly by professors that were connected to the CEM, such as Marelis Pérez, who is now the president of the Commission of Family, Women, and Youth as well as Nora Castañeda, who was the director of the CEM and is now the president of the Women's Development Bank.

Since then, the CEM has continued contributing to all the work done with women, which in this last ten-year period has grown substantially. Not only the work, but the way that 21st Century Socialism has understood the importance of the liberation of women in order to achieve total liberation, and the way that relationship is being constructed. There is still a long path ahead, but a very important step has been taken which is the opening of minds to feminist ideas and the importance that these ideas have for justice around the world. That is to say that there is no such thing as an egalitarian society if there is not equality in the home.

Affirmative Actions for Women

Many of these ideas that were implanted in the constitution of course were already being worked on for some time. For example, the subject of valuing the work done by women in the home, and this has now been amplified to include the care of children provided by women. This has always been a feminist concept, because here lies the essence of women's oppression. That is to say that when women are considered to be exclusively responsible for their children, what we have as a result is what feminist authors have referred to as the patriarchal dividend. This is a gain for the patriarchy, for a certain amount of work and energy put forward by women who have these responsibilities for the simple fact of being women, and remaining invisible within society.

The concept of affirmative action has its origin in the understanding that certain social groups have suffered historical setbacks, generally for ideological reasons. These measures of affirmative action were thought of first for African-Americans in the United States. The concept is that where there have been circumstances of negative discrimination, we should employ on a temporary basis forms of positive discrimination, or positive actions providing greater benefits to a group that has suffered historical oppression. For example, there should undoubtedly be something like this for indigenous peoples — and for women as well. Women have suffered centuries of patriarchy, a series of tasks that are obligatory if you are a woman, whether you like it or not, and a series of limitations on the actions that you can take in your life.

Madres del Barrio Mission

The idea of the Madres del Barrio Mission comes precisely from this understanding. Here in Venezuela, we have a situation in which 70 percent of those in conditions of poverty are women, in which the majority of poor households are those with women at the head of the family.[9] In fact, one of the greatest elements that drive women into poverty is the condition of being left alone to care for their children. There remains a high index, a bit less today, of irresponsible fathers. There is a strong socio-cultural establishment in our society where women are the sole caretakers of their children, rather than the couple, allowing for fathers to evade their responsibilities. When poor women are left with the sole responsibility for their children, logically they enter into a cycle of poverty because if you have two or three children to take care of alone, then your capacity to work is limited. So, the Madres del Barrio Mission is a social program directed at women who live in the slums, which is where we have the highest levels of poverty, with the intention of supporting them for a certain period of time so that they have a minimum income — a minimum income that allows them the opportunity to go about the process of acquiring a career while resolving the issue of how to feed their children. So the Madres del Barrio Mission is a program aimed at combating poverty, but with a gender perspective, because we discovered that within poverty the most poor are women. The program unites both visions, combating poverty with a feminist perspective taking into account the historical and personal setbacks experienced by women.

Furthermore, keep in mind that Venezuela has a high proportion of adolescent mothers, and this of course is a major constraint for the life and future development of these women.[10] Very often, these are women who have had very few opportunities to study. Today, female students who become pregnant can't get kicked out of school as has happened in the past. Nonetheless, there is a major limitation on one's ability to study when you have a baby to take care of.

Women enrolled in the Madres del Barrio Mission are provided with job training, but also education around their sexual and reproductive rights. We also do general empowerment work, helping them to achieve greater levels of autonomy; to make more well-thought out and informed decisions, to avoid falling into the same cycle of deeper poverty. According to the latest numbers, 200,000 women have participated in the program.[11] This still might be a small percentage, but along with our other institutions, such as the Women's Development Bank and the Ministry of Popular Power for Women and Gender Equality, we are confronting the problem of women and poverty on various fronts.

Law of Gender Parity

Gender parity is the idea that if all the societies around the world are constituted half by men and half by women, societal decisions should be made more or less within those same parameters. That is to say that injustice is evident when you look at the National Assembly and it barely has a representation of 18 percent from women. In terms of political activity, and what many of us noticed during the 60s and 70s, women always serve as an important grassroots base but are excluded at the point of taking on positions of power. We can even see this replicated inside some communal councils.

Gender parity, then, is another form of affirmative action, which establishes that all the spaces of political decision-making should be constituted equally by men and women. We are demanding this for all positions subject to popular elections and the boards of directors of state-owned companies, and that private companies be exhorted to do the same. This is being included in a law called the Organic Law for Gender Equity and Equality that is being worked on within the National Assembly at the moment within the Commission on Family, Women, and Youth.[12] Of course, this is a challenging law to pass since those that must approve it are in majority men, who know that they may not be in the same positions in the future if it passes. We believe that this is necessary, because otherwise the natural tendency is a delay in waiting for women to have the opportunity to take on positions of power.

A parity ordinance was pushed forward by the National Electoral Council (CNE) for our last regional elections on November 23rd, 2008 in which the lists of candidates being elected for our city councils had to have an equal number of men and women.[13] So now women's participation on a local level is much greater. However, since this was an ordinance enforced by the CNE just for this election, we are fighting to have a law established so that we don't have to battle for this in every election. Rather we want this to be the case for all elections from now on until there exists greater equality and we don't need a law to enforce it.

The President's party, the United Socialist Party of Venezuela (PSUV), is the only political party functioning within Venezuela that has sought to enforce parity within the party. While this hasn't been established within the statutes of the PSUV, it was agreed upon and in fact President Chávez pushed for this to be the case.[14] Although it is not a complete parity, it is very similar to what we are looking for, and it is an important achievement since it provides an important model to the other parties.

Women and the Bolivarian Revolution

There is now a philosophy that comes from the feminist movement that has permeated through the government and its public policies, and has resulted in a greater consciousness of what we are talking about, of the necessity for women's liberation to attain genuine socialism. While many out-dated mentalities still exist within the government, we have certainly advanced profoundly. First, in the ideological sense and in the public conscience. It is invaluable, for instance, that we now have a president who calls himself a feminist. There are women that criticize him for this, saying that in reality he is not a complete feminist. Well, that doesn't really matter. The important thing is that he declares it, which is a huge break from anything in the past. What a difference to go from the 1970s when to be a feminist was to be the worst of the worst, to now having a president that declares, "A socialist who is not a feminist lacks breadth."[15] It is an achievement because it provides a great example to others of the way that things should be.

Also, the President and the whole movement of transformation in Venezuela have greatly incorporated women. Women are participating everywhere in this process and there is hardly ever a speech given that does not talk about the importance of women's participation. Therefore, some feminist ideas have become commonplace. We have huge possibilities because the women's movement for liberation is now on fertile ground.

An issue that we still have that is incredibly hard to break with is that while woman are now more mobilized, they often fill up their time participating exclusively in social activities that are not focused on their interests as women, and which makes them forget about and delay their needs as women. For example, to give you an anecdote, I remember once participating in a workshop concerning planning policies for municipal councils with a focus on gender. And when we talked about a subject as simple as health, these same women that participated in a group where I was doing work, found it very difficult to see their own needs. This was most evident in the needs for pregnant women, because in this municipality, like in many, in order for a woman to properly give birth she must travel a long distance. While this is a very real need to respond to, when you raise it on a community level, often this becomes delayed in favor of a more abstract notion of health for everyone. Then one realizes that there is still much lacking for there to be a real gender consciousness that allows women to demand their rights and needs.

Violence Against Women

We have made important achievements in work around the issue of violence against women. We have one of the most advanced laws on violence against women in the world. Courts specifically dedicated to this crime have been created.[16] However, there have been situations where some judges have dragged their traditional, cultural, and ideological beliefs into the courtroom. I have heard cases of judges justifying violence because the culprit was drunk. Being drunk doesn't give you the right to hit anyone, nor does it make you innocent! We still have much impunity to confront. Of course, there is much work to do in terms of providing greater support for the victims of violence as well. This is also the case for prevention, because the idea is not simply to punish, but to prevent these situations from continuing to happen.

We have a long way to go in order for social conditions to be looked at realistically, because once you see the reality, you can see the need to focus on gender. For example, we have participated with an organization that does work with family members who are victims of violence, including police violence. But when you use the term family members who are victims of violence, this is simply a euphemism. These are not just any family members; these are typically women. Or when we talk about family members of those who are in prison, the reality is that 95 percent of those in prison are men, and their family members are women — their mothers, girlfriends, or wives.

Future Work for the Women's Movement

There are still many priorities that we have to address. In the first place, the connection between poverty and gender must continue to be developed and discussed. That is critical for a society seeking to do away with poverty. There is also still much work to be done around sexual and reproductive rights. Abortion is still penalized in Venezuela. This is an incredibly important feminist issue, because we can't claim to have genuine independence when we are not allowed to make decisions over our own bodies in the fear that we will be punished. In general, greater work must be done to improve attention to pregnant women, as well the prevention of unwanted pregnancies.

A very significant task that this process must confront soon is the introduction of the concepts of gender equality into public education. We have to work permanently to break from our socio-cultural models of domination that make women oppress themselves. As young men grow up, they often go about learning that they exist in the world in order to dominate, while girls are often taught that they need to seek permission for all their decisions. Well, these are two distinct models of education and provide two very different visions of the world. This culture must be challenged permanently because centuries of patriarchy cannot be overcome within ten years. We have an open door with great possibilities. There exists a greater symbiosis than ever between feminist ideas and socialist ideas, but we still have a long road ahead of us.

FOUR

Yanahir Reyes.

Yanahir Reyes,
Women's First Steps Civil Association

(Antímano, Caracas)

The metro station in the busy Antímano district is like any on the west side of Caracas. The streets are full of people buying and selling. *Buhoneros* hock coffee, *empanadas*, lottery tickets, and pots and pans every few feet.[1] Yanahir Reyes takes a fifteen-minute jeep ride up into the surrounding hills, then walks the final leg of the trip to teach where there are no schools. Only a few miles from the main road below, she enters a different world where there is no running water and where structures made with corrugated tin and cinder blocks house the hundreds of families that make up the La Pedrera *barrio* of Antímano. Yanahir is a feminist and a teacher who has been working here for three years. She says the best way to challenge sexism in Venezuela is through community projects empowering the residents with women at the helm.

Women have played a tremendous roll in the Bolivarian Revolution. They are at the heart of the communal councils, the committees, and various grassroots movements. Seventy percent of the people participating in the Venezuelan government social missions are women.[2] But despite their active participation in the decade old Bolivarian Revolution, *machismo* and an obsession with beauty maintains a firm grip over the nation.

Beauty is hard currency in Venezuela. It stares down at you in advertisements with curvaceous, light-skinned models selling everything from alcohol to cell phones. Beauty shops are everywhere, even in the poorest communities. Countless beauty pageants fueled by large corporate sponsors dump millions of dollars a year into the country. In 2004 alone, Venezuelans spent over $1 billion on beauty products making the country one of the largest consumers in Latin America.[3] Plastic surgery is commonplace and is often given as gifts for *La Quinceañera*, the right of passage for fifteen-year-old Venezuelan girls. Bandages covering recent surgeries are worn in public as a badge of status. There are even bank loans to fund such procedures.

This is not a setting ripe for feminism. In spite of that, Yanahir, 28, has become a young rare voice critiquing Venezuela's obsessions. Since 2005, she has worked in a community learning project called *Asociación Civil "Primeros Pasos de Mujer"* (Women's First Steps

Civil Association) that brings education to poor communities without schools. She also founded the feminist radio program *La Milenia Palabra de Mujer* (Millennium Women's Word) on Radio Perola, the community radio station in her neighborhood of Caricuao.

Yanahir Reyes

Becoming a Feminist

I became aware that I was a feminist when I started to see the injustice in the daily life between men and women. It started in my home when I realized that my father could go out and do whatever he wanted. He was freer, while my mother stayed at home, taking care of us — the girls — ironing, washing, scrubbing, and cleaning the house.

My father was in the guerrilla movement, with the *Movimiento de Izquierda Revolucionaria* (MIR - Movement of the Revolutionary Left).[4] I admired him for his views on politics and life, until I realized he was with my mother and also another woman. It happens to all of us. I felt betrayed; it was a betrayal of the whole family. Of course, I didn't want this for my mother. No one wants this to happen to your mother. The most incredible thing I realized was that my father was a coward, a chauvinist. He did us so much damage by not making a decision. He involved me with this other woman, as a friend, as a mentor; that helped me with my studies, since I was a bit undisciplined. She was going to set me straight, and it turned out that she was his lover.

That's when I became aware of the inequality between the sexes, like in my family. My father had the power to dominate the situation — to take care of my mother, and to take care of the other. I was thirteen. And now I'm part of the solution. I'm buying their apartment so my father is able to go and my mother can stay. Housing is very hard to come by in Caracas and sadly some women are forced to remain in demeaning situations because of it. They have lived this way for years and now finally they can separate and my mother can begin to heal.

Societal Norms

We are in a revolution yet the shopping malls are full. People are buying incredible amounts of cars, clothes, liquor. I don't think it's right. We give consumerism more outlets than humanism. It is difficult to admit to myself that overt sexism appears in our newspapers and everywhere. Still, in a country in the process of revolution, there is an element of denial that many of us have. This is the fault of [those in] the government, because it's their responsibility to make the laws to protect its citizens. This is damaging us. It is hard to imagine many of these people changing.

Will the youth or the elders who have seen this forever, be able to alter their consciousness with this consumerism pounding them? But what are you going to do? I support taking a hard stance against the evils of our society. We should crack down on the corrupt politicians and publicize it, so people see it on television. We pay the National Assembly representatives so much money, while people just like you and I have to work hard. Some, I will not say all, are wealthy just because they are representatives. Every month, they make so much money it's sickening. This has been accepted in our society for far too long. These are things that have to change.

I can see within my own family, we act in ways that don't help the revolutionary process. Because of this, I think change has to begin with the individual. This is what I'm doing. There are things, for example, like Christmas. Christmas here is converted into an event full of consumerism. Fine, let's resist. We won't buy anything. Christmas is for the family. In our family tradition, we don't buy presents. There are other presents: a hug, we go to the beach, we stay home with family. We're going to resist and if more families do this, change will come. The whole world needs these changes, but honestly it's so slow with the so-called "democracy" that the western powers promote. There are cycles that get repeated over and over again. The institutions get bogged down in their bureaucracy and this prevents the communities from reaching their full potential. When we permanently break the bourgeois elements of the state and empower the population we may see the changes. Without justice, there is no chance for democracy.

Breaking the Mold

My sister studied at the university, graduated, had a job, had a boyfriend, and went to the United States along with him. That was scandalous! She broke from this submission, and said, "I am going to do what I want. I'm older. I have the right to do what I want, to be a woman." In this society, my brother could do this, but not my sister. So, this example was important for me. My sister is a very authentic and determined woman. We had our differences as sisters, as is natural, but also a lot of coincidences in our lives. Maybe she's become a little more conservative, classy. She got married in the church, all these things. That's fine. It's what they've sold us. It's how we grew up, culturally speaking.

Her example early in life had a great impact on me. I knew that I wanted to be different. I wanted to study, and I wanted to get things for myself. I want to have my own apartment, alone. I want to travel, to do a lot of things without depending on a man. I knew my career had to involve women. I work with a lot of women and I see their discontent, socially and in the workplace. It was based on these experiences that I started to openly criticize how the chauvinist society does a lot of damage to us.

Working in the Community

When I started to work in the community I began to defend women's rights; noticing who had the children, who had to care for them alone. It's the women. We started this radio program that's called *En Casa* (At Home) that is still running to this day and my friend hosts it now. The focus of the program is on children, family, and also the woman. I remember when the founders of the radio told me that they saw me as a fighter in defense of women. They didn't call me a feminist though. This struck me. I asked, "What is the problem if we call it a feminist program?" They thought that feminism was the same as *machismo* but in the other direction. There has been a struggle for many years to define feminism as an ideology in Venezuela. Of course everything has its excesses and extremes, but the essence of feminism isn't the fight; it's not the ideology, it's the things that are gained by the feminist organizations and women's rights.

The people from Radio Perola whom I had known from the neighborhood proposed that I make a program geared towards women. On that day my sister and I decided to start *Milenia Palabra de Mujer*. She was with me for a year. My father attacked my program. He said that women's rights and violence towards women were themes that had been talked about too much already. He said it was a *tema trillado*, something that people talk about a lot. But everyday, a woman dies of violence; therefore, it's not spoken about enough.

Economic Dependency

We have not progressed as far as I would like to see after ten years with this government. There are many steps that have been taken. And, of course, there is resistance to these changes because for over 500 years our society has been ruled by a patriarchy, and later supported by capitalism. This is not going to change overnight. We, the women of Venezuela, have to take responsibility of our own struggles. However, it is important to identify the structural barriers that keep women in a state of oppression. *Machismo*, which we have discussed, often leads to woman being economically dependent on men. This is at the root of the problems women face.

When men leave women behind with children, or they have children with several women, we suffer. When women are in mentally or physically abusive relationships, we suffer. The opportunities are greatly limited for them. Even when school or professional development programs are available, many women cannot take advantage of them. Their responsibility to their children comes first. Some of these limitations may seem to be self-imposed; however, we must examine where they come from.

Women's rights and gender equality can't just be talked about as an issue between men and women. We need to recognize that there is a reason behind this that isn't isolated from the political and economic order that has been extending itself over our planet for centuries. We talk about the double exploitation of women. We have to begin the work of recognizing violence, but that shouldn't be disconnected from the political and economic realities in a nation or the world. The issue with the *maquiladoras*.[5] Who are the people working in the *maquiladoras*? They are women in the factories all over the world.

The idea is not that we as women just oppose men because they are *machistas*. The media, the means of production, the state, the Church, all play a role in maintaining inequality. And in the end *machismo* does not just harm women; it also turns around and harms men as well. At least here in Venezuela, in our *barrios*, the ones that die are men and the ones that kill are men, young men.

Women Led Popular Power

Women need to be accepted as leaders in the community. This is the path to change history. The work being done in La Pedrera is a wonderful example of women from a community organizing themselves into a collective to solve serious problems that they face. Another teacher, Milda Viña, and I were appointed by the Ministry of Education as teachers in the community. I met Milda at Radio Perola and she recommended me to work with her. Antonia Rivera and Lourdes Jiménez were the women from the community that started the project. We all came together to go out into the community to conduct a census to find out how many children were not in school.

In the first two sectors that we covered, we found that there were a hundred elementary school-aged children not receiving education. This number grew as we got out to more areas. There was no chance of a school being built in the short term, so in September 2005, we began construction to renovate some of the families' homes to use as make-shift schools. We added onto the living rooms of the shacks — houses made of planks of wood, tin, and some constructed with brick and concrete. In any case, these places have problems. When it rains, water and mud seep into the house. We did not anticipate the damage the water would cause, forcing us to also use the *ludoteca* that we had hoped would provide space for the youngest children and pregnant women. It is now a space for us to share and learn from each other.

The *ludoteca* is a concept that has emerged from the experiences of a few countries. For example, we have learned about *ludotecas* in the *barrios* of Medellín [Colombia] whose primary purpose has been to decrease violence. The term *ludoteca* etymologically comes from the Latin word for "play." But primarily, it is a space that is flexible, that responds to the needs of the community. In Europe there are *ludotecas* but primarily for wealthy people. The children go and play, but there is no ideology of transformation. In our case, we use the term and concept, but adapt them to our historical, political, and social context and needs.

The *ludotecas* are different from traditional schools, because they can take place anywhere in a community. They can be under a mango tree, a room in a *barrio*, on a closed-off street. The *ludoteca* isn't managed by the teacher or an institution, it's managed by the people. Mothers and fathers participate in the space. It's a place where the family comes together through the use of games. The family is part of the curriculum, of the learning process. Everything is planned with the interests of the children, the family, and the community. The games are for bringing about a different world. The *ludoteca* isn't just an area with a chalkboard and desks, but rather they are spaces that are constructed by the people.

The *ludoteca* also has the objective of strengthening the emotional bonds within the family and using play as a means of education — but an education for transformation. Not just a cognitive education, but also a social and emotional education. Early childhood education is absolutely political because these children are the ones that are going to ensure transformation in the present and future of our revolutionary process.

Our priority in La Pedrera was to open a space for infants. But we saw that there were many older children from eight to up to fifteen years old that had never had a formal education. Due to the violence in the *barrios*, the right to play is taken from children. They are forced to play at being adults. A seven-year-old girl is expected to take care of her little brother because her mother has to go work. So the children's creativity and imagination becomes repressed. Learning about the world through play, which is emotional and pleasurable, becomes repressed. These are stages in a child's life that need to be respected because this is what makes you healthy as an adult.

Popular Education

We supported the organization of the women in order to ensure the lasting legacy of the school to be administrated by the community, and to convert the mothers into teachers in their community. At that time I was finishing my bachelor's degree as an educator at the *Universidad Nacional Experimental Simón Rodríguez* (UNESR - Simón Rodríguez National Experimental University).[6] One of the policies that the Bolivarian government has developed is that upon graduating, university students should have a project based in a community where they are providing the community with support based on the knowledge they gained through their program. Some other students from the UNESR and I used our work in La Pedrera as our community project. So our work there was developed with our research and practices from the university, which was able to enrich the experience for the women in the *barrio* as well. This project was submitted to the mothers and they took ownership over it.

First the mothers would just bring their boys and girls to the spaces that we created. Later, they became more active in their relationship with the children. So rather than just being mothers, they became volunteers in the defense of the rights of their children. At the beginning there were ten women participating from different parts of the *barrio*. Now we have eight women — some have had to leave the organization because of work commitments or because they moved from the *barrio*.

The women were not trained in workshops or anything like that. They began by just observing what Milda and I did. But when the women began to participate as volunteers, they started learning children's songs, how to play the children's games, how to work with pregnant women. It wasn't about us teaching the mothers. They learned through practice.

The school pushes the community to organize, to solve serious human rights issues, like the right to water, education, security, recreation, nutrition, and other necessities. The *ludoteca* functions as a safe space, preventing the violence generated by the nature of survival and from the vicious cycle of patriarchy and capitalism. It is a space for women to unite and reflect on the impact of *machismo*. We need to re-think our children-rearing habits, because these are often *machista*, capitalist, and very conservative. Beginning when the baby is in the mother's womb, we start telling them how they should act. So we need to ask ourselves what messages we are giving to our son or daughter? Are we giving them messages for liberation or for being dominated?

The idea is that the space functions as a center for the investigation of popular education from the prenatal level to the primary level, which goes until age fifteen. For us, this is how popular education is spread, with the active participation of the family and the community in which the basis of instruction is the wisdom and hope of our community. This is how we challenge the oppression that we women have suffered.

This work was created by women, for women, and we are able to educate men as we do this. We don't want to say that men didn't help. They have grown as a result of this as well. We still want more participation from the men in the community because the responsibility of the children is still falling completely in the hands of the mothers; this inequality still exists.

First Steps

Now we are legally organized as a civil association, called *Primeros Pasos* (First Steps).

Primeros Pasos was created as an informal initiative. But we began to develop a more structured organization, recognizing that it was going to be necessary to have resources for our work to progress. We realized that this initiative could die because the mothers have their own needs to take care of — paying for their food and health costs for instance. So we started to look for a way to access resources so the women could resolve some of these needs and also meet some of the children's needs — because we needed to cover the costs for the children's lunches, transportation, or to take them on field trips.

We realized that there were institutions that were able to support us economically and morally. The Ministry of Education still did not really support us because they still have conservative and bourgeois education policies. They think that education only takes place in the classrooms and don't consider alternatives of how to work with the communities most in need, which is necessary. We know that a boy or girl that lives in a *barrio* on the tip of a mountain is going to have difficulty accessing education — so we are talking about inequality here.

But, we were able to receive support from *Fundayacucho*, which is a foundation under the Ministry of Education.[7] These are the contradictions we have in the government. The people inside Fundayacucho understand this project, but the people working directly in the Ministry don't. They provided us with 100,000 *Bolívares Fuertes*.[8] This was seed money to allow the mothers to continue working as volunteers. This made us all very happy because this also has to do with our self-esteem — we made a proposal that was taken into account and we got a response from a government institution that is difficult for people from the *barrio* to see. The relationship with this institution has been very good because there has been a lot of follow-through and accompaniment; not just with the funding but also with support in achieving the objectives of the project.

The Door has opened a Crack

With Chávez, these doors have opened. A new path is available to improve the lives of women. But really, our concern goes beyond the language of gender inclusion, and the political participation of women. The larger struggle is to change the culture. This is necessary for women to achieve real justice. We want to see a change in the "family load," meaning how our society values women and where responsibilities are shared between men and women. It must go to the heart of our culture.

We know that the Chávez administration understands the importance of creating policies that include the women of *barrios* and housewives because poverty has a greater impact on women than men. It is very encouraging to see the government embrace this new vision. The National Women's Institute was created; Banmujer is providing socio-productive loans. The protection for women and family has been strengthened since 2007 with the passage of the Law on the Right of Women to a Life Free of Violence. This process actually examined the different forms of violence established by patriarchy and *machismo* as a cultural and ideological system. The creation of The Ministry of Women and Gender Equality in March of 2009 was another very significant step. But I have to say that the bureaucracy swallows good intentions. I think it is a mistake to keep strengthening the institutions. The communities are ready to make the changes. The struggle continues to be the divide between institutions and popular power.

The Future

I see the progress we have made in my lifetime and it is encouraging. I also look to the future with fear. The blinders have come off which means we have no excuse for not achieving what we know to be possible. Economic dependency still exists which puts us in the crossfire of the woes of capitalism. I can see the boys and girls who are today isolated from the struggle in which I participated. The onslaught of capitalism and the values that come with it have made a mark on the younger generation. Popular education, with our own values, will bring us to the next level. Without that, we will not achieve the socialism that we are striving for — socialism with real democratic values. I believe we have the ability to achieve this if we are not derailed. There are many amongst us that call themselves revolutionaries though are actually reformists. We must continue to push and not let that element guide this revolution.

FIVE

Marianela Tovar.

Marianela Tovar, Contranatura

(Caracas)

I t only takes place once a year, but it is by far the most colorful march in Venezuela. A smiling lesbian couple walks by hand in hand, as cheerful rainbow-painted marchers dance to the music and wave at the dumbfounded passers-by. A flock of beautiful men extravagantly dressed in high heels and long flowing gowns do remarkably well to keep pace with the massive march as it winds through eastern Caracas towards Plaza Venezuela. A young bare-chested gymnast, Georgi Martinez Torres, flips his way down the street.

"[We are here] to show the community that we don't just go out at night, as many believe," he says. "And we are going to demonstrate how many of us there are. And that's what we want to show to the community, that we are growing and that people are becoming aware of this." Torres is an organizer with the gay rights organization, Lambda, one of the coordinators of the annual Venezuelan LGBT Pride March. Lambda is one of a dozen sexual diversity organizations that shot on to the Venezuelan scene shortly after Chávez took the reins in 1999.

In 2000, just a handful of marchers came out to the first Gay Pride March ever in Venezuela. In 2008, attendance had jumped to 40,000 people, and the parade was sponsored by the pro-Chávez Metropolitan Mayor's office of Caracas.

"The government has encouraged us to organize. There isn't the sense of repression that existed before," says Marianela Tovar, a long-time LGBT activist, and a founder of the sexual diversity organization, *Contranatura*. Over the last seven years, her organization has worked in the academic, political, and activist arena to promote LGBT rights in Venezuela.

The political situation for Venezuela's LGBT community has improved dramatically over the last decade, but "there is still a lot of homophobia, a lot of sexism, a lot of lesbiophobia and transphobia," says Tovar. Since their creation, Contranatura has taken their battle against homophobia to the university and the government — even confronting the "conservative positions" within the *Chavista* movement.

They have recently been fighting an uphill "battle" for the inclusion of sexual diversity issues (such as the legalization of same sex unions and the recognition of transsexual sexual identity) in the National Assembly's proposed Organic Law for Gender Equity and Equality. The community is also battling the rapid spread of HIV and AIDS. An estimated 40,000 Venezuelans are infected in the country and roughly 70 percent of those who are infected don't even know it.[1] Fortunately, the Venezuelan government provides medicine to HIV and AIDS patients free of charge. Despite leading an admittedly small organization that faces many challenges ahead, Tovar says she is "optimistic about the future."

Marianela Tovar

Personal History

I'm *Caraqueña.*[2] My mother is Mexican. My dad is Venezuelan, and I've lived here in Caracas my whole life. I'm part of the generation that was born with the petroleum boom. I was born in '73. And since I've been politically conscious, I've been an activist among the ranks of the left.

Since I was in the university, I was never in the closet but I wasn't an activist. I had a partner in the university, but I never hid it, and afterwards I had partners and I never hid it. But I wasn't an activist in any sexual diversity organization because, first in the 1980s, the organization that existed then, *Entendido*, was practically all men. The other organization in 1990, *Movimiento Ambiente* (Ambient Movement), was also led by a man.[3] So I didn't identify with the organizations enough to be active in them.

The group from the 1980s lasted only a short time because many of its activists fell sick with HIV. This obviously affected the politics of the LGBT community here.

I graduated from the university in 1986.[4] First I was an activist with the Communist Party, and then I started to work in the office of propaganda. And I also saw the very misogynous, sexist behavior of the employees and activists in the party, and that had a lot to do with my break from the party.

In 1993, I went to the United States to study and to work, but remained unconnected from political work. I had lived there for a year when I was seven. My dad went to do a doctorate at Harvard, and in a way, I think I wanted to see the monster from the inside.

It was in the United States that I met LGBT leftist activists. We met and I didn't hide my sexual preference, but I still wasn't active in any LGBT organization, because at this time I thought that activism for social change was more important than sexual diversity.

This was an important experience because I saw that not everyone on the left, not all of the left-wing activists in political parties, where homophobic. That it wasn't like here. There, the left-wing parties had adopted the feminist agenda, and the agenda of the sexual diversity groups instead of rejecting them. It's been like this in Mexico and in other countries in Latin America, but not here.

Here, the women have even had to leave the left-wing parties in order to push the women's agenda. The only party that included the women's agenda, and which had a feminist group, was the *Movimiento Al Socialismo* (MAS - Movement Towards Socialism), which divided from the Communist Party.

I came back from the United States at the end of 1996, and I wasn't active with any organization at this time. The sexism and the homophobia had started to affect me, as well as all of the discrimination towards sexual diversity. And like today, I'm not going to be active in a party where they are not combating this. That would be taking a step back for me.

Forming Contranatura

In 2002, two friends, Rodrigo Navarrete and Carlos Gutiérrez, and I decided to form Contranatura, because although there were some sexual diversity organizations, there was a problem with the theory and the political education, so we felt it was necessary to create an organization focused on education and theory.[5]

It began as a study group, and we started to meet weekly to study and discuss what we read. At that time we had as many as twenty people in the group, who came together each week to study. The majority of these people were students at the university, and not just lesbian, gay, and transsexual, but also heterosexual. We organized various events, and all of these activities were connected to the academic arena. It's in just the last few years that Contranatura has moved towards political activism and outside of the university.

Perhaps the most significant thing we have done was to participate in the proposal of the Constitutional Reforms, which took place in 2007. Throughout the whole year we were working so they would include various articles to guarantee the rights of the LGBT communities. Like a change to the article on marriage, because the article in the constitution says that marriage is between a man and a woman. We wanted them to change it to marriage between two people in order to open the door for us.

Article 21 guarantees us the right to not be discriminated against, but we wanted it to speak explicitly to the non-discrimination of sexual orientation, as well as gender.

We wanted the National Assembly representatives to include gender identity in the article on the reform proposal. We also supported the feminist agenda and wanted them to speak specifically to the decriminalization of abortion and to guarantee payment to the housewives. Remuneration is already written in article 88, but it hasn't taken place in practice, and we wanted the explicit compensation for domestic work. We also wanted adoption rights for partners of the same sex. These were many of the points that we brought to the table during the discussions on the constitutional reform.

We did university forums, activism, got the word out and painted the streets with graffiti. We met with National Assembly representatives. We met with everyone possible to promote our agenda of sexual diversity and feminism. We came together in a coalition that was called *Grupo S*, which was formed for this purpose and for this year alone.[6] As soon as the process of the Constitutional Reform ended with the defeat of the proposal, we went our separate ways.[7]

Now we are creating a degree in sexual diversity at the Central University. It's the first such degree at the university. It has never been done before for both undergraduate and postgraduate students. We have also taught sexual diversity courses in the women's post-graduate studies program, which is the first time this has also been done.

We participate in all of the political activities that the sexual diversity groups convoke. We do investigative work. We have been published in university magazines. It's not just political work in the streets, but rather we penetrate academia. The themes of sexual diversity and feminism should not be secondary themes, but rather they should be themes that the university takes into account.

Contranatura, above all, has done various workshops about sexual diversity in the National Women's Institute (INAMUJER). We made contact with [the director] María León. She has supported our agenda of sexual diversity, but we believe that the employees that attend to the problems of Venezuelan women have to be sensitized towards lesbians, transgender, and the transsexual, because at some point they are going to come to them with a problem, and there shouldn't be a discriminatory response on the part of the employees. So we did some workshops around this, we also did some workshops in the Madres del Barrio Mission, because obviously there are also single lesbian and transsexual mothers in the *barrios* that need economic support from the government, so we held the workshops to sensitize the employees so they aren't going to shut the door just because they are lesbian or transsexual. We believe that these are very important areas, because the missions and institutes, like the National Women's Institute, work with vulnerable populations and they need to be sensitized to sexual diversity.

Government Openness to Sexual Diversity

Really our relationship with the government has been positive. I don't have complaints. I think that, in the sense that you present yourself as an activist and have an attitude that is respected — not someone with fears and insecurities and with attitudes of victimization — the government bodies are open.

I have to be honest that the organizations that have been created under Chávez have not shut the doors. They open the doors. We do the workshops, but there is no policy of continuity. That's the problem. I think that INAMUJER should have a small group of employees specialized in working with lesbians and sexual diversity, because obviously not everyone is heterosexual. I believe that the same goes for Madres del Barrio, and various government organizations that work with vulnerable populations. The only one that had an office for the LGBT community was the Metropolitan Caracas Mayor's Office under Juan Barreto, which ran out of the Office of Citizen's Attention.[8] This was a good initiative, and it worked well, but now with Mayor Ledezma, they closed the office.[9]

Chávez & Growth of the LGBT Movement

Chávez won the elections in 1998, and took office in 1999. It's significant that sexual diversity organizations began to flourish after the year 2000. A dozen have been formed, from the year 2000 till now. This is significant, because it is a sign that there was a change in the political atmosphere before Chávez and after Chávez. Why didn't these organizations appear before? Why did they only arise at exactly the moment that Chávez took power? Because, obviously, there is a climate that sponsors political organization in the country, which has sprung up since Chávez came to power.

The new constitution may be a factor, but I don't think it had the biggest influence. I think that it was the new political climate created in the country after Chávez. There was a political spark. Before there was apathy and indifference towards politics; there was a very pessimistic attitude towards the future of the country, but with the arrival of Chávez this changed. There was a very positive attitude that things are going to get better; that the country is going to have a better future; that there is going to be social change. There was an interest in politics that didn't exist before, a new necessity to organize.

It's not that the government has a policy towards sexual diversity or feminism, but the government has encouraged us to organize. There isn't the sense of repression that existed before. Of course, there is still a lot of homophobia, a lot of sexism, a lot of lesbiophobia and transphobia, but there is a feeling that we can organize and we aren't going to suffer consequences for being organized.

It's also important to point out that many of these [sexual diversity] organizations aren't *Chavista* organizations.[10] The majority of them are anti-Chávez. They are in the opposition. They don't explicitly come out against Chávez, but when they speak they openly express their posture towards the government. Nevertheless, this hasn't meant any type of repression.

Why are they anti-Chavista? I think they have bought the anti-Chávez discourse for various reasons. Without political education, many have let themselves be dragged down by the influence of the mainstream media. Others are profoundly conservative and anti-communist. So regardless of Chávez, if you put someone else on the left there, they'd be against that person, too.

They don't see the benefits that have been achieved in many vulnerable populations, economically as well as with women, Afro-Venezuelans and indigenous peoples, but rather they are only worried about the problems that affect sexual diversity. So these people are anti-Chavista simply because they are conservatives.

Venezuelan LGBT Pride March

There was no gay march before Chávez. This is part of the new climate that was created with Chávez. There weren't many people in the first march though, and it has been growing. Now a lot of people go. I didn't go to the last one, but they told me there were something like 40,000 people there here in Caracas. The only march in Venezuela is held here in Caracas. The last two marches before this year were sponsored by the Metropolitan Mayor's Office of Caracas including the stage and everything. They were openly involved in the organization of the marches. Now with the new mayor, Ledezma, this has changed. It's not going to be the same. Of course, I have my differences with these marches because I think that they are very de-politicized. That's why I didn't go last year. It's like a parade with a big party, but it doesn't have political content.

Sexual Diversity Groups in Venezuela

The majority of the groups are still dominated by men — groups like *Acción Afirmativa* (Affirmative Action), *Alianza Lambda de Venezuela* (The Lambda Venezuela Alliance), and *El Bloque Socialista Homosexual* (Homosexual Socialist Block). *Bloque Socialista Homosexual* is a group of homosexual young men that are active in the PSUV. The majority of them are male. Fortunately transsexual organizations have arisen, like *Transvenus de Venezuela* and *Divas de Venezuela*, which didn't exist before. And there are lesbian organizations like *Reflejos* (Reflections) and *Colectivo Lesbiana Josefa Camejo* (The Josefa Camejo Lesbian Collective), and there's us, *Contranatura*. We are not identified as specifically lesbian or gay, but rather sexual diversity. We accept all sexual diversity among our members including heterosexuals, because we believe that otherwise you are very limited.

The 1999 Constitution

During the constituent assembly, the sexual diversity groups put together an agenda of articles for the new constitution, which was obviously set back by the political right-wing and the Catholic Church. The pressure from the Church and the conservative groups was very strong, although the conservative position in terms of sexuality isn't just from people on the right. Within *Chavismo* there are some very conservative positions in terms of sexuality and sexual diversity, very conservative.[11]

The Organic Law for Gender Equity and Equality

The Organic Law for Gender Equity and Equality is a project that has been launched within the National Assembly, specifically by the Commission of Family, Women, and Youth, which is directed by Marelis Pérez Marcano, who is in the PSUV. It is a law that touches on everything that has to do with inequality between men and women — issues dealing with reproductive rights and domestic work — things that have been espoused in the constitution.

The sexual diversity groups, building off of the proposals made by the Assembly representative Romelia Matute, felt like it was important to incorporate our demands — specifically the legalization of civil unions between people of the same sex and the recognition of the sexual identity of transsexuals. Romelia Matute's proposal included the requirement that the government pay for sex change operations. When she made her proposal public, Marelis Pérez Marcano immediately pronounced herself against the inclusion of that article.

So we began to battle on various fronts — in the media, in academic spaces, including going into the street to protest. How can an organic law talking about gender equality be approached from such a hetero-centric point of view? As if we have nothing to do with that law.

We organized a march around mid-August 2009 along with various sexual diversity organizations. At the end of the march a proposal was taken to Marelis Pérez Marcano. But she has clearly responded that the demands of sexual diversity groups will not be included in the law. She made the excuse that this issue was not discussed at the World Conference on Women in Beijing.[12] We had to remind her that it was discussed there and also in all the following international conferences. But, regardless it's not like we should just stay stuck in Beijing, like everything ended there! We also told her that these issue had been included in the laws of various countries concerning gender equality.

This is an issue of political pragmatism because she is worried that evangelicals and fanatics from the Catholic Church are going to come out against her, and that she will lose their votes. This is also an issue of her own prejudices, of her own homophobia and transphobia. She doesn't make any political or legal arguments. Venezuela has signed onto international agreements that obligate it to recognize these things. So we should be consistent with these international conventions. When you approach it from a political perspective, there is no argument. This is a personal problem of hers.

The law has now been frozen. They haven't returned to talk about it. I don't know if this is because they know that we will protest again or if the National Assembly is just interested in other issues right now... maybe they consider other laws to be more important right now. But our sense is that we will not be included in the law even though there are other representatives in the National Assembly who have publicly supported us.

Chávez & Sexual Diversity

On *Aló Presidente*, Chávez said that you couldn't discriminate against homosexuals. From what I have heard or read, he has never made an openly homophobic comment.[13] Many *Chavistas* that are with him have. Nevertheless, I don't believe that he has a significant policy towards sexual diversity. I mean, he is simply not homophobic, but nor is it an issue that interests him, nor is it a priority, nor is it on his agenda.

PSUV & Sexual Diversity

Within the PSUV there are many, many leaders who are homophobic; that have made homophobic comments. One of them is Mario Silva, who is the host of *La Hojilla*.[14] On his program he has made homophobic comments, he has joked above all, about a journalist that has a program on Globovisión, but he joked by making a reference to this journalist's sexual orientation. I think Silva and others' positions are incoherent, because they attack the homophobia of the groups on the right, in the opposition, but they too make homophobic remarks. So, Silva shows it, he criticizes it, but he doesn't appear to see his own homophobic comments.

I'm not saying that everyone is homophobic. Many of the activists in the PSUV lack education with respect to feminism, gender theory, and even more so, sexual diversity. They don't see that there are contradictions in their socialist discourse and their homophobic and sexist positions.

Sexual Diversity in the Government

Yes, there are LGBT people in the government, in public positions of great responsibility and leadership, but they are in the closet. There is no one who is openly gay. It's as if they continue to think that these are private issues and not public. There is a lesbian that has a high office in the government, a female minister, and everyone knows that she is lesbian, but she doesn't say so. She should say that she's a lesbian because to say so is a political act, and in a way it would combat that general misconception that lesbians don't exist.

Changes in Respect for Sexual Diversity

Venezuelans talk more about the issue now. And you see, above all, the young men with much less fear. They are bolder, they express themselves more and openly show their sexual orientation. Nevertheless there is a lot of homophobia. A lot of homophobia. I think we Venezuelans have progressed little in this. They aren't going to attack you directly, but yes, there is homophobia and rejection.

Discrimination in the Workplace

There is still workplace discrimination, and this shows you the weakness of the sexual diversity organizations, that everyone is still doing their work on their own. We are fragmented, divided. We don't have a broad base. I mean, we are two or three people, and we don't have this solid connection with the LGBT population. We are in the minority. We are working in a disconnected way, without a clear political agenda and without impactful work with the LGBT population. This means that people don't feel protected. Lesbians and homosexuals are the object of discrimination, which they don't dare denounce — workplace discrimination, sexual assault, violence. In other words, these acts of discrimination happen and they go unpunished and unrecognized because they are not denounced. Very few cases of this type are denounced, because people are not going to expose themselves to say that someone has discriminated against them because they are homosexual.

Many Closets

There are a lot of closets here. The problem with the closet is really serious. It's very big. Not just with the lesbians, but also with the homosexuals. This is a problem that the organizations have. The people use excuses not to leave the closet. There is a huge fear to be identified as a lesbian or a homosexual. So it's very difficult for us to do political work.

I have been discriminated against for my physical appearance because I am not a feminine woman, and you know that here in Venezuela, that's a crime. It's practically a crime against humanity not to have make-up on, nor have high heels, nor have gone to the beauty salon. So I have received disrespectful comments. Fortunately, I have not suffered direct violence as other lesbians have. But yes, disrespectful, rude comments, disapproving looks in the women's bathroom, even women that have been frightened thinking that I am a guy. They laugh, this type of thing.

I don't think that they have openly discriminated against me at work. I imagine it's because of my attitude, which is not of fear, nor of humiliation, but rather it's as if people know who they're messing with. That's why I say that the people who are in the closet don't know the harm that this does. The closet kills, because when you are in the closet, the only person who believes that you are in the closet is you. Everyone else knows your actual sexual orientation. They attack you, and discriminate against you without regard because since you're in the closet, they know that you're never going to do anything. On top of this you feel your own homophobia, the feeling of humiliation of being homosexual and lesbian.

Violence Against Transsexuals

Right now most of the violence is directed against transsexuals, from the police and from the clients of many of the sex workers. Many of the transsexuals feel forced to do sex work. Why? It's the only way that they can be their true gender identity. I mean a female transsexual cannot exercise her work with her new gender identity because they don't accept her. I know of a female transsexual who was a nurse, and couldn't work as a nurse because they demanded that she present herself as a man. So many feel forced to work in a hair salon or as sex workers, because in order to work in what they would prefer, they would have to violate their gender identity, and they are obviously not going to do this, because for them, their gender identity is a matter of life and death. The police assault them in every way — rape, beatings, sexual harassment, but where are they going to go to denounce it? In fact there's a problem right now, because a short while ago they killed five transsexuals here in Caracas, but nobody cares, and it wasn't even in any newspaper.

Media and Sexual Diversity

Yes, there have been changes. Right now, we lesbians, homosexuals, transgender and transsexuals appear more in the media and they call us for interviews for special programs much more than before. It's not all the time, but at least they listen to our point of view. Not like before. Before, you could count the number of times that a homosexual appeared on an opinion program or in an interview. It was really rare. Now it happens more frequently, so in this sense there has been a change. Nevertheless, the media also broadcasts homophobic messages and homophobic positions of the homosexual male stereotype. They continue in their traditional attitude and only open the door to us sometimes in order to be politically correct, but we take advantage of these cracks that they open for us, and at least they hear our voice every once in a while.

Weaknesses in the Movement

The few sexual diversity organizations on the left with a political foundation share visions and strategies with Latin American organizations, in a common agenda. But I think that the sexual diversity movement here is very weak, quantitatively as well as politically, in comparison with similar movements in Mexico, Argentina and Brazil. And compared with the capacity of these organizations to convoke and mobilize, I would say that ours is laughable. These groups have a large number of members, a great number of action alerts, and clear political strategy, while the majority of us don't.

We don't have enough work in the grassroots. We are still too isolated from the people we are supposed to represent. You can't just be an activist on the Internet or on Facebook. You have to do work in the street. Some of the only outreach work that gets done, in the case of some of the male gay rights groups, is to go to the bars to pass out condoms… which is good. But that is just a palliative measure to prevent the spread of STDs. The organization *Reflejos* has various programs, like providing psychological consultations, but not political work. Political work would be going to the bars and trying to get people organized.

Connections with Social Movements

We have been meeting with a new group that we are form-ing called *Sexualidad Liberada* (Liberated Sexuality). There are two men, but it mostly has a feminist focus. There is a member from the landless movement, members from the Pachamama Front, members from the Ezequiel Zamora Campesino Front, and other social movements. I mean, they are not people who belong to the sexual diversity or feminist movements, but rather they are from the *campesino* fronts. So we are establishing these connections now. There is going to be a meeting of the Ezequiel Zamora Campesino Front and we are going to participate by bringing these gender is-sues to the table.

HIV Politics Under Chávez

The quality of help for people who are HIV positive and with AIDS has changed. For example, the state gives those infected the medicine free of charge, and I think this is significant. It is not like in other countries where HIV positive patients don't have access to medicine. Here there is free and universal access. There has been a clear policy by the Ministry of Health, and there are many organi-zations that are exclusively dedicated to working with HIV/AIDS patients. In this case, there has been a significant change. On the other hand, preventative policies haven't changed nearly at all.

Sex Education

There are sex education and prevention policies but not with the aggressiveness there should be, given the large number of sexu-ally transmitted diseases that the population has. Also a large amount of the population has HPV, the Human Papillomavirus, and this is obviously because they don't use a condom. HIV is very high in heterosexual women as well, which is transmitted to them by their husbands and boyfriends. So I think there are no overwhelmingly bold, aggressive polices and massive sex education. In this case, the state has an unresolved debt, not just to prevent HIV, but to help prevent all of the sexually transmitted diseases, and to also prevent unwanted births. We are the country with the highest number of pregnant teenagers in all of Latin America. This clearly tells you that the policies of sex education are practically non-existent.

In the high school curriculum, they are working on the subject of sex education, but this is an issue that still doesn't touch sexual diversity. I imagine that it must come up in class, but it's not part of the curriculum. Above all, the curriculum is oriented towards sexual and reproductive rights — how to use a condom, and these things. Within the universities, it is only recently that groups like us have been raising these issues of sexual diversity.

Contranatura & the Future

I am very optimistic about the future. Despite conservative positions on sexual issues, as much from the people who define themselves as *Chavistas* — or from the left who are critical of *Chavismo* — as well as the right, I feel very optimistic about the future. I believe that there have been very important changes in the country; changes not only in the economic situation of a large part of the population, but I believe that the conditions are also ripe for a change in mentality.

Cultural changes and changes in the perception of the world are always much slower. They take much more time, but I believe the conditions are right. Perhaps I will not see these changes, but I believe that we have a contribution to make by investigating the theory and to continue participating in political activities, such as the legislative initiatives, and to continue proposing changes that help to remove the discriminatory situation of the sexual diversity population.

Well in the short term, we are working to open up a permanent chair of sexual diversity in the university. We are speaking with the publisher, *El Perro y la Rana,* so that among the books they publish, they release a line of work about sexuality. And in the long term, to continue pushing so that the issue of sexuality, gender, women, and diversity is taken as a top priority on the political agenda of the country. And other projects will come up along the road. We are not going to end with homophobia, but we are going to make our small contribution.

Part III:

WORKERS & LABOR

SIX

Félix Martínez & Richard La Rosa.

Félix Martinez & Richard La Rosa,
The New Generation of Workers Union of the Mitsubishi Motor Corporation

(Barcelona, Anzoátegui)

The barrage of freight trucks barreling down the asphalt streets of central Barcelona form an incessant stream of traffic. They speed past the monotonous backdrop of auto parts stores and body shops that line this concrete jungle, carrying cars and every imaginable auto part to the multiple ports along Venezuela's northern coast in order to be transported to the rest of the world. The heat is unbearable, and is only accentuated by the freight trucks' bursting fumes. There are very few sidewalks in Barcelona's Los Montones Industrial Zone — just factories surrounded by little more than streets and dirt.

While Barcelona may be better known for its beaches and well-preserved colonial architecture, its industrial zone is rugged and working class. With its dilapidated buildings and congested streets, it is now becoming notorious for its insurgent workers movement emerging from the automobile and auto parts manufacturing plants clustered here. In recent years, the workers in these companies have maintained a rhythm of constant action, organizing a relentless wave of marches, strikes, and factory occupations to challenge attacks on their collective contracts and attempts at weakening unions through the use of subcontracted employees.

Taking up President Chávez's call to create a socialist society, they are confronting their own companies as well as government bureaucrats in their attempts to make socialist rhetoric a reality. Even amidst government policies supporting the poor and working class, labor activists in Venezuela have been met with opposition in the form of both bureaucracy and bullets. But the greatest obstacle that these workers face is a fractured union movement that has prevented them from establishing a truly united and dynamic federation. Félix Martínez and Richard La Rosa, two leaders in the *Sindicato Nueva Generación de Trabajadores de Mitsubishi* (SINGETRAM - New Generation of Workers Union) at the Mitsubishi Motors Corporation plant in Barcelona, are convinced that only through developing a "new kind of union" that overcomes the internal bureaucracy plaguing past unions will workers be able to develop such a federation.

The *Confederación de Trabajadores de Venezuela* (CTV - Venezuelan Workers' Confederation), the primary union federation prior to 2003, had dominated the Venezuelan labor movement for nearly half a century, often through a clientelistic relationship with Venezuela's dominant political parties. When President Rafael Caldera turned towards implementing neoliberal policies in 1995, the CTV remained passive in the face of deteriorating labor benefits and the privatization of industry.[1] Félix and Richard become visibly angered talking about the sense of disregard they felt under their former CTV - associated union at the plant. "Even with a law in place to protect us, and with a union at the factory, we would see our rights being violated," says Richard.

Witnessing the demise of its political power with the downfall of the Punto Fijo Pact and Chávez's ascendance to the presidency, the CTV leadership bitterly attacked the new government. In an act of betrayal to their working class constituency, CTV leaders allied themselves with Venezuela's elite business federation FEDECAMARAS in supporting first the 2002 coup attempt against Chávez and subsequently the oil lockout carried out by the management of the national oil company, PDVSA. In 2003, those union leaders supportive of Chávez regrouped to form a new labor federation, the *Unión Nacional de Trabajadores* (UNT - National Worker's Union), after recognizing that the CTV was out of their control and beyond repair.

With over 1,200 delegates in attendance, the UNT's first national congress overflowed with an ecstatic outpouring of proposals and projects committed to creating a new union movement based on a truly working class and democratic foundation.[2] But the foundation was born divided into various labor tendencies holding distinct viewpoints on goals and their relationship to the national government.[3] These divisions have only deepened with time as one of the labor tendencies, the *Frente Socialista Bolivariana de Trabajadores* (FSBT - The Bolivarian Socialist Workers Front), has now called for the creation of a new union federation.[4]

Impacted by their experiences in challenging and eventually replacing their old factory union, workers like Félix and Richard seek to unify the working class into an independent and united force by creating a participatory union. They belong to the *Corriente Marxista Revolucionaria* (CMR - Marxist Revolutionary Current), an organization that has predominantly engaged in the occupied factories movement in Venezuela, but is now attempting to create a space within the labor movement by promoting this concept of a "new type of union." The defining characteristic of this "new type of union" is a horizontal structure driven by the rank-and-file with a strong base in the local community through links with the communal councils. While it is a marginal faction within the UNT, the CMR has brought significant attention to itself through the bold actions of affiliated unions such as SINGETRAM. The workers at the Mitsubishi Motor plant have now become an important point of reference and respect amongst workers throughout the country as their struggle has led them to confront both bullets and bureaucracy with chants of "We are not afraid!"

Félix Martínez & Richard La Rosa

Personal Histories and History of the Union

Félix Martínez: My name is Félix Martínez, Secretary-General of the union. I am the quality control inspector in the production line and, what can I say, we have been in this struggle since 2003. I am originally from Caracas, from the Carapita *barrio*. With a lot of effort, I got my high school diploma, but my experience attempting to enter the Central of Venezuela was very difficult, because it is challenging for someone from a low-income background to enter the University. After taking a test to enter the University, and being one of the people that passed it, the rector of the School of Languages, where I was applying, called me into a meeting. He asked me who my family was. This was an incredibly demoralizing question because what it made me understand was that if I was not from a prominent family, it was going to be very difficult for me to enter into the School of Languages. He told me that I should go study at a private institute instead, but I had no way of paying that. My parents could only offer me so much. They are *buhoneros*. They sell *hallacas* and juices at a stand in the El Cementerio market in Caracas.[5]

Well, after working at a clothing store for a long time, there came a moment when I decided to move here to Barcelona. My father is originally from Carupano, here in the eastern region and my mother is from Colombia. I told them I was coming here because we had family and people we knew all around, and I was hoping to get a job that was Monday through Friday because I was tired of that

Sunday to Sunday kind of work that's the most common in Caracas. When I first arrived, I got a job at the Hotel Maremares, which was a really abusive job. I worked there for about six months and was let go because of a staff reduction due to the low tourist season. I began to work with Mitsubishi Motors Corporation later that year. I began working in the labor struggle towards the end of 2002 when the oil strike was taking place. Starting around January 2003 the company began trying to attack our labor rights. They tried to force a 50 percent wage cut on us, which the union we had at that time permitted. The union tolerated all kinds of threats and unwarranted firings. It was a part of the CTV and was directed by somebody who had been a union leader when Ford Motor Company was originally running the factory. We saw that this union was ceding the rights of the workers, not defending our rights.

On the other hand, we heard the things being said by the national government: that no company can lower labor standards or fire an employee without just cause. We saw the contradiction between what the government was saying and what this company was trying to do, as well as the attempts of these business owners to attack the government, a government that we consider to be the only one to support the working class and the poor. So we decided to confront the union officials and we began to identify who could take up leadership roles amongst the workers. In a meeting we held amongst 800 workers of the factory, only 186 decided to organize and confront the union. Under the old union, we didn't have the democratic freedom to have internal elections, so we decided to form a parallel union. The company was trying to fire some of us and we had to find another way to protect ourselves. So we united to form a new organization, which we now represent, the New Generation of Workers Union.[6]

Richard La Rosa: My name is Richard La Rosa. I am the Press and Communications Secretary for the union. I also come from a humble family. My father was a farm worker and my mother was also a *buhonero*. I have six siblings. My parents separated, and my mother was the one that took care of all six of us. She sold *empanadas,* hot dogs, as well as clothing on the street. I dropped out of high school a year before graduating, and began to work on my own. I told my mother that I would put forth the same kind of effort that she did towards raising us towards my siblings who were all younger than me. So I started to work really hard. I worked in construction for about four years, which was hard work. Afterwards, I was able to get a job with Vivex, a company that produces windows for automobiles, where I stayed for nine years. I always saw the manager's awful treatment of the workers and I didn't tolerate it. I would always speak out against it. So the supervisor had me fired just for not tolerating that kind of treatment. Afterwards, I got a job with another company called Macusa, an auto parts factory, which makes armchairs for Mitsubishi. I lasted about four months there before I was dismissed for the same reason. I saw the appalling treatment of the workers and would talk to them, saying, "Listen, *compañeros* we can't continue accepting this kind of treatment. We need to do something. We need to organize ourselves!" But can you imagine? With the fear the workers had, they would prefer to go on accepting that awful treatment and low pay, rather than risk losing their jobs. At that time there was no union in that factory.

I went without work for about five or six months, after which by chance I got a job at the Mitsubishi plant. I worked as an operator on the assembly line with Félix, and the tremendous exploitation at the plant became very clear to us. Even with a law in place to protect us, and with a union at the factory, we would see our rights being violated. We had no right to make demands or complaints. When we would go file a grievance with the union, the leaders would simply tell us, "You come here to work. There are plenty of people out there that would like your job and you can be replaced." It was horrible! We had to put up with this! Félix and I would always talk and we asked ourselves, "How long can we keep putting up with this kind of treatment? Is someone ever going to come and organize to get this union to do something?" And Félix said to me, "Listen, we have to do this ourselves." This was such a delicate discussion that we always had, that we could lose our jobs over. Félix said to me, "We have to form a group of workers that are reliable." Félix would ask me who I trusted in my assembly line, where there were about fifty to sixty workers. I would look down both sides of the line and I couldn't say that I trusted anybody, only myself. It was terrible. If the workers heard someone talking about organizing, they would go to the supervisor or the union, and that person would be fired.

At that time, the company had us working only half time. To give you an idea of the magnitude of the exploitation we were living, we were still expected to produce the same amount as in a whole day but were only paid for half the workday. But I say, if God permits things to happen it is for a reason, because the free time that we had gave us the opportunity to meet, debate, and talk to the other workers. The majority of workers were not with us at first. There was a lot of fear, because of threats from the union. But with effort, we went about winning the workers over little by little.

Creating a New Type of Union

Félix: Our union constitution committed us to not develop the same customs as the old union, which had been led by people that would come to the factory at a certain time, eat, and then leave afterwards. Or if they didn't leave, they would go to their office, smoke a cigarette, and read the newspaper. When somebody would go to them to solicit a complaint, they wouldn't pay any attention. We couldn't continue with this kind of attitude. Our goal was to have constant meetings and generate discussion amongst the workers during our breaks. We created a plan of action and an orientation different from the last union. As a result, the majority of the workers affiliated themselves with our union within six months. Having the majority of the workers in our union allowed us to be officially recognized by the Ministry of Labor. This allowed us to begin to fight for the workers' rights and begin to recover all that had been lost. In this way, the workers began to gain confidence in our positions and ideas. We were with the workers constantly, responding to them, protesting for their rights. This carried us, regardless of the strategies being used by the company to debilitate us. They were offering us what we called an "unhappy salary package" so that the workers themselves would decide to quit. Around 200 workers left the factory around that time. Of the 600 that remained, about 25 people affiliated with the old union stayed behind. Some of those in the old union negotiated with the managers, behind the back of the workers, for a sum of money to leave the company. The contract expired in 2002 and it was time to bargain for a new one. At that time, only four directors from the old union stayed behind. We negotiated the new collective bargaining agreement and these four accepted the new benefits we obtained.

After winning the new contract in 2004, we asked ourselves, "What actions do we take now as an organization?" We proposed the idea of inventing a new type of union. We asked ourselves what the vision, mission, general and specific objectives of a new kind of union should be. Through this process, we developed our constitution. While the union has a vertical structure on paper, it does not function that way. It functions completely horizontally, with a coordination team. The coordination team has three secretariats: the Secretary-General, the Secretary of Records and Finances, and the Secretary of Coordination. Being the three principal secretariats, they have to constantly work with the other committees. We have four committees apart from the coordination team made up of union members.

We have a Sports and Culture Committee, which includes twenty-seven workers. They discuss and debate what the union should be doing around culture and sports for the rest of the workers. We have the Press and Communications Committee, where Richard is, which includes another group of twenty-seven workers from various production lines. They are responsible for collecting information about the situation within our union, and other unions, and compiling that into publications which the workers can use to read, analyze, debate, and present their own ideas and proposals. We also have the Health and Welfare Committee, which is in charge of occupational health and safety, with people focused on injury prevention, but also with any social problems affecting the workers. The workers go to them if they are having problems at home, for example if their children are sick. They also support workers with disabilities. We have the Contract Enforcement and Conflict Committee, with the participation of another group of twenty-seven workers. They are in charge of monitoring that the company is complying with our contract and helping workers to get organized in order to file any grievances. They also support the ideological education of the workers. We have 150 workers in the union participating and working together.

Building Democracy Inside the Union

Félix: We now have six years organized as a union and we are discussing moving to the next stage. The current union representatives were elected through a process of debate within worker assemblies organized by production line, but we didn't have an electoral structure with direct and secret voting. Since 2005, we have been developing this step by step. We want to legalize the structure of the union by reforming the union statutes. We believe that for this structure to be real then what we have on paper must surge from debate amongst the workers, from the experience of the workers. It is necessary that the workers now debate, strengthen, and decide in an assembly what statutes they want the union to have. The process of reforming the statutes should be as democratic as possible. At the end of the year, we are going to have union elections, where 150 representatives are going to be elected from the 1,200 workers we have in the factory. These are "representatives," in quotation marks, because we simply lead by obeying the orders of the workers. We want the workers to be vigilant of the union leadership. Any decision by the workers to immediately revoke someone from a leadership position will be possible. Our goal is to truly democratize and strengthen the working class movement.

Developing Ideological Consciousness

Richard: One of our main concerns as an organization is the ideological formation of workers as a class. We must fight against this capitalist system, but with a clear consciousness of why we are in this struggle. We are looking for a truly just system where we have equality, health, and decent housing, but how do we achieve that? By educating the working class. Since we are the ones that produce and generate wealth we need to liberate ourselves, and take control of the companies and the political power.

Félix: We believe that we mainly have to know who we are as a working class. Undoubtedly, we have to develop a historical analysis of the working class struggle. We believe that one of the tools that the working class must study is Marxism. We have to study the Communist Manifesto, historical materialism, without forgetting the essence of our reality: who we are in this country and Venezuela's historical conditions. We are strengthening ourselves with all of this. We have done a lot of research using the Italian worker model of occupational safety and health in order to look at these issues and defend ourselves in the factory.[7] We believe that one of the weaknesses of the working class here in Venezuela is that we don't have a strong federation that unites us and elaborates on these kinds of tools that we need.

The Fight Against Subcontracting

Richard: One of the things that we have strongly attacked is the subcontracting of the workforce. On top of violating our contract and the rights of the workers, Mitsubishi had also hired 135 workers to do maintenance work through a subcontractor called

Induservis. These 135 workers do the same work as the regular employees working directly for the company. While the regular workers make forty-six *Bolívares Fuertes* (Bs.F) daily, the subcontracted workers only make twenty-six Bs.F.[8] The Constitution of the Bolivarian Republic of Venezuela states that if you do the same kind of work for a company, you should make the same salary.[9] It is only just that these subcontracted workers should make the same amount as us. The outsourced workers saw that the company was also violating their health standards, so they decided to organize.

They chose three delegates to represent them in matters of health and safety before the governmental institutions. The law states that these workers have the right to organize in this manner. Since the company doesn't like organized workers, those three delegates were fired. The other Induservis employees struck in support, also demanding compensation owed to them by their company. One of the conditions that Mitsubishi had placed on Induservis was that their employees could not have contact with us, precisely because of the work that we do in the union. Before this, those workers would always avoid speaking with us. But afterwards, they decided to take the risk and work together with us. Mitsubishi then decided to terminate their contract with Induservis, because their employees were now a problem for the company and because the workers were going to defend their rights.

Being clear about the struggle we are in, we held a discussion amongst the Mitsubishi workers. We told them that this situation had to do with our own job security, because one of the strategies being applied in the automobile sector in Venezuela is to convert the assembly workers into independent contractors. This is where we begin to lose our stability, the contractual benefits that we have won. These subcontracted workers don't benefit from the collective contract and are unable to organize themselves into a union. We took the position that we should make a decision in defense of these workers because we could not permit that 135 family fathers be put out on the street. What happens to these workers inevitably hurts us also; we are brothers of the same class. So we went to the Ministry of Labor with a list of requests, which, apart from mentioning the various complaints and contract violations, also included the conflict over our fired *compañeros*. We demanded that these 135 outsourced workers be absorbed by Mitsubishi as regular employees of the company since they do the same work we do.

Félix: We had two meetings at the Ministry of Labor with representatives from Mitsubishi and Induservis, where they made a mockery of the institution and the workers. The company representatives attended the first meeting, but did not bring the necessary documents that the Ministry asked them to bring for the meeting. They did not even show up to the second meeting. By the following week, no decision had been made and it was clear that the Ministry of Labor was not going to take action.

Occupying the Factory

Richard: Afterwards we had an assembly and took a vote amongst the workers where it was decided that we would not go back to work until the situation with the Induservis contractors was resolved. Only the administrative personnel continued to work, but those on the assembly lines didn't return. However, the company didn't respond to us. It was essential for us to escalate our actions. All the decisions that we made came from discussion amongst the workers, so they themselves could decide what was best. We, the workers, and the unity of the working class, are the only guarantees that our rights will be respected. The workers asked themselves what effect a strike outside the factory would have. What matters most to a business owner are their machines, their property. So as a result of another consultative referendum, 860 out of 883 workers decided that we needed to occupy the factory.

We planned everything out — how we were going to occupy the factory. You should have seen it! We waited for one worker to open the main door while another worker drove a car into the opening to keep the door from closing. When the car was driven in, all the workers ran into the factory and we took over the whole plant. All the managers and the administrative personnel were kicked out. Only the workers stayed inside. This was January 20th, 2009 when we started the struggle from within.[10]

The Murders of January 29th

Félix: Representatives from the company approached the doors of the factory on two occasions and we told them that we were open to sitting down and talking with them, but only with the presence from the Ministry of Labor. They had nothing to say about their unwillingness to fulfill their responsibilities so we continued refusing to leave the plant. The third time they approached the plant is when two of our *compañeros* were assassinated — José Marcano and Pedro Suarez. January 29th was undoubtedly a massacre, a massacre against the working class. The whole thing was planned and premeditated in order to end this project that union leaders on a national level recognize to be completely unique. We have proof that there were snipers with infrared beams outside of the factory that day. What were snipers doing there that day?

We have harshly criticized the governor, the Anzoátegui state attorney general, as well as the police commander. How could the same governor, who participated in a resolution that decreed in 2005 that no police forces could hold weapons at protests, allow state officials to have guns at this peaceful demonstration? We have many right-wing elements in Venezuela, such as those in the judicial system and in the police structure, who continue defending the bourgeois state and the companies. These elements are taking advantage of the silence of the reformists permeating the government institutions. We are convinced that the only way we can redress the murder of our *compañeros* is by detaining and imprisoning the masterminds behind their assassinations. The police may have shot them, but they are only partially responsible. They themselves have been misled and some are simply doing what they are told to do. But those who paid for these murders to be committed are the ones who should be in jail.

Richard: Within this capitalist system and within a country that maintains a bourgeois structure, we still have laws created by the business class that are meant to defend them and perpetuate their system. Between the bourgeoisie, the bureaucrats, and the reformists we are not going to be allowed to take the place of the business class. But those who are in power know that if we continue advancing with this project and we continue mobilizing, in the future we will displace them. If the communities and the workers see what we are doing and the support [that] we are providing, whom are they going to believe? They are going to believe in the true leaders — leaders that are rising up from below and struggling with them.

Political Pressures on the Union

Félix: We had occupied the factory for sixty days. We left the factory due to political pressures, especially from the current directors at the Ministry of Labor, the Minister María Cristina Iglesias and the Vice-Minister Ricardo Dorado, who told us that the factory could not continue to be paralyzed and we had to come to an agreement with Mitsubishi. The minister herself expressed to me personally that this could become a bad example for other unions. The state has a great weakness in that it uses a large number of contracted workers in clear violation of Article 77 of the Organic Labor Law, which reflects the situation we are experiencing with Induservis.[11] Every ministry, including the Ministry of Labor, has many contracted workers. We have pointed out that our own government is setting an example to these transnationals to outsource their labor. Imagine, we have contracted educators, contracted medical staff, we also have contractors in PDVSA and SIDOR.[12] So clearly, our example was going to be a serious problem for them.

The President had recently participated in an international event where he signed various economic agreements as a response to the global economic crisis in order to bring more investment into the country and manage the national budget.[13] One of the countries with whom an agreement was made was Japan, and principally with Mitsubishi. An occupied Mitsubishi plant was going to create a bad image for the Japanese with whom our government was going to begin negotiations. The Japanese Embassy was laying considerable pressure on Venezuela during the occupation.

Ending the Occupation

Félix: By way of another labor leader, we were told that if we didn't leave the factory the National Guard would be called in to take it over and the Ministry of Labor would permit the company to go through the procedure for our dismissal. It was a very difficult situation. Now we had the company, the reformists, and the private media all working against us. On March 21st, we came to an agreement in which not all of our demands were satisfied, but we believe that 85 percent of the grievances that the workers had with the company were resolved. We made the company commit to no longer outsource jobs to subcontractors, and forced them to renew their contract with the Induservis workers. Our goal is to continue with this struggle. Once the Induservis contract expires, we see no other option than for Mitsubishi to absorb these workers as regular employees of the company. We will continue to maintain this position.

Our constitutional law does not require companies to compensate workers after a strike ends for the time that they were not working.

We were able to force the company to pay the salaries and provide all contractual benefits that the workers stopped receiving during the months we were on strike. The company must provide this because it is their fault that we had to take these actions in the first place. This was an important development and a reference point for the whole working class. The company also had to respond to a number of other violations to our contract. For eighteen years, the company did not compensate workers for vacation and days off that they were forced to work. They have now been forced to recognize those work-days and pay for them, as well as provide days off in compensation.

Uniting the Labor Movement

Félix: Undoubtedly, one of the major weaknesses that we had was the lack of united political leadership amongst the working class, [leadership] who would truly defend our ideas. There was silence on behalf of the pseudo-leaders that supposedly represent us in the labor federations: the CTV, UNT, CUTV, and the FSBT.[14] Imagine what kind of strength could have been generated by a confederation! We have a major task ahead of us, which is to build unity amongst the working class within our state, in the automobile sector, and on the national level. This is the only thing that will allow us to take a genuine leap forward and break away from the state structure in order to build what our President is constantly calling on us to do.

We are part of the UNT Confederation of Anzoátegui State. We have internal problems that originated on the national level but have had an effect on the regional level. We are working to resolve those problems by convoking a regional congress and a national congress, or constituent assembly, to truly bring the country's work-ers together to discuss what kind of a confederation we want and the program of the working class struggle. We strongly criticize the national leaders of the confederation who we don't feel are repre-senting us because they have not submitted themselves to the will of the rank and file. We ask ourselves, "In what factory do they work? Who are the workers to whom they respond, day to day and hour by hour?" We want to have a horizontal structure that truly allows the rank and file to have autonomy.

Within our union, we have some workers who are commit-ted to a particular ideological position and are part of one of the labor tendencies and there are others that don't participate in any labor tendencies. I am particularly an activist with the Marxist

Revolutionary Current. But that doesn't make any difference between us because we believe in open debate, and that the decision of the majority must be respected by all of us regardless of any disagreements. I have criticized all the different labor tendencies, but I think that we have all learned from each other as well. We must have unity in action because our struggle and destiny as the working class are one.

Uniting Labor and Communal Councils

Richard: We also have a project of integration with the communal councils. We have provided social services in the *barrios* where it is difficult for them to receive vaccinations or dental work for example. In the same way that the people must come together through the communal councils, we the workers must also unite with them. The workers are like the heart — the motor that moves this country and the whole world for that matter. Through our activities and our struggle, we are a union that has developed a strong relationship with the community. The people in this region have come to identify themselves with us.

We are deeply thankful for the role that the communal councils played on January 29th. There are four communal councils surrounding the factory. They heard all the noise and the gunshots. The people from the community formed a human chain so the police couldn't enter the factory and attack us. Another group of people from a *barrio* next to the plant stopped a freight truck and took the keys from the driver to block the road to the plant. We now have a regional committee that meets with the communal councils and other local unions. We have a meeting planned during which we are going to discuss the global economic crisis and the role of how the unions and the communal councils can work together.

Building Socialism

Félix: We are absolutely convinced that the only way of creating a socialist state is to have a planned economy with control in the hands of the workers and the communal councils, that the people are the ones who truly elaborate this socialist project in order to satisfy their principal needs in health, housing, food, education, and security. We support proposals that will deepen this revolution. There are many divided unions that have not put forth a working class political project, but rather have simply fought for their collective bargaining agreement. We don't discard that. We have to fight for collective bargaining agreements in a capitalist state, but in a transition to socialism we should propose ideas as well — ideas that move us towards the state that we want. We have come to learn about proposals from the communal councils that they have put forward to take over an abandoned industrial park here in the state of Anzoátegui. They want to provide the maintenance for it and recuperate the closed factories. This is the kind of work where the union and communities can move forward together.

The left is going to have to organize a joint plan of action along with the masses, and the President is going to have to defend it. After the February 15th referendum, he committed himself to supporting what the majority decided. All of this demands the working class to overcome the labor bureaucracy and find its new leaders. We already see the social movements, like the *campesino* and communal movements, with the strength to debate, to struggle, to guide their own development without submitting to any bureaucrat.

The people's ideas are there, but where is the leadership that listens to them and brings those ideas into fruition? The only leadership we see is from Chávez. But for God's sake! One man for the whole country? We believe that the President needs other revolutionary leaders and we are here to struggle so that this process has that leadership, and so this socialist project can be brought into reality.

SEVEN

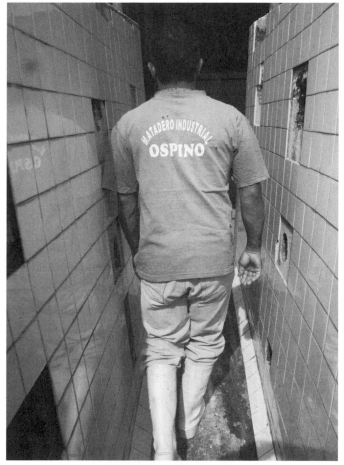

Candido Barrios - Entering the Factory.

———

Candido Barrios & Manuel Mendoza,
Pedro Pérez Delgado Cooperative/Industrial Slaughterhouse of Ospino

(Ospino, Portuguesa)

The crisp morning air has already started to give into the humidity that dominates Venezuela's countryside when the workers of the Industrial Slaughterhouse of Ospino begin to change into their white uniforms, rubber boots, helmets, and goggles. While telling each other jokes, they sharpen their foot-long knives as naturally as if they were regular sized dinner knives. They take their routine positions on the assembly line as the cows begin to file in. *La matanza*, as they call the slaughter, is carried out efficiently and almost ceremoniously every workday except during worker assemblies.

The slaughter is not a pretty sight, but the workers constantly talk about how beautiful their experience of taking over its operations has been. The workers, now members of a cooperative managing the factory, talk about the incompetence and carelessness of the private companies that had operated there before them. Little maintenance was provided to the installations. The workers safety and well-being was clearly not a priority. After years of seeing their workplace and their working conditions deteriorate, they came to a breaking point when five of their friends who were working for months as contractors were going to be fired — all this after winning a significant legal battle that should have forced the company to keep them as regular employees.

Manuel Mendoza was one of these contractors, who as a day-laborer came to the slaughterhouse almost every day to see if they needed a few extra workers. He proclaims that he never expected to be part owner of a factory; he just wanted to keep his job. But, the workers knew they could run the slaughterhouse better than the private company and that their so-called managers were in fact destroying their livelihoods.

On May 1st, 2006 the workers of the Industrial Slaughterhouse of Ospino took over the factory and formed a cooperative named after the legendary Pedro Pérez Delgado, also known as *Maisanta* and Hugo Chávez's great-grandfather.[1] Today, 150 workers run the factory. There are no bosses. There is no management. The associates of the cooperative work on the assembly line alongside their *compañeros* in *la matanza*. They decide together how they will pay themselves and if they can at all.

The financial hardship of the economic crisis has hit them as the price of cowhides upon which they greatly depended has dropped to under 10 percent of the original price. Cooperative member Candido Barrios looks annoyed as he glances at the immense piles of cowhides buried in salt. The cowhides are purchased by automobile manufacturers for use on their car seats. But with the slump in international car sales, their demand has ground to an almost complete halt.

But Candido insists that they do not want money from the government to pay themselves, as other cooperatives have done. They simply want their cooperative to be recognized as the operator of the slaughterhouse so that the members can apply for loans to maintain and expand their installations in order to sustain their business. While they have run the slaughterhouse for over three years, their cooperative has yet to be recognized as the legal concessionary by the government. Municipal governments own most of the slaughterhouses in Venezuela and providing their cooperative with the concession to operate it should be a simple task. However, the workers at Ospino believe that their predicament is an example of the entrenched interests inherent in a corrupt, self-serving bureaucracy and local government.

The situation confronting the workers at the Industrial Slaughterhouse of Ospino is one example of the many challenges that have faced the occupied factories movement in Venezuela. The movement was officially born with the worker occupations of *Venepal*, a paper factory located in Carabobo State, and subsequently of *CNV*, an industrial valve manufacturer located in Los Teques, a city roughly thirty kilometers outside of Caracas.[2] After their respective private owners abandoned the companies, the workers organized to demand that the government nationalize and re-open the companies under a "co-management" scheme in which the government and the organized workers manage the factories together. As Chávez began to declare his commitment to socialism in 2005, he responded to the worker mobilizations by expropriating Venepal in January of that year, (renamed Invepal) and CNV in April (renamed Inveval).[3]

Chávez followed with a warning to other private business owners that their businesses would also be expropriated should they attempt to close down their operations without justification. Seeking to build upon these advances, the workers of Inveval launched the *Frente Revolucionario de Trabajadores de Empresas en Cogestión y Ocupadas*

(FRETECO - Co-managed and Occupied Factories' Worker's Revolutionary Front) in 2006. Learning from their own conflictive experiences in attempting to develop a co-management model that allowed for worker participation in decision-making, the Inveval workers realized that such an organization was necessary to push forward their demands, while supporting other workers seeking to take over their factories. Co-management continues to be a conflicted term that in practice has taken on various manifestations in the factories where it has been implemented.

Whereas some in the Venezuelan government view co-management as simply a model in which employees have partial ownership of an enterprise, FRETECO has chosen to promote what they call "revolutionary co-management," which they see as a path for workers to eventually take full control of factory operations. Rather than owning the enterprise, however, FRETECO members want ownership to remain in the hands of the state, seeing worker ownership as simply another expression of capitalism. While the workers at the Industrial Slaughterhouse of Ospino are not official members of FRETECO, their goals and beliefs are congruent. They want the slaughterhouse to remain under government ownership, while continuing to fully manage it themselves, as they have done for the last three years. The Ospino workers reject the idea of having a private company take part ownership of the concession again, even though this is the only proposal that a representative from the local government has presented to them.

Many occupied factories are still waiting for greater support from the government, arguing that a corrupted bureaucracy has stifled the true potential of their movement, while others continue demanding that the state expropriate their companies from their former owners who abandoned them. Amidst all of this, Chávez is now adopting the language of workers' control as well. After nationalizing a number of iron and steel producing plants in the Guayana region in May 2009, he proclaimed that these factories, while owned by the state, would eventually be placed under full workers' control.[4] The workers at the Ospino slaughterhouse are hopeful, but they recognize that if their project of determining their own economic destiny continues unsupported, it may very well fail. They fear that if this occurs, there will be dire consequences for the future of economic transformation and workers' control in Venezuela.

Candido Barrios & Manuel Mendoza

Personal Histories

Candido: My name is Candido Barrios and I was born in Sabaneta in the state of Barinas, the same town where President Chávez was born. I came to Ospino at a young age, where I was allowed to work as a minor. I have been working since I was seven years old because my father left my mother for another woman. There were six children in the family and I was the oldest so I had to work to support all of them. Later I moved to Caracas where I worked for four and a half years, and then I returned to Ospino. Shortly afterwards, I got married and began to work in the slaughterhouse.

Manuel: My name is Manuel Mendoza and I was chosen to be one of the legal representatives of the cooperative. I grew up here in Ospino and came to the slaughterhouse as a contract worker. I had been unemployed for some time. I would often come to the factory to wait and see if they needed extra people to work that day. Some days they would take us and other times they wouldn't.

Candido: I started working here before a single animal was slaughtered, when this was practically an abandoned shed. The building was recuperated and the first company operating here was launched on November 9, 1998. That company was called *Consorcio Industrial Ganadero Ospino* (CIGO - Ospino Industrial Cattle Consortium) and it functioned for about five years until they were removed by Amilkar Pérez, the mayor of Ospino who just recently left office. The mayor bid to become concessionary of the slaughterhouse, but publicly he was only an associate — not the official president — so that he would not appear to be controlling the business. In reality, the official president was a front man he had appointed. This company was called *Frigorífico Industrial Portuguesa* (FIPCA - Industrial Meat Processing Plant of Portuguesa).

This company continued to exploit the workers in the same way as the first company, but they made conditions even worse because they did not maintain the facilities. The first company did not treat us well, but you could at least see that they were investing in the slaughterhouse. They repaired the meat lockers and took care of the machinery, for example. But with FIPCA, there were many times that our operations were stopped for two or three days because of damaged machinery. Under the private companies, we were never paid very well, and when they increased the slaughter they never raised our wages to complement our extra work, either. We were constantly being threatened and at that time we had no way of defending ourselves. Under FIPCA, we didn't even have social security benefits any more. The companies bought all the labor inspectors that came to check on our work conditions.

Manuel: The company was slaughtering dead animals at that time, which is illegal. When a cow is dead it needs to get quarantined and examined by the veterinarians, not slaughtered! That's something that you have to be very careful of, because the cow could be infected and it could infect the whole herd. But they would just put the dead cows in the line without being concerned that the meat might harm the community. All they cared about was slaughtering the animals and making money. And if we tried to challenge the company, they would just tell us to keep our mouths shut and that it was not our problem. They also never complied with the security norms enforced by INPSASEL (National Institute for Prevention, Health, and Labor Security).

Fighting the Company

Candido: There came a point where I was so infuriated by all of this that I realized that I needed to defend myself, my co-workers, and of course my own family. So I began to organize and started fighting with the company, to the extent that it was possible. Even though I had little education because I never even received my high school diploma, I knew enough to realize this: my work at the slaughterhouse was considered very important by the companies here. I was in charge of removing the heads from the animals, which is something that anyone can do, but not with the level of quality that I was able to provide. So the managers didn't want to get rid of me. Even though I would always make a fuss, they still wanted me to produce for them, rather than hire someone that might still make a fuss but not produce.

We got organized and registered a union within a year of the second company's arrival. This was a challenging process. We always had to wait for the production manager to go to the office and then run into the bathrooms to meet quickly to sign all the necessary forms and legal documents. We would tell everyone what they needed to contribute and what still needed to be done. My family runs a small market and I would use the money from our family savings to register the documents when we didn't have enough funds. When the other guys here had money they would help me out.

Manuel: Candido was the president of the union. The company would call Candido into the office and offer him thousands of *Bolívares*. The boss gave him blank checks and told him, "Write the amount you want on there." He offered him cars for him to get rid of the collective contract. But Candido defended that contract for all of us.

Taking the Factory

Manuel: All of these problems took us towards the decision of occupying the factory. There were many of us who worked here as contractors at that time. After working at the factory for five months, the management wanted to fire me and four others, to prevent us from becoming regular employees of the company. This way they could just hire new contract workers to replace us. We went to the labor inspector to fight this. We fought for six months and finally won the right to be rehired. But the labor inspector didn't have the power to order the company to hire us back. The managers simply said, "No, we don't want to rehire them!" Because there was a sense of camaraderie amongst us, that same day the rest of the workers — including the regular employees — decided to occupy the factory. We all entered the factory together on the evening of May 1st, 2006. We ate and slept here. The president was called and told that the workers took the factory. Since that day, we have not seen the president. The company simply disappeared.

Candido: When we decided to occupy the factory and form a cooperative here, many people told us that we were crazy. They said, "How can you believe that you can just take that factory from those people?! Those people have too much money!" There was one rancher in particular that told us that we were crazy, and we told him that once we had control of the slaughterhouse we would invite him to bring his cattle here. Later he came back and said, "Wow, you guys really have it together here!" Very few have done what we have achieved here. We have supported ourselves and have succeeded. We realized that if we didn't produce we would have caused great damage to the local food chain, so from the first day we took control of the slaughterhouse we have continued to operate it as a cooperative. Our operations have not stopped for a single workday!

Financial Challenges

Manuel: The financial situation at the slaughterhouse is very difficult. We always depended on the sale of cowhides here. Many cowhides would be purchased by automobile manufacturers, for use on their car seats. But the global financial crisis has lowered automobile production. Before they were selling at 100 or 120 Bs.F per hide and now they are selling for as low as 15 Bs.F. That is a decrease of over a 100 percent. Cowhides aren't even being purchased now. We have 2000 hides just sitting there! When the private company was operating here, they made a lot of money off cowhides. But they would just pocket the money without investing in the facilities.

Candido: Unfortunately, we can only operate as a service slaughterhouse. Without resources, we cannot purchase animals to directly sell ourselves. The cowhides were like the band-aid for the cooperative, and for the whole region for that matter. When we had a slaughter of 600 animals a month and the cowhides were selling at 120 Bs.F a piece we were able to buy a new steam boiler, new water tanks, we fixed the corrals, we painted the buildings, and we fixed all of the motors here. Now we are slaughtering up to 2,400 animals a month and barely getting by.

Seeking Recognition from the Government

Manuel: We have submitted a variety of projects to the Ministry of Agriculture and Land and other institutions in the government, but they haven't been able to support us because we don't have a legal base. The majority of the industrial slaughterhouses in Venezuela are already owned by the municipal government, including this one. But they are essentially privatized because the concessions are provided to private companies. FIPCA still officially holds the concession to this slaughterhouse. The last mayor, Amilkar Pérez, didn't want to recognize us because he was the majority stakeholder in the last business. Now we have a new mayor and governor here, both from the United Socialist Party of Venezuela who we supported during their campaigns. They came here with a coordinator from PDVAL (Venezuelan Food Products and Distribution Company) and proposed that we become a joint venture where we would essentially work for PDVAL and the company would be partially owned by the state, the workers, and a private enterprise.[5] We told them that in the eleven years that this factory worked under a private company, hardly anything was fixed. We have been the ones to invest in the maintenance of the facilities.

Candido: We have been operating here both legally and illegally. Legally, because when we took over the factory we received recognition from INDEPABIS (The Institute for the People's Defense in Access to Goods and Services), which at that time was called INDECU (The Institute for Consumer Education and Defense).[6] They told us that they would recognize us if we took on the responsibility of the plant's operations. From the first day, we took on that responsibility. We are illegal because we don't have a legal document stating that the cooperative is legally operating this slaughterhouse and that the concession has been provided to the cooperative. But we don't believe that a single document can impede the kind of process in which we are engaged.

Manuel: What we need is support from the government. We are not looking for money for the cooperative or its members. We simply need a loan to maintain the facilities since they are essentially still owned by the state. What we need is an investment from the government to find more forms of income. We need ways to create product of added value. For instance, we can use the animal fat that is wasted here to make soap. We just need the equipment to be able to do this. We also need transportation to get rid of our waste here ourselves, which would help us generate more income. It is the responsibility of the government to provide us with this assistance since the slaughterhouse is owned by them.

A Mixed Record for Mixed Socialist Enterprises[7]

Manuel: I don't think that the mixed socialist enterprises in Venezuela have been working. I have seen with my own eyes mixed enterprises that have failed. They haven't been able to even cover their own operation costs. They are just another burden on the state, which is what we want to avoid. We visited a slaughterhouse in Quibor in the state of Lara, which had a cooperative but only in name, since the government bureaucrats essentially managed it. The administrators had no experience managing a slaughterhouse and the workers were exploited. It was run totally inefficiently. The workers would just throw away many animal parts on which slaughterhouses depend. But because they received funding from the government regardless, they just didn't care. The workers didn't have a sense of ownership over the slaughterhouse. They eventually had to shut it down because it incurred too many costs, and they had all the resources they needed to run it. I think that they want to eliminate workers' control here.

Candido: We have demonstrated that here, in Venezuela, we are one of the few cooperatives that has been able to support itself on what it produces alone. To this day, there has not been a single government institution that has invested in this slaughterhouse to allow it to operate at 100 percent capacity. Governors, mayors, ministers, National Assembly representatives have come here and made us offers, telling us that they will submit our proposal to the government institutions so that we can receive funding. But we have received no real response, only promises. We know that they make us promises in the hopes that we will eventually get tired and quit, so that this factory will be left on a silver platter under the control of two or three capitalists.

But to be honest with you, we have remained calm. We have figured out how to support ourselves and we hope to continue doing that. The state officials and the ministries don't want this process to advance. So we ourselves have to push forward. There will be a moment when the President will see what is happening here with his own eyes and we will see what actions he takes against those so-called revolutionaries at his side. There are a lot of people who are revolutionaries during public events, and afterwards… well we don't know what they are. Of course, there are some good people in the government as well. I'm not criticizing everyone. But of those who have come here, not one has been of any use.

These bureaucrats are playing dirty with the working class, telling us that this revolutionary process is the most transparent. We are not going to say that this process is bad because we have made progress. But this is one of the most important issues we are facing, because not everything in this economy can be based on petroleum. About 150 tons of meat are consumed in the state of Portuguesa every month. The thing that I don't understand is that this slaughterhouse is so strategic. Ospino is like the gateway to the *llanos*. We are right next to the region that produces the most animals, the state of Barinas. The slaughterhouse is located fifty meters from the main highway so we know the animals won't suffer so much in the transport; we know that it will be a quick arrival. And we know that we have one of the highest quality facilities compared to other slaughterhouses in the area.

Managing the Cooperative

Manuel: When we first started, we had a president and treasurer but that didn't work well because those titles went to the workers' heads. They began to give orders without contributing to the work, and making decisions without participation from the cooperative members. So we got rid of those positions. Now we have a legal commission consisting of eight cooperative members that have authorized signatures to financially represent us at the banks. All decisions are now made in an assembly amongst all the workers. Nobody can make decisions affecting the cooperative, not even the legal representatives, without the participation of the rest of the workers. Decisions are made with a simple majority.

We don't have bosses here, but we do have responsibilities. We make all the decisions ourselves. It was very difficult at first to remove that boss mentality from our heads and to recognize that we are the operators of this factory. We had to realize that each one of us must take responsibility for everything. We are liable for any necessities and have to cover the costs of maintaining the facilities. We figure out how much money we have in the bank and how much we can pay ourselves depending on the economic situation. When the factory was in the hands of the company, we didn't know anything about these things. They would just pay us our salary and we would commit to a work schedule and that was it. Of course it was exploitative because they would make us work longer hours without reimbursing us fairly. This has been a very challenging but beautiful experience.

Everyone here earns the same amount, except for the veterinarians who are registered with the Ministry of Health. As medical doctors, they receive professional remuneration for their work. Although they are registered with the Ministry, the government has not assumed the responsibility to pay their salaries, so we have to pay their salaries as well as their benefits and Christmas bonuses.

Supporting the Community

Manuel: Our goal is not just to avoid being a burden on the state, but also to be able to provide for our community. One of the things that we do here is buy five or six animals from cattle ranchers and slaughter them to provide low cost meat for the community. We sell the meat at the price at which we bought the animal, without making any profit. This is part of the social labor that we can provide.

Candido: We do that to show the community that it is possible to eat for cheaper, but that we all have to take a risk and we all have to rise up against capitalism. The major capitalists don't want to see us succeed because imagine what would happen to them if we did. We have also been able to provide loans with very low interest to our cooperative members so that they could buy their homes. We have had members who have gotten sick, and we have donated two or three thousand Bs.F to pay for medicines, without asking for the money back. We have donated to an elderly home in Ospino, providing them with fans, a television, a blender, a domino table, a dining table, about 500 Bs.F worth of food, and lazychairs for people to rest on. We painted the building and installed water tanks for them. Overall, we provided them with a donation of around 7,500 Bs.F in merchandise alone. We provided refrigerators to all the local schools. No schools in Ospino had any refrigerators before that. In one school we built an entire bathroom because before their was only a hole behind the school building for them to use.

The Struggle Ahead

Candido: We are afraid that this cooperative could die. We know that if the workers' necessities are not met here, then they will have to move on. If our cooperative doesn't survive here, then I'm afraid that cooperatives in Venezuela may not be around for much longer. I have traveled around and I have seen too many cooperatives subsidized by the government. But the day that the government doesn't have money to give to those cooperatives, they are going to die. The difference here is that we have been supporting ourselves. But supporting ourselves is not enough, because we need to think about our children's futures and taking care of their needs. Some workers might feel forced to accept another private company here. And it seems like that is the only thing in which the mayor and governor are interested, because they can make more profit with fewer owners, rather than having a whole cooperative supporting itself here. It's like having a birthday cake made for fifty people, rather than just for ten. They want the cake to be for ten people so that they can have bigger pieces. But what we want is a cake for fifty people where everyone has a small piece, but is happy with it.

EIGHT

The Founding of the National Cooperative Councils (CENCOOP).

Alfonso Olivo,
Leufogrup Cooperative

(Barquisimeto, Lara)

I f the slogan of the May 1, 2005 Worker's Day March in Venezuela was "Co-management," by the following year, it was "Cooperatives." The 2006 pro-Chávez May Day March began at the head offices of the former Ministry of Popular Economy and the National Training and Education Institute, INCE, and wound its way across Venezuela's bustling capital, Caracas.[1] The same month, hundreds of cooperative members from around the country met in Caracas to lay the foundation for the cooperative councils, which they hoped would quickly grow into an autonomous movement that could support the needs of Venezuela's rapidly growing cooperative sector.

In 2001, President Chávez passed the new cooperative law, and within three years, the Venezuelan government had established the Vuelvan Caras Mission to train thousands of individuals in technical skills and cooperativism, enabling them to set up their own worker coops.[2] President Chávez began to champion democratic businesses as a tool for overcoming capitalism. In addition to training and technical assistance, his administration provided coops with funding, tax credits, and other forms of direct support. The Vuelvan Caras coop job-training program empowered thousands to take charge of their own lives to lift themselves out of poverty. By 2007, after the first three years of the program, nearly 300,000 individuals had graduated from Vuelvan Caras forming nearly 8,000 cooperatives.[3]

By the beginning of 2009, just over 260,000 cooperatives had been officially registered in Venezuela over the last decade, up from fewer than a thousand coops when Chávez was first elected in 1998.[4] The number puts Venezuela as the top country in the world with registered cooperatives, and hundreds of thousands of Venezuelans are finding their way to these democratic enterprises. They are changing many lives, despite the fact that according to the Venezuelan government's own statistics, less than a quarter of total registered coops are actually functioning.[5]

The Venezuelan state of Lara lies roughly at the halfway point between Caracas and Mérida. A hilly, rural, agricultural region, Lara is considered by many to be the heart of Venezuela's cooperative sector.[6]

The traditional coop sector grew over the last century in consumer, health, funeral and financial cooperatives. For years, the traditional cooperatives were organized in state federations and then through a national coop federation known as CECONAVE.[7] With the advent of the new *Bolivarian* worker cooperatives promoted by the Chávez government, some Chávez supporters discarded the traditional sector as being of the *"Cuarta República,"* meaning that they were essentially capitalist or dominated by Venezuela's political opposition.[8] Their differences cut a rift between the two sectors, which has been difficult to overcome, but some coops in Lara state have succeeded in wedging a union between the two groups.

Alfonso Olivo is a middle-aged, fast-talking member of the six-year-old ten-person administration cooperative, *Leufogrup*. From his cooperative's tiny two room windowless office in downtown Barquisimeto, he straddles the line between the old and new coops, and has an uncommon vantage point of Venezuela's cooperative movement. Olivo has been highly involved; from his father's fishing cooperative to his studies at the Central University of Venezuela to his eight years with Amnesty International, predominantly focused on Central America solidarity work in the 1980s. He has been a *cooperativista* for two and a half decades and is now the coordinator of the three-year-old Lara State Cooperative Council. The cooperative councils have been formed nationally, regionally, and locally all across the country. In very few places, however, are they as organized as in Lara state, where they also have the peculiarity of including individuals from both the old and new cooperative sectors.

Alfonso Olivo

Background

My background comes from my father. My father is a *cooperativista*. He's still alive. Right now he lives in the United States, but he lived for a long time in the eastern part of the country, and he started a fishing cooperative in the small town of Marigüitar in Sucre state. I always saw my dad in these activities, organizing people, bringing the fishermen together, trying to coordinate projects with different people in the community: fishermen, workers, artisans.

In 1976, I moved to Caracas and began to study at the Central University of Venezuela (UCV), and I got involved in the movements in solidarity with the people of Nicaragua, El Salvador, Chile, and Colombia. So I began to see and learn and understand what it means to have a position on the left, to be progressive.

I wasn't born to be a millionaire. Yes, I like money, and I like to do quality things, but I like to make money without exploiting everyone else, without stealing from everyone else.

I'm not saying that I'm Gandhi or Rockefeller. I don't want to be any of that. I am Alfonso Olivo, a citizen, a *cooperativista*, a fighter, and I believe that this is a feasible way of living. It's possible, when you have the will.[9] That's why I believe so much in cooperativism. There are people that don't understand. The radicals on the left say that we are just petty bourgeoisie, that cooperativism is still a form of property. And the capitalists say that we are socialists. So we're in the middle; cooperativism is in the middle of the system.

Venezuela Cooperative History

Here in Venezuela, the cooperative movement was born around 1902 or 1904. There are two theories: one tells of some cooperatives in Margarita, in Porlamar, that were formed in 1902, and the other speaks of a cooperative that began in the Andes in 1904. This is the origin of our cooperative movement. This cooperative movement that arrived to Venezuela came with this European theory, and this was the cooperativism that they taught us. Ok, so who were the promoters of this cooperativism in Venezuela? They were the Jesuit priests. They were the ones that saw cooperativism as a way of helping the poorest communities. They were ones that came here to our region.

This also came to our country from the United States as a response to the triumph of the Cuban Revolution. In 1959 or 1960, this revolutionary movement spread in Latin America. So the United States dictated its Latin American policy in which they saw cooperativism as a way for people to see that there are other ways of freeing themselves of poverty without revolution or war.

So the priests came here to our region — we're talking about the 1960s — and at that time this was a primitive cooperativism, that looked more like Europe than us. For example, they taught the people that cooperativism was to live in a state of absolute poverty in really tiny communities, to wear old clothes, to be humble, and to produce to survive. But it was not a cooperativism that considered the development of the state and the country.

That's when our great cooperatives here in Lara were born, like *La Cooperativa el Dia*, like *La Cooperativa Fecoseven*, like *La Cooperativa Alianza de Sanare*, *Cecosesola* which supports 40,000 people a week with produce, and *Cecocoro* from Coro, with medical services. These cooperatives transcended the limited space of the coop members and went to the streets.[10]

Then came the new era, the era of Chávez, in 1999, and this process launched a new cooperativism. In a way it was a rejection of the cooperativism that existed, which they saw as a closed cooperativism. The state saw it as a non-solidarity cooperativism. So the state created the new cooperativism through the Vuelvan Caras Mission, which created around 1,500 cooperatives just in Lara state alone.

The Vuelvan Caras Mission

This movement was born with a lot of strength, and with the support of the state, but looking back, it hasn't borne the fruit that was expected. Of these 1,500 cooperatives in Lara, some 15 percent have been effective. The rest have fallen apart, broken up, withdrawn, or dispersed. They committed many mistakes, the biggest was not to have prepared these people to become *cooperativistas*.

Each individual has his or her own interests. People respond to their particular situation in their community and the idiosyncrasies from where they come. Looking back, these groups were united while they were studying, while they received a scholarship to study, but when they launched the cooperative and received funding and began to work, the groups divided. And this happened with the Vuelvan Caras Mission. But the remnant that remains has been positive. We've helped some of the coops that survived this phase. We've advised a large group of them here in Lara, and they have survived and are working to come together in the end.

This experience was good. It was really good. It told the state that there is receptivity. The people are looking for this. You need to also remember that when the revolution began, we took over a country that had 12-15 percent unemployment, and there were a lot of really needy people. There was a lot of poverty, and that's why the missions were a success, because they responded to these needs, but they were momentary answers. They were short-term answers and not long-term.

The Communal Councils – A Revolutionary Step

After initiating the Vuelvan Caras Mission, the state launched the communal councils. Why do I mention these? Because there's a cooperative within the communal councils. The communal council is a structure that has three branches: an executive branch, a social auditing branch, and a financial branch.[11] The financial branch of the communal council is a cooperative. It is different from the traditional cooperatives, in that it is a cooperative of collective or social property, which in a way belongs to the community.

This cooperative, or communal bank as the state calls it, is in charge of administering state funds. The state transfers a certain amount of funds to the cooperative, and the coop passes the funds to the community, to fix a street, or build a school. In this way, the communal councils begin to be government. That's the revolutionary step. I would say that that's the most revolutionary, transformative act of the Chávez government —the creation of the communal councils, because they take the capital from the bureaucracy, from the mayors and council members, and pass it directly to the people for them to administer.

Cooperative Councils

The National Superintendent of Cooperatives (SUNACOOP) is a government body that coordinates policies for the cooperative sector. But SUNACOOP gives the orders, provides trainings, and writes the laws. It does everything, and that can't be. You have to allow the movements to have their own autonomy. Look at the experience of Uruguay, Argentina, and Colombia. These are experiences where the movement has its own direction, which is not the case in Venezuela.

Remember that until the year 1998, there were only 760 cooperatives in the country, and in five years we jumped from 760 to 150,000. Now there are nearly 280,000 registered cooperatives in the country, yet there is no structure that can respond to the needs of this growing sector. Carlos Molina, the ex-superintendent of SUNACOOP, and a visionary sociologist, said, "The answer here is for the cooperative movement itself to have its own dynamics, its own direction. Let them organize." And he began to propose that the movement guide itself and that's when he proposed the creation of the cooperative councils.

The idea is that within a Venezuelan state, you set up a council for the parish, for the municipality, or for the state. Here in Lara state, we have three structures. We have the state cooperative councils, the cooperative councils from one of the municipalities and a cooperative council from a parish. So that's three expressions.

Why do we do it like this? Here we have parishes that are really remote, some 150 kilometers from Barquisimeto, and the cooperative members almost never come here. So, for example, these local cooperative councils act as an intermediary with these remote cooperatives to help them acquire funds, so they can begin to produce. Also these councils can provide workshops and training for these local cooperatives.

The cooperative councils can also serve as a link between the cooperatives and the state organization, which is the Superintendency. That's what we're talking about. We don't want to be the government. No, we want to work little by little, acquiring the space so that the movement has its own identity.

For example, the cooperatives are being beaten by the issuance of a document, which is called the Certificate of Fulfillment. It takes a long time to receive it, and almost no cooperatives have it. Why does the Superintendency, which is the government, have to issue this document? Why isn't this document issued directly by the cooperative movement? Twenty years ago, a cooperative needed five steps to be contracted by the government, and now twenty steps are required, twenty procedures, twenty requisites. This can't be possible. So on one hand, you talk about supporting the process and the cooperative movement and on the other hand you block it with the bureaucracy! That's why we have to fight the bureaucracy, because this bureaucracy is not interested in the movement being autonomous.

Composition of the Coop Councils

The majority of the members of the cooperative councils are new, with only four or five years in the cooperative movement. The older cooperatives, that could actually contribute with the highest level of knowledge and understanding, ended being up left out. Here in Lara, we have the peculiarity in that we all coexist together; the old movement and the new movement, which expresses itself and converges here in the Lara State Cooperative Councils.[12] We have this reality in Lara, and I believe something similar is happening in Falcon, Bolívar, Zulia, and Táchira, which are the emblematic states. In the other states, things have been more reactionary; the movement doesn't have the unity for reasons that I was explaining.

Bolivarian vs. Traditional Coops

These Vuelvan Caras cooperatives were created with the very good and healthy intentions of the government, and you have to take advantage of this experience in order to implement the new co-operativism. You have to learn discipline and experience from these old cooperatives, which have their traditions, and their struggles, and their ways, and their human and economic capital. How did they come together to build this wealth? And we endow these lessons to a cooperativism with a more social vision, which perhaps was what the old movement has missed; this commitment to the development of the community. That's the fifth cooperative principle, the commitment to the community.

So, I believe that we need to complement these two visions of the state, so that in the end we can release a product that will simply be called a cooperative without the last name.[13] A cooperative is a cooperative, but this has to be the product of discussions. It has to be the product of training. It has to be the product of trust. You have to believe in the people.

Revolutionary Change

It is not enough for someone to say in the streets, "This is a revolution. I'm a *Chavista.*" That doesn't matter. What matters is what you are doing to transform this country of ours, which we have to change. We had to change the way in which they had been governing, with exploitation and theft. This is what the people want to change. There are two ways of changing. One is transferring power to the people. The other is dressing things up so that everything stays the same.

Perhaps in another country things are different. If you compare us with Cuba or with Nicaragua, those are different situations. For fifty years we lived beneath an *Adeco-Copeyano* government that exchanged power every five years and the people got used to this way of life.[14] The state gave the people crumbs and kept them busy until the people realized that they were worth more than that — that the profit produced by the petroleum reserves had to go directly to the people, who are the owners of these natural resources. When the people understood this, that was when they revolted. Now, how do we tell the people that at the same time as the natural resources belong to them, they need to use these natural resources rationally, and they need to help conserve them, in a system of equality and justice. The cooperative is an instrument whose job it is to do just that.

Cooperativism as Development

We think that cooperativism is a grain of sand in the creation of this consciousness. When a group of businessmen detach themselves from some of their profits and transfer them to society, that is a form of solidarity, it is a form of socialism. We believe that cooperativism is an ideological tool that allows you build this consciousness, but on the other hand, countries can't live without productivity. You have to produce.

This is a country that depends a great deal on the petroleum income, and all of the state investment comes directly from the wealth from the oil profit. Now, what do we do to grab this wealth and take it to the people and transform this wealth into other products? So that when this petroleum boom is over, our future generations can continue to live in a wealthy country, or at least in a country where the people can live together without want.

Contradictions & "The Middle Class Revolution"

The government has good intentions in this process. President Chávez, at least, has demonstrated good collective and social intention. Now, where are we failing? In the team that is accompanying him. There are definitely members of the government that prevent us from developing this new economy, because we can't lose sight that this revolution is being driven by the petty bourgeois sectors of Venezuela, I mean the middle class.

These are the contradictions that we have right now in this government. Who is driving this process? The middle class sectors of the populations. And they want to drive it without affecting the capital, the large national and multinational businesses, and without affecting the large landowners. I am a revolutionary and I am a *cooperativista*. I don't like the way they are driving this development because the consequence may be that we once again return to the same system that we had overcome.

Ten Years of the Bolivarian Process

The government cooperative policies over the last ten years haven't been a resounding success, but nor have they been a failure. They have served to propose the construction of this alternative. They have served to transform and spread the collective spirit, because perhaps before someone only thought of individual goals, like buying a car and getting a new house, and then suddenly wait a minute: "Lets go ask for a school, and look for work for everyone." In that sense it has been useful. It's been a success.

Socialism

Living in socialism is much better than living in capitalism. Isn't it better to share things? To have a public hospital service that cares for everyone instead of paying for a private clinic? To have free education for your kids, rather than paying for a private university? Socialism is much better, but people still don't understand it and there are sectors that take advantage of the lack of understanding. There is a conflict of interests. The government in itself is not socialist nor visionary. The government is guided by a leader whose name is Chávez, who has a socialist vision of development and of our people. But the rest of those around him don't have the same vision. You have to differentiate this. So what do we do? You have to support the ideas that move us further along, the radical ideas, in order to offset and counterbalance the other, petit bourgeois vision, which is also advancing.

Cooperativism is there in the middle. What do we do to spread these policies so that they germinate through the rest of society? We tell people, "Organize yourselves in groups." Call them what you want: associations, societies, organizations, but the people need to organize. They need to organize and begin to demand, not only their rights but also their responsibilities. The majority of the failures of our people and of our revolution are because the people don't have this level of consciousness and maturity to allow them to understand that they are the ones that do this, not one man. And you can't follow men, you follow ideas. You follow the good ideas. That's what we're talking about.

This movement must continue to exist, because cooperativism is a life-long project. It's not for one day, or for one government; it's for your whole life. Now, where does cooperativism work better? In socialism, of course. For us a socialist government is much better. Right now, we can count on a government that supports the cooperative movement. A government like Chávez's is much better than a capitalist government which fights against us. Before, in 1964, we were insignificant. The people didn't believe in us, and the cooperatives were merely for cleaning the streets. Today we have people who are forming cooperatives, who believe in cooperativism. This is positive. So this isn't going to end. Regardless of what happens, we are going to continue.

Venezuelan Democracy

The transfer of power through the communal councils is the most revolutionary measure that this government has taken, because it is transferring to the communal councils what the mayors and the governors did before. The people are capable by themselves, without the involvement of the state or the bureaucratic officials. That is democracy: a system which is in discussion each day, which is fighting in the streets, which is speaking with the students and the workers. There is a wide diversity of opinions, and this enriches the discussion. I am sure that we are on the road to acquiring a state which, if not socialist, will at least be profoundly democratic — in which there is a depth in democracy and not just an election once every four years without any expression.

Remember, they also spoke about democracy here under Betancourt, Carlos Andrés Pérez, Caldera, but it was a democracy with representatives.[15] Now the people participate in these decisions and that's why the president speaks about participatory democracy. Now we talk about deepening democracy, expanding political action, going beyond voting, and getting involved in the economic, social, and political interests. That is socialism. This is socialism.

Now, of course, this isn't all rosy. There are four million Venezuelans here that are in the opposition, and they have their own vision of democracy. They are people who used the former democracy to get rich: to have large mansions in the United States, chariots at their doors, four cars of the latest models, and forty servants at home. These people are used to this kind of life and that's not right. You have to take this away.

You've seen Caracas full of shacks. Here in Lara, we also have shacks in Barquisimeto. These people work in a factory, or they are *buhoneros*, or workers in the informal sectors in the street.[16] They go to work and sleep in their shacks. They don't have water, perhaps they have electricity, but they don't have education services. They don't have anything; yet they are still Venezuelan. That's where the state needs to direct its efforts. To include this population. That is what we call profound democracy. And this is called socialism. It's as simple as that.

Part IV:

COMMUNITY MEDIA, ARTS & CULTURE

NINE

The San Carlos Free Barracks of Popular Power.

———

Negro Miguel, José Ñañez Ibarra, & Hector Rangel, Captain Manuel Ponte Rodríquez Foundation, Cuartel San Carlos

(Caracas)

There are no longer prisoners here, but the cold hallway on the second floor has changed little. Gates still guard the rooms although they are no longer locked. The Foundation uses the third room on the left as an office, just next to the cell where Hugo Chávez Frías was held shortly after his failed 1992 coup attempt. They don't touch the room at the end of the hall, where Manuel Ponte Rodríguez was left to die after the failed 1962 rebellion in Puerto Cabello. The view through the bars on the windows overlooks the courtyard, now basking in the hot morning sun.

In the back, sections of the thick stonewall are slowly crumbling. Thigh-high weeds blow softly in the breeze, and cover the rubble where jail cells once stood. Much of the complex was recently renovated, but the *Cuartel San Carlos* (San Carlos Barracks) still whispers loudly of its long tumultuous past, a history that covers four centuries, and is still at the forefront of Venezuelan politics.

Named after the King Carlos III when the Spanish began construction on the barracks in 1777, its builders had little clue of the illustrious role it would play. At the time, the barracks were simply the last line of defense in a string of fortifications winding up the Avila Mountain and down to the Caribbean port town of La Guaira.[1] At the end of the 16th century, Caracas had been sacked once in a bait and switch by the English pirate, Amyas Prestón.[2] They weren't going to let it happen again.

For the next thirty years, the installations would be used as a fort and military barracks, until 1808, when the Spanish converted it into a prison to hold members of the resistance junta that rose up against them. After a long struggle, on July 5th, 1811, a Constitutional Congress led by Francisco de Miranda declared Venezuela's independence from Spain and a week later the new Venezuelan flag was hoisted over the barracks.[3]

The Spanish reacted quickly. As the war of independence waged on, they were recovering lost ground in Venezuela when on March 26, a massive earthquake leveled cities across the country, killing 15,000 and partially destroying the Cuartel San Carlos. It was eventually rebuilt and became one of Venezuela's most prominent prisons in the 20th century, holding presidential assassins, political prisoners, leftist guerrilla fighters, and U.S.-backed terrorists.[4]

In 1994, then incoming-president Rafael Caldera closed the Cuartel San Carlos prison shortly after he pardoned Hugo Chávez for leading his 1992 rebellion. The site was declared an historic monument. Under the Chávez administration a decade later, the Ministry of Culture began to renovate it with plans to convert it in to a museum. But rather than preserve its history, the cooperative that was hired for the renovation began to sell off the barracks' century-old architecture.[5]

A group of ex-political prisoners quickly jumped into action to stop the pillage, and on July 26, 2006 a dozen of them occupied the barracks. The former prison and military barracks is now *Cuartel San Carlos Libre de Poder Popular* (The San Carlos Free Barracks of Popular Power), a cultural center "at the service of the people."

The ex-prisoners have now launched a school for political education here. Members of the Madres del Barrio Mission hold their meetings here, as do some PSUV battalions. Last year, a wing of the Political Secretariat of the Caracas Metropolitan Mayor's office, held training sessions here for community members to support and form communal councils. The community has held free concerts and events, including an extraordinary meeting of the Venezuelan National Assembly in celebration of the fifty-year anniversary of the overthrow of Pérez Jiménez.

Lining the corridors of the barracks are dozens of large black and white images of people who were disappeared, tortured, and assassinated during the 1960s and 1970s. Many of the images are of students. One young man with short hair and a sport jacket, stares out of the picture without expression. The caption reads: "Luis Rafael Tineo Gamboa, Disappeared, October 25, 1965. *Campesino* social activist, detained by Captain Edito Ordaz, who accused him of collaborating with the insurgents. From the moment of his detention, [Venezuelan security forces] began barbaric torture, after which they ordered him to dig his own grave, into which they threw him after they had cut off his ears, nose, hands and genitals. The place of his burial was found after a 13 month search showing signs that he had been buried alive."

"A people without history are lost," says Negro Miguel, whose real name, Enrique Velásquez, he can finally reveal after fifty years. Miguel is an ex-guerrilla combatant with the Armed

Forces of National Liberation (FALN) who fought against the *Acción Democrática-Copei* governments of the 1960s. Miguel was imprisoned here in the Cuartel San Carlos for two years. He is one of the hundred ex-prisoners and family members that took back the barracks two and a half years ago and now manage the former prison.

The Cuartel San Carlos is just one of numerous such autonomous experiences which have sprouted up across Venezuela over the last decade, like the *Casa de Cultura* of La Pastora; the political-cultural collective, FRAPOM, in Valencia; and the cultural NUDE *Tiuna el Fuerte*.[6] All are putting "culture" directly in the hands of Venezuelans.

The Chávez government has prioritized culture and the arts. Over the last five years, communities across the country have formed hundreds of cultural committees to help organize cultural and sports activities, and record community history among the residents. Community radio and TV have also gotten involved. Members of Catia TVe's ECPAI program interview their communities about their history. Before formation, each communal council must carry out a community census. They are also expected to write a history of the *barrio*, in order to rescue the hidden and forgotten past. And that is why the ex-prisoners are here.

"I was in every one of these jail cells," says Barlovento resident José Ñañez, who was a construction worker in 1960 before he joined the urban guerilla wing of the FALN. He worked out of Caracas for many years before he was shot, captured, tortured, sentenced by a one-day military tribunal, and imprisoned. The year was 1966.[7]

Hector Rangel walks out to the side of the barracks past a group of six teenagers who are learning how to stilt-walk, and up the stairs to what was "the hole." Tiny jail cells, three feet wide, are still there, the metal bars now rusted. Phrases are etched into the black cell walls into which prisoners carved their sufferings decades ago. "He who stands up is he who writes history," says one.

Next door, Rangel points out the lookout tower of what used to be the offices of the Armed Forces Intelligence Service (SIFA). The building is now gone. The *barrio* has grown in and around the only remaining tower. "That was the torture and death center," he says, "when they detained you, they took you there, and that's where they tortured you. They disappeared some of them, or transferred them, or tossed their bodies into the hills there. Others went to the military tribunals, where they were sentenced and then went to the prison, next door."

Rangel was an activist with the Leftist Revolutionary Movement (MIR) and spent time here at the Cuartel San Carlos, although not for long. He was convicted of military rebellion ("without being a solider," he adds) and quickly transferred to half a dozen prisons before spending two years on the island of Tacarigua in lake Valencia. "We called it the Rafael Caldera concentration camp," he says.

Miguel, Ñañez, and Rangel are all now members of the secretariat of the Captain Manuel Ponte Rodríguez Foundation, which was set up by the ex-prisoners and there families to oversee the barracks, and fight to preserve this history in danger of extinction.

Negro Miguel (Enrique Velasquez)
José Ñañez Ibarra
Hector Rangel

History of the Cuartel

Miguel: I can tell you that this place where we are standing today is a little more than two centuries old. They began construction here in 1777. Its first *naves*, which is what they call the area, were finished in 1784. It has been barracks as well as a fort, a hospital, though it has mostly been a prison. For instance, in the epic history of the push for liberation against the pro-slavery Spanish, this was a barracks, but in the time of independence, it was a prison. Some historians say that even the founding fathers of our independence were imprisoned here.

Many years later, at the beginning of the twentieth century, this was a prison for those who carried out the assassination here of the presidential candidate, Carlos Delgado Chalbaud.[8] In the 1960s, as a result of the bad governments, we were imprisoned here as guerilla fighters for going against the governments who were clearly ordered and organized by the United States.

Since we were primarily an oil producing country — in fact, at the time, they even said we were mono-producers, because we only produced petroleum — the people from the countryside made an exodus for the oil fields, and in consequence this brought the North American interests. We began to fight against this, with guns in hand. I'm talking about just a short while ago, almost fifty years.

There were various civilian-military movements, which were at the time defeated. For example, there was the civilian-military movement called El Porteñazo, which was in Puerto Cabello, a city here in Venezuela. There was the Carupanazo, in another city in the eastern part of the country called Carúpano. There was the Barcelonazo, in Barcelona, a city that is also on the eastern side of the country. These movements were civilian-military, but the soldiers at the time, the few that were patriotic, always had their hands tied; they were tied by the people who had sold out to the foreign interests. That's why we were defeated. As a result of the Porteñazo — which was the most important civilian-military movement in the country — we began to organize as a guerilla force, and we formed the Armed Forces of National Liberation.

We are survivors of this era. Perhaps when you passed by here, you saw the galleries of our people who were killed; in ten years of struggle, we lost more than three thousand people who were tortured, disappeared or killed. Because don't forget one thing: they put the teachings of the School of the Americas into effect here. They began to apply the teachings of how to torture here, in this country. The practice of the political disappeared came about here; the practice of putting them in a helicopter and throwing them out; the practice of burying them alive; the practice of cutting off the hands of the prisoners. This evolved here.

I would say that the last of the romantics who was in prison in these barracks is the current president of the republic. He was in prison right over there in that cell and then he was transferred to Yare and from Yare he was freed. These barracks, where we are sitting right now, had a very rich history. A history very connected to the idiosyncrasies of us as Venezuelans. And now we are here, as members of the Manuel Ponte Rodríguez Foundation, more than anything else to preserve all of this history that I am telling you.

Along the Halls of the Cuartel San Carlos

José: Because of the many years we spent here, along these halls of the Cuartel San Carlos, we feel as if we were born here. We feel that in the soul, so we'll defend this at any cost because this rightfully belongs to us, because this is a process in history, and they wanted to erase it; they wanted to tear down the Cuartel San Carlos, which we couldn't allow, because we are part of it. I am proud to be a man who is part of this living history. We are still living and we want to live longer to continue to tell more.

These barracks have a long history. They rose up here in 1945, with the October 18, 1945 massacre, and these were the last barracks to surrender. This is part of our historical memory, because this is part of the history of Venezuela.

I spent thirteen years of my life here. I was in all of the jail cells that were here. The torture was terrible. They tortured us, but not here. When we got here we said, "Now we are saved, they're not going to kill us." But when they got you, there was torture of all sorts. They put plastic bags around your head to make you suffocate, they held you underwater in the toilets, they beat you, they shot me in the chest and they tortured me with the wounds, they offered me money, they offered me a passport, everything to make me tell who and what. I always denied it, and now I don't deny it because I am free. I feel free because this process that we have now gives us the freedom to say many things that we never wanted to say before faced with the repressive apparatus of the enemy.

Negro Miguel

Miguel: My complete name? I can say it now after fifty years. My full name is Enrique Velásquez. Even these comrades here that have known me for years, it is only now that they know my name, because we used pseudonyms. And they always called me Negro Miguel, and my old friends continue to call me Negro Miguel.

The Occupation

Miguel: We have been here for approximately two and a half years. It's not that we long for the torture, nor do we long to be in prison here, nor to make us out as victims, or any of that. But for a while we have been making excuses that it is the Fourth Republic — the people we have been fighting against — who erased the historical memory. So, we can't stand in solidarity with people that say they are *roja rojita,* with people that say they are revolutionary, and they have the same process as the Fourth Republic.[9] When we saw these people, these *rojo rojitos,* begin to destroy these barracks under this government, then on July 26th, standing before the tomb of Jorge Rodríguez, there in the cemetery, we decided to come here.[10]

It wasn't easy. It wasn't easy because when we got here, they had a hundred *lanceros*.[11] These *lanceros* didn't understand that we just wanted to preserve this history. They thought we wanted to take away their bread.

José: There were a number of us, something like twelve or so, and the private security was there. We went in through the back, and we were armed with pistols. We were going to take this, no matter how. One person stood watch here as the reserve. We said "We order you to stop all of this. You're not going to move anything else here. This is occupied."

Well, this tiny guy, very aggressive, of course he saw dollar signs here. He said, "OK, if it's like that you're going to have to kill me." I told him, "We'll kill you right here. Right here we will kill you. We have to defend this, and if we have to kill you, we will."

Well, we lost the original architecture here. They robbed it. They stole everything they could. They took the tiles — the originals — that were 200 years old. The floor was made of terracotta; they carried it off in truckloads. They took the bars and the windows. They dismantled it all. They looted everything.

Miguel: Of all of those 200 years, there's only this door left and two others. Their intention was to take everything on the inside and make everything look right on the outside. But in the end, they took it all. They put these doors and windows in there, and they are metal; painted; and they took the two hundred year old wood.

As a result of all of this, we complained to the Ministry of Culture, because they were in charge of protecting this national heritage site, but they were destroying it. So we complained to them, especially because we had just come from the grave of Jorge Rodríguez, and it turns out that the person who had ratted on him — and as a result of this, the DISIP killed him — is now the current Vice Minister of Culture, Ivan Padilla Nolasco.[12]

This deeply disturbed us… how is it possible that they are destroying our historical memory and above all, the Vice Minister of Culture is an informer? Are we a revolutionary government? Are we a new type of government or what are we talking about here? The national government needs to know these things, because — while we are with our *comandante*, who is the closest to our dreams — it appears that there are things that aren't clear there.

Cuartel San Carlos Libre

Miguel: This was a place of death, of tears, of family separation. But once we took this over, we decided to call it, *Cuartel San Carlos Libre.*[13] It is free for whom? For the organized people. For the communities. For all of the movements that are in support of not just socialism, but the historical development that our nation demands of us.

So in a way, we have become custodians. Fortunately, they now want to give us an allocation of funds for all of this, but until now we've paid out of our pockets for the secretariat, the maintenance people, and the janitors. With part of this allotment, we recently opened the school of revolutionary education; we believe that this ideology is what this country currently lacks in its consciousness. We know that the empire and socialism don't mesh, because one is based on the interest of the individual as a person, and the other is based on the goods that can be acquired above this individual. This is incompatible, and you have to teach the people why. If you don't teach this to them now, you run the risk that in the future, you won't be able to solidify it.

Culture

Hector: The culture of the people is very broad. History doesn't exclude culture. The fact that we want to have a training school here says that we want to make culture also. What we don't want is to characterize this as a grotesque museum, as a center for just culture not of discussions, or of forums. This is culture, but it should be with a revolutionary orientation. And we believe that an installation such as this should be at the service of the people. The people are the ones that make the decisions here. That's our intention, to make this a place of dissemination of revolutionary thought.

The Captain Manuel Ponte Rodríguez Foundation

José: Manuel Ponte Rodriquez was a *compañero* who rose up in Puerto Cabello. They grabbed him, they brought him here, they gave him a heart attack and they left him to die. As he was a military officer who later joined the side of the FALN, the soldiers took revenge and left him to die. And in name of this great comrade we named this the Captain Manuel Ponte Rodríguez Foundation to which we are very proud to belong.

Hector: We have been working, and we have a lot to do still. We just recently inaugurated this really nice room over here, which is the revolutionary school of political education. Right now we have approximately thirty or thirty-five students. We are trying to deepen the understanding of the revolutionary process and ideological stability for those that attend. And we want this to multiply; we want these people to leave here from these courses and for them to be multipliers of revolutionary thought. We want to give them an ideological foundation in order to fight for the revolution with consciousness, with clarity. To understand what the revolution is, what socialism is, from this theoretical point of view, because there is no revolution without theory. That's the incentive. Our president has said that we need to create a thousand and one schools of political education, to sow consciousness, because when there is consciousness, you build clarity. And we are doing this, and we hope that at some point not so far away, we can multiply these centers of revolutionary education throughout the country.

We have financial limitations to carry out the projects, but we are also working on a proposal that we have already presented to the legislative assembly about the crimes that have remained unpunished. Just like other countries, Uruguay, and Chile, that have worked so that this memory does not die so it is not lost, and so that justice is done for those that lost their life. A law of moral reparations is what we need. We need a law of moral reparations, not economic reparations, because the life of the revolutionaries has no price. These revolutionaries died fighting.

Here, we are trying to do these things. We are planning to set up a community radio and a community television to spread revolutionary thought to the people. This is the work of the foundation. And above else, to maintain a clear memory. We are determined that the historical memory will not be forgotten.

Losing Historical Memory

José: They have hidden the historic roll of the Cuartel San Carlos and all of us that have lived here for a long time. The youth don't know. A lot of people don't know who is who, and why we are here, what it means for us to be here, and why we did this. This history is not told in the street. People don't know the sacrifice and the suffering. You abandoned your children, your wife, your family; you went hungry on top of all of the things that can happen, because a revolutionary gives everything for what he believes — everything. You even leave your family for this. We sacrificed all of this.

The youth of today don't know this. They come here and, "oh, how pretty this all is," and we tell them that this looks like a convent, the way that they painted it.

There is no connection that enables them to come to us. Now we are spreading the word, not only nationally, but also internationally: who we were, who we are, and what we are going to do. This has already been spread across the world. The Cuartel San Carlos is an opening, a point of convergence in Venezuela.

Bolivarian Process

Miguel: The Bolivarian process is the closest thing to this dream that we had when we were young when we began to put our lives at risk here. Many of our comrades were left along the way. The Bolivarian process has rescued this and has given us, the *viejitos*, the opportunity to continue dreaming.[14] As a philosopher comrade once said, "We always wanted to touch the sky with our hands," and how far we were from this. But now we see that with this, we have taken another breath; that's why we set up this school for revolutionary education. And I know that at any moment my clock may stop to tick, because it's the law of life. So, I don't want everything to end up sterile. I don't want the effort of my comrades, the effort of the others, those that were left along the way, to end up…

This memory has to be maintained. We need to share the little knowledge that we acquired, because people without a history are lost. That's that.

José: This history wasn't born the Fourth of February. The first stories of the anti-imperialist revolutionaries here are of our native peoples against Spanish imperialism. During our era, in the 1960s, we left behind more than 50,000 dead, and they don't recognize our true history. I am proud because I am part of history, all of us are, and that's why this grows. As my *compañero* here says, this government that we have now, is better than any other, and since it is better than any other, we are going to defend it with the little life we have left. We are prepared to defend it.

Miguel: We continue to be dreamers, we continue being reflective. We believe in what we have always said, and today, more than ever you see the proof of our goals, because now they speak of imperialism, now they speak of a North American government that comes to put its Yankee boot here. We've been saying this for fifty years and they called us "that group of whackos."

José: They have always called the great men crazy, in any era, in whatever country. They have always called them crazy because they were revolutionary. They called Chávez crazy. They called Bolívar crazy. They called us crazy because we fought against an internal and external army, but the *locos* of today are the connection to tomorrow. We are those of tomorrow and we will continue to be of tomorrow.

Contradictions in the Process

Miguel: I'm going to tell you something. Even the people in the present government don't like us. Why not? Because we know who they are, like the Vice-Minister of Culture. There are others that have been ministers or governors and they were our repressors during the Fourth Republic. I'm not going to say names… but they know who they are. Of course they are *rojo rojito* and they cross the street and they see the comrade Ñañez and they don't like him. Or they see Negro Miguel and they don't like him.

We know they don't want us. These were the people who generally had us covered up. But we don't pay any attention to them. Why? Because we are right. We continue to be right and until today, we have held a stance within the realm of what you can call a revolutionary.

I admire my comrade here. Others say they admire me, because for fifty years I've had my ideals; fifty years not dressed in red, fifty years, of which I spent three in the mountain, twenty-four hours a day, putting my life at risk with nothing in return except for the satisfaction of fighting for something. And now, I paraphrase the words of our Liberator, "Now I can die at ease." With this movement here, I can die in peace.

TEN

Wilfredo Vásquez: "Don't watch it, make it!"

———

Wilfredo Vásquez,
Catia TVe

(Catia, Caracas)

"Don't watch it, make it!" That is the mantra of the western Caracas community television station, Catia TVe. The station is located just down the hill from Venezuela's presidential palace, Miraflores, past crumbling walls spray-painted with murals, and across from the polluted Guaire River that winds its way through most of Caracas. Inside the brightly painted headquarters of Catia TVe, the atmosphere is laid back and bustling. The front lobby of the station is alive as community activists head off to record interviews or return from the free community media-training program offered by the station. The four-month ECPAI (*Equipos Comunitarios de Producción Audiovisual Independiente* - Independent Community Audiovisual Teams) program, has trained dozens of neighborhood collectives to be community journalists. The groups exit the program with the skills to produce their own digital video, some of which is aired at the station.

The station's gregarious co-founder, Wilfredo Vásquez, waves his arms enthusiastically as he questions guests on his weekly program. He is a longtime community activist and a passionate member of the Catia TVe collective. On air, he describes how their programs contrast to traditional stations, and jokes about the "un-Venezuelan" stiffness of national broadcasters. He finishes an interview with a group of foreigners living in Caracas, and the sound engineers quickly mic up five Venezuelan university students about a confrontation that has just occurred on their campus. The station is always on the pulse of community news, constantly creating an urgent buzz throughout the facility.

Catia TVe was born out of the *Cineclub Manicomio* (Manicomio Film Club), and the struggle of the 1980s against a repressive police force — a force which responded to the Caracazo uprising by violently hunting down community leaders and carrying out mass detentions and disappearances. Wilfredo and a group of friends began to film during those uncertain times. They used rudimentary cameras and interviewed their neighbors about their lives. The community enjoyed seeing people they knew on the screen. Wilfredo and the community media activists ran with it, spurred on by their belief that Venezuelans needed to see local people talking about local issues.

Operating legally since 2001, Catia TVe was one of Venezuela's first community television stations. It is now part of a vibrant nation-wide community media movement that —with support from the Chávez government —has swelled over the last decade to hundreds of local community radios and more than a dozen community television stations. Catia TVe guarantees that 70 percent of its news is produced by residents of the Catia neighborhood, and their signal now reaches most of the city.[1] The station is a reflection of the community it serves and like the people of Catia, isn't afraid to voice its opinion.

Media in Venezuela has become a highly contentious issue. From early on in the Chávez government, the president faced harsh criticism from the four major private television stations: *Venevisión, Globovisión, Radio Caracas Televisión* (RCTV), and *Televen*. The Venezuelan state attempted to respond by broadcasting its perspective through the state channel *Venezolana de Televisión* (VTV), but it was often little match for the breadth of the private stations.

In 2002, Venezuelan media became even more polarized as the private channels ramped up their anti-Chávez campaign, supporting opposition marches and calling for the overthrow of the president. The short-lived 2002 coup d'etat has been called the first "media coup" in history, with mainstream private media implicated in the event.[2] During the coup d'etat, community media helped to spread the word that the Venezuelan people weren't getting the whole story. Catia TVe played an integral part in disseminating the news that Chávez had not resigned and that he was being held against his will.

Once back in power, the Chávez government quickly moved to support community media with equipment, broadcast licenses, and at times, funding. Over the last seven years, the government has also opened several new public television stations, such as Telesur, Vive, and Avila in order to counter what it calls "the media war."

Then, in May 2007, after repeated violations of the Law of Social Responsibility in Television and Radio, the Chávez government decided not to renew the public broadcasting license that RCTV had controlled for fifty years.[3] International reports condemned the action as a Chávez "power grab," and said that the Venezuelan president was censuring press freedoms. The opposition said it was retaliation for the station's criticism of the Chávez government. Chávez supporters saw the move as a radical step towards democratizing Venezuela's airwaves by sanctioning a station that had consistently violated the law. Others said it was a legitimate recourse against a private company that acted to deceive the public during the 2002 coup d'etat. Despite the non-renewal of the broadcast license, RCTV is still available on cable, and as of 2008, more than 75 percent of Venezuela's television and radio airwaves were still in the hands of the private media.[4]

Nevertheless, dozens of community television stations, like Catia TVe, are putting media directly in the hands of Venezuela's citizens — a story that often gets overlooked in the mainstream media. Venezuela's community media have seen an unprecedented growth during the Chávez era, and Wilfredo Vásquez has been involved from the beginning.

Wilfredo Vásquez

The Beginning

I was raised in the Simón Rodríguez *barrio* in a part of the Pastora Parish, known as El Manicomio, particularly in an area called *Las Barracas* (The Shacks). That's what our houses were — shacks. They had tin roofs and the walls were made of plywood and scrap wood. The floors weren't covered... they were just dirt. We didn't have functioning bathrooms in our homes. We had outdoor bathrooms that were collective.

There were lots of trees and space at that time. The *barrio* was practically built on Avila Mountain. There was lots of green space. Now all of that is just houses. My father was a police officer when Marcos Pérez Jiménez was in power, under the dictatorship.

In that *barrio* there were a lot of old Communists. I had an old friend named Pablo Muñoz, who is dead now. He went by Carlos Rojas... a lot of these old guys would change their names. He was an alcoholic, he drank a lot of liquor; but he would listen to you and guide you. I would have little sparks of understanding whenever I spoke with him. I learned a lot through those old guys.

Political Education

But my real political education in the *barrio* began when I entered the Luis Espelozin High School in Catia, which they called "the tiny University of the West." In the early 1980s, the leftist organizations, like *Ruptura*, CLER, PCV, MAS, *Bandera Roja* were very strong in the factories and in the high schools.[5] A lot of the activists from the left, who had been students there before, became teachers — there was continuity. Of course there were *Adecos* and *Copeyanos* as well, but the influence of the left in that school was fundamental. In the classroom we learned through school pamphlets about theater, about Stanislavski, Brecht.[6] We studied them and implemented their ideas in the workers' theater, street theater.

I was part of a student group that won the elections for the student center. We made connections with collectives in other high schools and worked with people from the *Movimiento Revolucionario de los Trabajadores* (MRT - Revolutionary Worker's Movement) at the Central University (UCV).[7] At that time, we would say that the university needed to come to the streets and in those years the university really came to the streets. This is how we met Blanca Eckhout.[8] She came from the UCV to incorporate herself into the *barrio*, to strategize with us. The academic with the popular movements: that was a really interesting mixture and I'm a reflection of that experience. We would organize protests together every Thursday and classes would be cancelled. The police always knew to expect a protest on Thursday. This even started happening nation-wide.

From all of these experiences, we created a collective called *Grupo Conciencia* in Catia. In the same way that university students were calling for their universities to go out into the *barrios*, we also called for the high school to go out into the *barrios*. We were all kids. One of the people in that group was Ricardo Márquez. He is also a founder of Catia TVe and was the president for about four years. Now he's the president of Vive TV.

Our goal was to eradicate the delinquency and drug dealing going on in the *barrios*. The *Adecos* and *Copeyanos* would just turn a blind eye to these issues. We started a newspaper called *Toma Conciencia* where we would denounce all of the issues in our communities and discuss proposals. We generated discussion. We would wake up at dawn to distribute the newspaper to all the homes in El Manicomio to create that consciousness. This is where we started doing the work of little ants that led to the creation of the *Casa de la Cultura Simón Rodríguez* (Simón Rodríguez Cultural Center).

The Simón Rodríguez Cultural Center

In the cultural center we held study circles every Monday and a lot of *compañeros* from Caracas would attend. We talked about political theater, national politics, and we also analyzed international politics. We created movement with culture, but always to insert the social and political discussions. The form of expression and protest for the people at that time was theater. It was the cultural form of pointing out that there were problems in the government and in our community. It was then that we decided to learn about our past, and get to know our own *barrio* in order to gain support. We saw that we could teach each other. It was like a community committee. We got to the bottom of the issues that affected the community.

We had enemies that sent us to jail; they knew what we were looking to do through theater. I was taken to jail from the cultural center a lot of times and the people in the community would get angry and support us. At that time, you had the main political parties, the *Adecos* and *Copeyanos*. They had a lot of power. They controlled the *jefatura civil* and the *junta parroquial,* and were behind all the repression.[9] Once, when we were heading to a film-forum in the La Pastora Plaza and the *jefe civil* arrived and asked if we had a permit.[10] We told them no so they surrounded us and put us up against the wall to ask for our papers. Since we were young and long-haired, they often confiscated our equipment and hauled us off to jail. We fought this. We did a lot of workshops with Amnesty International at the Simón Rodríguez Cultural Center, and we became a human rights organization ourselves, within La Pastora, so they backed off.

Many *compañeros* that came from grassroots organizations were educating themselves and they created a human rights commission right here in La Pastora. At this time there was abysmal repression from *Acción Democrática* and *COPEI*-you can't forget that for every protest you had in the street, there were detentions, raids, and disappearances. This was happening constantly. For each flagrant violation committed by the police, we went out with the people and demanded our rights. But even with this, it was a constant siege by the police, the National Guard, the Venezuelan Military Intelligence. This was happening all over the country.

Here, in El Manicomio, the repression was especially harsh: they locked me up, they shot me. It was really rough. But regardless of what they did, they could never stop the dreams of this community.

We wanted to see a different country; to see the democratization of knowledge; to raise the voice against an oppressive, exploitative, murderous system. We challenged this so-called system of representative democracy that existed at the time. Many *jefes civiles* knew the people, and went after them, and if they were community leaders, they sent them to jail.

From Cineclubs to Community Media

Out of the Simón Rodríguez Cultural Center we began to organize the *Cineclub Manicomio* with all the *cineclubs* around the country, through the *Federación Venezolana de Centros de Cultura Cinematográfica* (FEVEC - Venezuelan Federation of Cultural Cinematography Centers).[11] We got involved with FEVEC through Marcos Ford, a friend who also arrived to Catia from the Central University. He actually stayed in the *barrio* and still lives in La Pastora. He was a theater instructor and he was the person who opened our eyes to *cineclubismo*. He worked for FEVEC, and later became their Secretary-General. FEVEC united all the *cineclubs* in the country and they would organize national film forums. There were a lot of *cineclubs* throughout the whole country at that time. *Cineclubs* were about art, culture, and politics. But not party politics — protest politics. FEVEC was a government foundation that was financed by CONAC.[12] It was made possible by a left-wing current working within the government of the Fourth Republic. The left at that time always controlled the cultural spaces.

FEVEC was a very interesting experience but it dissolved because a lot of the *cineclubs* like ours began to develop into community radio or television stations. Catia TVe was born from Cineclub Manicomio. From the *Cineclub Cara En Contra* came Radio Perola in Caricuao. Radio Ali Primera in El Valle used to be a very famous *cineclub*, called *Cineclub Guaraira Repano*.

Through Marcos Ford we got our hands on a Bell & Howell 16mm video projector. We did film-forums in a centrally located sports complex. We showed the Mexican Golden Cinema, like *Cantínflas*. We showed films that we got from the Cuban and Belgian embassies. We even showed Korean films. Even though they weren't translated, we understood their ideas, and people liked them. We began to connect with some young Venezuelan film students, and directors connected to the FEVEC. These were films that had social content. We found short and long-format Venezuelan films and we showed them in different *barrios*. But before showing the film, we held assemblies to talk about the movies. These debates went well beyond the films and spurred people to organize.

Next, we got behind the camera and started to interview people from the neighborhood. At first people where shy when we asked them to talk about themselves. So, we asked them which baseball team they supported to help break the ice. This really got things moving and before we knew it, they were going on and on about there lives, their families, and the oral history that had been passed down to them. We decided to show our documentary to the community and we again took advantage of our national obsession with baseball.

We advertised our debut along with the big game between the *Leones* of Caracas and the *Magallanes* from Valencia. We got the word out all over the neighborhood and had a huge turnout, nearly 2,000 people. We started by splicing our short films onto the large screen, and then went back to the game. We took advantage of any breaks in the game to show more of it. When the crowd saw people they knew on the big screen, they went wild. They became more interested in our production and they demanded that we continue to show it and forget about the game. That was it. We knew that our people wanted to hear the stories of regular people. Our dream was coming to life.

The Caracazo and the Rise of Chávez

Contemporary history in Venezuela exploded on February 27th, 1989 with the *Caracazo*. It was not just in 1989. We must remember the student deaths that continued between 1989 and 1992. In Caracas, there were approximately twelve students that were killed by the police and the National Guard. This happened before Chávez, before February 4th, when he came onto the scene. The students were fighting for preferential reduced-price student transportation passes. People couldn't take the system of domination any more. They couldn't take the neoliberal plan of globalization any more. It opened up the floodgates and out came the voice of the people. It's important to say that the first country in the world to rise up against neoliberalism was Venezuela in the *Caracazo*.

To the Venezuelan people in the coup attempt in February 1992, Chávez appeared to right the wrongs of the government — the government that turned guns on its own citizens in the *Caracazo* and continued to do so. When he came out of prison and began his campaign for the presidency, we were traveling around the country holding film screenings. Then Chávez won and we were meeting with groups doing work similar to ours. We had partners from all the different states that we had connected with through the *cineclubs*.

Bringing Catia TVe to Life

In 1999 we started working in a project called *Fundación Catia Constituyente*, which was created to work with the victims of the Vargas tragedy who were left homeless.[13] Through this we supported a lot of people with getting new housing. I was involved with the cultural part and we organized *Radio Orejita*, which later became *Radio Rebelde*. It was a *radio parlante* directed at four warehouses filled with 2,000 victims of the Vargas tragedy.[14]

It was at this time that a member of the team in *Fundación Catia Constituyente*, Ricardo Rojas, was working with the *Fondo Único Social* (The Single Social Fund), which proposed to fund one of our projects.[15] So I had a discussion with Blanca and Ricardo and we decided to found a television station. That is really the moment when Catia TVe was born from all of the experiences we had accumulated. They provided us with 47,000 *Bolívares* and we were able to buy an antenna and other equipment. We needed a lightning rod too because the building that we used for the antenna didn't have one. We realized that we needed to place the antenna in the highest place possible in Catia and that was the Hospital de Lídice "Jesús Yerena." We approached the director of the hospital and they gave us a small space there for the channel. We started broadcasting in 2000 on UHF Channel 25 without a permit.

We were kicked out of our space in the hospital in 2003 by Alfredo Peña, the Mayor of Greater Caracas, who started out as a supporter of Chávez, but really ended up being on the far right. The doctors there were all *escualidos* and they told the mayor that we were working with the Bolivarian Circles and that we were bringing pistols and machine guns into the office, when they were just guitars. We're still going to court to denounce all of this. We didn't function for a year until we received the space we have now. But during that time we were giving media workshops all over Caracas. We got our current building donated to us by the Ministry of Justice. The building was a wreck but we fixed it up. It was a warehouse for the trains that used to stop here at the old Caño Amarillo station.

Legalizing Community Media

On March 30, 2001 we legally went on the air. We were the first legalized community television station in Caracas. We had invited President Chávez to come to Catia TVe before, but he admitted that he could not come to inaugurate the station until we had a legal permit. President Chávez didn't talk about community and alternative media at that time. Blanca Eckhout explained to Chávez what the vision of the community television station was and he understood her. It's not until then that he started talking about community media. It's not just by chance that she is the Minister now. She is a key piece now and with her in MINCI we feel like we should be moving forward with everything that we have been talking about.

We initiated the discussion about creating a regulation to help legalize other community radio and television stations. We argued that there was no structure to allow community media to become legalized. This was something that we promoted and the government supported us. Chávez told Diosdado Cabello, who was the president of the *Comisión Nacional de Telecomunicaciones* (CONATEL - National Telecommunications Commission) at that time, to work with us to create the *Reglamento de Radiodifusión Sonora y Televisión Abierta Comunitaria de Servicio Público* (Regulation on Community Television and Radio Broadcasting).[16] We began having various meetings with CONATEL in 2002. Chávez mobilized these people because there were still people that didn't believe in what we were doing — they thought we were crazy. CONATEL didn't really listen to us at the first meetings we had with them. They would say that this was all new for them. They didn't know what to do on the legal level for community media. We had a lot of discussions and meetings before having the regulation that we have today.

A lot of community media participated in those discussions: people from Teletambores, Telerubio from Táchira, Radio Perola, Colectivo Radiofonico from Petare, and a lot of other groups from all over the country. This was all new for us too — using the bureaucratic tools of the state. That regulation gave many community radios and televisions the legal permit to broadcast, many that were functioning clandestinely for a long time. This was fundamental. Many have continued receiving legal permits thanks to that regulation.

Community Media Challenges the Mainstream

Many *compañeros* say that the private television corporations do not cause us much trouble, but I think they are very aware that we are a problem for them. The mainstream media have a hegemonic structure of power and we, the alternative and community media, even though we operate on low power frequency and cover smaller areas, are practicing participatory democracy. We are really doing it. We don't use women as objects to sell products. People see that. Unfortunately, we are limited. We don't yet reach the national level. Nonetheless, we do reach very specific areas. The private media know perfectly that we are a threat to them.

The private media's logic will never change. Their logic is to consume and to sell, that's it. "If I sell more publicity, people may consume more of the products I am selling, therefore, I make more money." That is essentially what they do. They continue exploiting women as sexual objects. They promote racism.

One must remember that in April 2002, when the coup d'etat took place, it was the community media that went on the air to inform the people of what was really going on. This is a very concrete example of community media standing up to private interests. We set the people free. We broke the chains of the television and other private media. After the coup, the work of the community media was recognized because we were the ones who restored the Channel 8 broadcast signal.[17] Community media was a part of the history. The private media is threatened because people want to be part of their own history, and they want to see themselves reflected in the media. They want to be a part of the crew in the studios, write their soap operas and their news, and this is happening.

Who Controls the Airwaves

Thanks to the people's participation and to the Bolivarian process, the communities know that the airwaves belong to the communities and to the people of Venezuela. The media was traditionally controlled by three families in this country. They made so much money that they have become transnational enterprises. Exploiting the people is not a problem for them. Their objective is to calculate how much they sell, and how much people consume. The private media do not believe in a socialist country, they don't believe in equality of conditions or justice, they don't believe in any of that. The only thing they believe in is their own personal wealth.

So when the renewal of the broadcast license to RCTV was rejected, they intensified the attacks against the government and President Chávez because a handful of families, the owners of RCTV, stopped receiving revenues of approximately $14 million a year and they are angry about it. When RCTV along with other major networks betrayed the Venezuelan people by lying to us during the coup, they lost the right to the public airwaves. It is as simple as that.

The Fourth World War

The private media is constantly bombarding the Venezuelan people. They do this throughout Latin America and the rest of the world. The modern war is different because it is essentially a media war. When the people sit down to watch TV, they promote consumption: "Don't think. Don't create." People have become ignorant, and unfortunately some people tend to believe the private media. This type of war is much cheaper: there are no ships, there are no bombs. They set up satellites, cameras and broadcast through television sets. The people involved in the coup d'etat in April 2002 organized a media war. It was not a conventional coup. The large private media corporations of Venezuela and the world were accomplices in the overthrow of a legitimate and democratic government. They consider us their enemies and vice-versa.

Internationalism

The relationship of Venezuelan community media with other community media from around the world is completely different from the private media. Our relationship is based on brotherhood and solidarity, it is not a relationship solely based on information. For instance, we are connected with our *compañeros* in Argentina and Brazil, where they do not have a law that protects them.[18] They are clandestine. So we have a relationship with different organizations around the world. We have had the opportunity to travel to other countries, and we welcome many people from abroad that want to know what is happening here in Venezuela, and about the process of Catia TVe. We are always in contact internationally. This protects all of us.

Not Going Back

We are going through an interesting process here in Venezuela. I say that with or without Chávez, going back is not an option. Sometimes the people have to learn lessons through misery and ignorance. All of the community media that we have in the country now comes from that struggle beginning in the 80s — from that desire to create, to see ourselves reflected, to be protagonists in our history so that we actually write our history rather than just have it told to us. Chávez has been an instrument to make all of this legal. He is the product of our experiences, of the demands the people were making during the *Caracazo*. The Bolivarian Revolution is a process, and we are part of it. Therefore, we are responsible for what can happen in our country. With Chávez or without Chávez, it is better to die on your feet than to live on your knees.

ELEVEN

Radio Libertad: Valentina Blanco, Raúl Blanco & Arturo Sosa.

Valentina Blanco, Raúl Blanco & Arturo Sosa, Radio Libertad, ANMCLA

(Boconó, Trujillo)

Valentina Blanco arrives at the station early. A cool breeze blows down from the mountains and through the empty streets. She knocks on the green metal garage door and it takes her brother, Raúl Blanco, a few minutes to open it for her. He greets her quickly and runs back to the soundboard where he's lining up the songs for the morning program before Arturo Sosa, their sound engineer, arrives.

The converted garage is cluttered but stylish. Wooden paneling covers the tiny studio. Valentina and her brother fill in each other's words as they show off the station. It opens into three rooms, with a sound board, a pair of microphones and a relatively new tower of electronic decks and equipment which is pumping this tiny station's signal up to the antenna on the roof and out into this quaint mountain town of Boconó and the surrounding valleys and hills of eastern Trujillo State.

"Here in Boconó, people listen a lot to *campesino* music, and our farmers don't miss this program. You can walk all over and you hear it," says Valentina.

In late 2002, *Radio Libertad* (Freedom Radio) was one of the first community radio stations legally permitted in the state of Trujillo under the Chávez government. They received their radio transmitter through the *Convenio Cuba-Venezuela* (Cuban-Venezuelan Agreement), whereby Venezuelan products such as oil are sent to Cuba in exchange for support from Cuba's medical professionals and other goods.[1] They still receive technical support though the Lara state office of the government-run *Red de Transmisiones de Venezuela* (RedTV - Venezuelan Broadcast Network).

The twenty-four hour Radio Libertad is just one of more than 240 legally operating community radios formed since Venezuelan President Hugo Chávez came to power in 1999.[2] Many of these radios have since set up their own networks, such as the *Red Venezolano de Medios Comunitarios* (the Venezuelan Community Media Network). Radio Libertad is an important member of the seven-year-old *Asociación Nacional de Medios Comunitarios, Libres y Alternativos* (ANMCLA - National Association of Free and Alternative

Community Media), and acts as the headquarters of ANMCLA – Trujillo.[3] ANMCLA has been an active and autonomous catalyst for community media organizing since 2002. More than 200 community media outlets participate in the organization. They have often joined with other Venezuelan social movements such as the Ezequiel Zamora National Campesino Front, the Urban Land Committees and the indigenous Wayúu to support each other's autonomous struggles.[4]

The energetic Father Edmundo Cadenas is one of the founders of the radio and a member of the thirty-five person collective that runs the tiny station. Cadenas pops in for a few minutes, before running off to a local coffee cooperative and a funeral a few towns away. He's one of only a half-dozen radical catholic priests who still preach Liberation Theology in Venezuela.

After a few hours, Valentina needs to leave. "You have to make a living and you have to do something to survive. Wow, you need to eat, pay rent, do this and that," she says. Radio Libertad was paid to broadcast an advertising spot from the Ministry of Communication in the first half of 2007, but those funds dried up a long time ago, and the radio coordinators, producers and sound engineers mostly do their jobs for free.[5]

Valentina, however, has many mouths to help feed. She has two daughters, a three-year-old granddaughter, and she also takes care of her aging mother, whose feet are not what they used to be. Valentina has worked in sales and graphics design for twenty-five years, and since 2000 has been producing the Boconó map and Carnival tourist guide. Although she has years of experience, both her and Arturo only just recently received their high school degrees through Venezuela's Ribas Mission, which has helped hundreds of thousands of middle-aged Venezuelans finally get their degrees. Valentina is now studying law through Venezuela's Sucre Mission.

Here, high up in these western Andean hills, Trujillo is a long way from Venezuela's capital, Caracas. Communities here can be hours from one another, with some *pueblos* only reachable on foot.[6] It was in these hills that revolutionary Venezuelans, such as Boconó's own legendary Fabricio Ojeda, led their guerrilla struggles against the repressive Venezuelan governments of the 1960s and 1970s. Raúl and Valentina's mother was one of those who took up arms.

Valentina Blanco
Raúl Blanco
Arturo Sosa

Revolutionary Roots

Valentina: My mom was born in Boconó. When she was sixteen, she moved to Caracas and started to work at the National Library, and that's where people like Fabricio Ojeda used to meet — people that were here in Boconó and then moved towards activism, and the guerrilla movement. She began when she was pretty young, and she was active for many years. She went to military school in Cuba for a year in '59 or '60. Along with my father, she was in charge of the guerilla telecommunications work, and they sabotaged commercial radios and national broadcasts.

She went to prison when I was five. Us kids were like the cover for them, so they didn't appear to be in the guerrilla. They were urban guerrilla fighters, so they were in various places, in Barlovento, in Caracas. I think they had an apartment behind Miraflores, and that's how they could interrupt the national broadcasts. My father was always a radio broadcaster. He worked at many radio stations, and was married many times and had a lot of kids.

So, yes, I think it is in the blood. It must be contagious or genetic or something.

So I imagine that some of this was the inspiration for Radio Libertad, because Raúl was the precursor of this dream of setting up a community radio.

Valentina Blanco

Valentina: I was born in Caracas while my mom was living there. I came here to Boconó in 2000, nine years ago. My mother is from here in Boconó, and I came here for six weeks to pick up my youngest daughter from her. And as great as people are elsewhere, it's not the same as being with your family. So, when I arrived in Boconó, it had been fourteen years since I had been here, and I saw my brother and he had this project and I got excited about it and I stayed.

Arturo Sosa

Arturo: I had never worked with radio before. I'm a student of *Misión Ribas*, and this is a school for me. I've learned from my *compañeros*. No one is anyone else's boss. Raúl isn't my boss. Valentina isn't my boss. We are all *compañeros*, and we work as a team, the same with the program producers, with everyone. The community has a radio here that always has the door open to help with the needs of the community, and I am very happy to be with this team and to continue to work to consolidate this process to raise people's awareness.

Radio Libertad – The Beginning

Raúl: Just before the year 2002 and the coup d'etat, we began to discuss the possibility of forming a collective among some long time revolutionaries to set up a community radio. I asked CONATEL, the *Comisión Nacional de Telecomunicaciones* (National Telecommunications Commission), which is the telecommunications regulatory body of Venezuela, for support and they required us to be a legally registered community foundation in order to create this radio here in Boconó, Trujillo.[7]

So little by little we got oriented and in 2002, roughly in August, already after the April 11th coup d'etat, we were able to get organized and hand in all the materials that CONATEL required, like the legal, technical, social and economic proposals. We passed them everything they required and we began to set things up. The most important thing was the legal recognition. But we also needed to legitimize it in the community. We began to carry out a community census to see about the possibility of setting up a community radio — if they agreed, if they were willing to work with us, etc. Meanwhile, we were consolidating internally as a collective. We continued to build the community radio project, Radio Libertad, and after a technical feasibility study, they gave us the frequency 99.3 FM.

In the beginning, there were many difficulties. There still are, but we have been able to overcome many things, and the support that we have received from MINCI, the Ministry of Communication & Information, has been important.[8] ANMCLA also really helped. The National Association of Free and Alternative Community Media helped us to believe in our proposal and also believe in our political position.[9] There are a lot of opportunists who want to do community radio because now they can, but it turns out that they end up doing religious radio or commercial radio, or radio in opposition to the process.

In our case, this is a radio that is supporting the community to understand the true sense of the revolutionary process in which we are living. The media war is impossible to fight if we don't have our own media outlets where the community is an active participant, where it has a voice that is truly heard. There have been many weaknesses, above all on the ideological level, and also in terms of political consciousness. The collectives are debilitated in this sense.

This community collective is called Burate Arriba, and the station is Radio Libertad 99.3 FM from the Boconó Parish of Trujillo State. We were also able to get support from some government bodies, and we have become multiplying catalysts for the other collectives from different Parishes in the Municipality of Boconó. We were able to offer support to five community radios that also wanted to do something similar, and our experience served as a launch pad for each of them to begin their work in their own Parishes. Boconó is a very large municipality in Trujillo state — it has twelve Parishes, and there are roughly five community radios here that are trying to solidify and consolidate. Some of them are already on the air, and others are in the process of getting set up. And well, we are a team and I make up part of the collective.

Valentina: We can't complain, because after the long struggle and everything we went through, we were one of the first community radios to be legally permitted, enabled, and set up. Of course it cost us trips to Caracas, without having anywhere to stay, without food, with *compañeros* that went and sat and waited in government offices. But we had the support of ANMCLA at the moment that the President put the pressure on. Chávez said that he wanted ninety community radios enabled within a certain date, so the government workers began to travel to the various regions and we benefited from this initial push. In the end, not all ninety were permitted and set up, but fifty-three were and we, as Burate Arriba Community Foundation, as Radio Libertad, can't complain.

"Our Path is the Road of the Community"

Valentina: People sometimes misunderstand the idea of community radio. Sometimes they have the idea that community radio is *chabacano,* or badly done. But I can tell you that the Libertad community radio enjoys wide respect from the listening audience in Boconó municipality where it is heard. At times our signal even reaches to some corners of Trujillo through the valleys within the mountains. And so, the people hear it and they care about it, because the message from Libertad is always positive, inviting you to develop. It is also a critical message — critical, because the voice of the community has a station here that exposes the faults. Sometimes, those people there in the establishment call those of us in the community radio *guarimberos*.[10] They call us counterrevolutionaries. But the people don't buy it. They know that we are with this process and our path is the road of the communities. That's one of the phrases we also repeat in ANMCLA: "Our path is the road of the communities."

We are hand in hand with the communities and the communities know that in Libertad they have support to resolve their problems, to communicate, and I think that these are achievements that you don't measure by how much you have in the piggy bank. They are achievements that the people care about, and which are measured by another vision that every one of the listeners of 99.3 FM can feel.

It seems to me that the community gets involved when they have their communal council meetings. So they come here and let the community know what is going on over the radio, and they know that we have a large listening audience. One of the programs with the highest listenership, which airs between 2 and 4 in the afternoon, is the *campesino* music program. Here in Boconó, people listen to *campesino* music a lot, and our farmers don't miss this program. You can walk all over and you hear it being played.

Raúl: And that's here in Boconó. Imagine in the rest of the countryside...

Valentina: ...where there are little communities. Where one house is separated from the next by 300 meters, or where there's only one house every few acres. They are all synchronized on the dial to Radio Libertad, listening to the music that is the product of our very own *campesinos*.

Programming

Raúl: We try to avoid playing the music that is played on the commercial radios that doesn't leave us with anything. That music doesn't educate us. It doesn't help us to grow. Of course we play *rancheras,* which the community likes. We play really good salsa, *campesino* music, reggae from Caricuao, from Caracas, national and

Latin American production from various different places; from Argentina, Chile. Well, we play a lot of music from Latin America, Venezuela… Our music, including the music from the *Golpe Larense,* the *llanera* music, and all of this music we play between our own programming, together with programs from community producers, independent national producers who produce their program here in Radio Libertad.[11]

Arturo: There are about thirty programs each week. Some are pretty solid, others come and go, but the good ones always stay.

Raúl: That's right. It would be good to clarify that in the beginning there were a lot of programs, something like fifty a week, and about ten a day, but many of them came with an already shaped idea. And now they had to, unfortunately, unlearn the only experience they had had, in order to be able to begin again in a more original way to do a new type of alternative radio. In this sense, ANMCLA has the job of supporting the process as well as doing something different, something more original, something that is better adapted to our revolutionary, transformative politics.

ANMCLA

Valentina: ANMCLA is a national association, which has participation from collectives of collectives. We all think in different ways, but we always have our common points of agreement, and meetings where we discuss the ideas and are able to arrive at a solution. So this is unity within diversity. In ANMCLA, there are alternative media, as much press as radio, websites, and audiovisual. I believe that the more we are able to organize as communities, each of us in our own battle trenches, and to communicate amongst each other and link each other together, we can defeat the mainstream media that do no good for our people.

In ANMCLA, there are also technological platforms, schools of grassroots communicators; there are cooperatives of radio transmitters; printing, ink and paper coops; graphic design workshops; audiovisual edition and audio edition workshops; and workshops for community radio production. Really, there are limitless possibilities that we have been inventing based on the beliefs of our Liberators, based on the slogan of Simón Rodríguez, *"o inventamos o erramos."* ("Either we invent, or we err.")

Community Radio

Valentina: Radio is a tool — a tool that gives you voice, and people out there listen, so you can replicate your message. What do we want? To raise the level of consciousness in our communities and to share understanding within our own communities, because our people are very wise; our people have a lot of knowledge and understanding and sharing it through the community radio helps us to grow each day, little by little.

I believe that basically when you listen to community radio, you are listening to the voice from the heart of every one of the people that has come to the radio to speak through the microphones. It is not a radio that is constantly telling you what to buy or where to go. Listen, the commercial radio stations here in Venezuela — according to the CONATEL stipulations, which is the government body that regulates the airwaves — have fifteen minutes of publicity for each hour of broadcast. These commercial radios abuse this, and rather than fifteen minutes each hour they take twenty-five minutes for their commercials.

Mainstream Media

Valentina: The mainstream media have all of the technology, they have all of the economic resources to be able to run their commercial media, and all of the brains sitting there who are very well paid to fabricate all of these lies, and we are tiny. It's not that we're tiny. No, because our people are very large, large in understanding and wisdom and many things. We are building. We make mistakes and we fall, but we get back up, and we share our knowledge, but of course we don't have the equipment that they have.

We, the people, are the owners of our airwaves, but look at how the Venezuelan airwaves are distributed here among the FM radios. I'm not an expert, but almost all of the FM frequency is in the hands of the commercial stations, and they are very competitive. Their transmitters broadcast much further. Sometimes there are community radios that don't even have sufficient reach with their own Parish because CONATEL assigns us a signal that can't be heard completely throughout the area. Are they afraid to let the communities speak? Afraid that the communities will really say what they want? We are all inhabitants of Venezuela, and all of our voices need to be heard, together.

There are a lot of interests within the mainstream media that have people infiltrated in these government institutions that block us. They put the breaks on this process, but no one can stop this. Even if we have to acquire a transmitter through our own efforts, hide it in a bedroom, and send the signal out from there even without a license. We are going to learn to activate transmitters wherever possible because our voices need to be heard, and we have to make these connections amongst each other because no one is going to stop this process. You can't stop it.

The Enemy Within

Raúl: There are many traitors in this revolutionary Bolivarian process in Venezuela. And little by little they are unmasked, revealing themselves, and you see who doesn't agree, but is only pretending to agree, and is really just disrupting the process.

We have received support from the government through bodies like CONATEL, MINCI, but unfortunately governors or some of those responsible in these institutions are against the process, and regardless they hold public offices. This is an issue that we, along with many other organizations, have been denouncing. And because we have been critical, we have been looked upon negatively. We have continued to question and critique, and because of this they have made our lives pretty impossible.

Valentina: Sometimes we feel like they play with our communities, and play with us. They ask for a ton of documents, and then they file them and they get stuck there in the bureaucracy. These public officials who have thirty to forty years in the same job but haven't retired don't have any sensitivity and they don't attend to the needs of the communities. That's why the people get annoyed, and they go looking for other options. That's what we do in ANMCLA. We exhaust the regular channels, but we won't think twice about starting a ruckus and carrying out nationwide demonstrations and marches.

RCTV

Valentina: The last march in 2007 to this respect was to support the non-renewal of the TV broadcast license to *Radio Caracas Televisión* (RCTV). ANMCLA had a lot to do with the initiative, and the media strategy. We did various activities. On March 27th, 2007, we carried out the march, we held a vigil in front of RCTV, and we painted the walls, although they called us savages and whatever. We had a great time writing thousands of things to *granielito*, Marcel Granier. There was a stage, a cultural act, they débuted a video about the need to not renew the Radio Caracas Television broadcast license, because our airwaves belong to all us. The airwaves belong to the people and they were being badly administered by a group of people with economic interests different than the interests of our revolutionary process. I believe, at this moment, the voice of the people was heard, and in this moment there was real organization between the government, the people, and the community.

Chávez & Community Radio

Valentina: It's a lie that the community media in Venezuela are all in the pockets of Chávez. In fact, there are a lot of community radios that are only "community" by name. They are vile commercial radios dressed up as community radios. They don't do anything for the communities. They survive with advertisements. They play the same music as all of the commercial radios. They have nothing to do with the community.

I believe that the majority of the community radios are independent. Of course, the true community radios are with the [Bolivarian] process, because if this process didn't exist, we wouldn't exist as community radios. There is freedom of thought, and they are critical of the process. And even more, the people are sincere and say what they think. They criticize, "Look, this is isn't right. What's going on here? We need to fix this." I think that we have matured in this sense. Some people, especially in the state of Trujillo, are sometimes a little shaky because the authorities sometimes take reprisals, but in general the community radios are pretty authentic. The people say what they think independently of what can happen.

Is There Freedom of Expression in Venezuela?

Raúl: There is absolute freedom of expression in Venezuela. Absolutely.

Valentina: Completely. Of course.

Raúl: There is even the possibility for the enemies to express their truthful information in the community media, but not to continue the media war. We have to resist from our own angle, because it is very intense, because they have the economic power and they are trying to misdirect and confuse the people.

We're better off without RCTV, although it's still on cable and some 5 percent of the population still continue to watch it, with all of its lies, with its slander, violating the laws — the Law of Social responsibility in Radio and Television and the rules under the Organic Law on Telecommunications. In the case of the community radios, there are many of them that don't understand, and are violating the laws of radio and television broadcasting, and non-profit community television. These legal mechanisms are being violated, even with this whole consciousness raising process.

So, of course, with respect to the question: is there freedom of speech? Well, I believe there is too much freedom of speech. So much that they violate the laws and continue on the air. They should be closed. In any European country, in any industrialized country, in any developed country, these stations that don't obey the laws are sanctioned. Not here.

Overcoming Fear

Valentina: I have a message to anyone who has the dream of setting up a community radio. The first thing you have to do is overcome the fear, the fear of this technological equipment. We have to overcome these fears: these fears that don't get us anywhere, these fears that paralyze us. And wherever you have a community radio running, there are *compañeros* there that are willing to teach you, to tell you how to do it. With everyone organized, we can activate the transmitter, and turn on a radio to cut through the airwaves of our skies and arrive in each of the homes, offices, work places, or even the countryside where people are working the land. That's how powerful even a simple radio is, because you have the possibility to hear other things.

Because a community radio is like having access to a window that shows you how the world is — the world that we want and which we are constructing, the world we all dream of in the depths of our hearts, as inhabitants of this planet. Because we have love for our planet; for our fellow mankind; for all of the men, women, girls, boys, adolescents who are part of this population. The world is united as one, regardless of music and language barriers. There are so many things to broadcast on the radio that allow you to dream, that caress the senses and lift the most diverse feelings in you — like anger, fury at the injustices — and wake up the need to change within you; to change things; to transform them. And it also awakens within you the need to change yourself, because while you are changing and overcoming these fears, you are transforming your reality, and transforming the reality around you, and this is like a spark, which burns and grows, and it is very beautiful to share with everyone. What else can I say?

Part V:

INDIGENOUS &
AFRO-VENEZUELAN MOVEMENTS

TWELVE

Warao Students - The Indigenous University of Venezuela.

Mecheduniya & Wadajaniyu, Indigenous University of Venezuela

(Tauca, Bolívar)

A Ye'kuana elder slowly recites the lyrics to an ancient story in his native language while he weaves a hat made from long, green palm leaves picked from the surrounding forest. Mecheduniya, a young Ye'kuana Indian, carefully writes these lines down in the written form of his language, which he has been learning over the past few years. Another group of young Ye'kuanas is getting dressed in bright multi-colored ceremonial costumes made only from leaves and feathers to practice for a presentation of an ancient play that they will be performing the next day. "We are teaching in the jungle here. In the jungle we learn how to sing the traditional songs and to tell our stories," says Wadajaniyu, a rector and one of the founders of the Indigenous University of Venezuela.

The university lies in the vast territory known as the Guyana region, which sprawls southwards below the great Orinoco River that cuts a nearly perfect diagonal line through the center of the country. To most Venezuelans, the Guayana remains only a place in photographs. Nearly 90 percent of the Venezuelan population lives in the northwestern half of the country, while indigenous peoples make up nearly fifty percent of the population in the giant southeastern state, Amazonas.[1] In the early colonial era, the myth of *El Dorado*, a land of gold, enticed Spanish *conquistadores* to organize expeditions into Venezuela's interior by sailing down the Orinoco. Little gold was actually discovered, but the region's abundant natural resources and wildlife are still the stuff of legend.

Like in the rest of the Americas, colonialism brought devastation to Venezuela's native peoples. As Venezuela entered the modern era, they continued to suffer the loss of their traditional cultures and lands as evangelists and development encroached upon their communities.[2]

Located four hours outside of Ciudad Bolívar, the capital of Bolívar State, and a two-kilometer hike down a dusty weather-beaten road, the Indigenous University of Venezuela is the indigenous movement's response to this devastation. The university seeks to be a focal point for indigenous peoples in Venezuela, using culture as a primary instrument in advancing their cause. This university has few classrooms as most of the teaching takes place outside under the thick forest canopy. The indigenous students at this university sleep in hammocks in the small villages divided amongst the varying ethnic groups.

Representing around 2.2 percent of the population with approximately twenty-eight ethnic groups located throughout the country, indigenous peoples form a small part of the Venezuelan population and historically remained marginal in the national politics of the country.[3] While other governments in the region were beginning to codify a new set of liberties for indigenous peoples in the 1990s, Venezuela languished with one of the most politically backwards constitutions with regards to indigenous rights. Still, Venezuela's indigenous peoples slowly found ways to organize themselves and insert their political goals into the national agenda through forming regional and state-level organizations such as the *Federación Indígena del Estado Bolívar* (FIB - Indigenous Federation of the State of Bolívar) and the *Organización Regional de los Pueblos Indígenas de Amazonas* (ORPIA - Regional Organization of the Indigenous Peoples of Amazonas State).[4] This local organizing began to consolidate nationally through the *Consejo Nacional Indio de Venezuela* (CONIVE - National Indigenous Council of Venezuela), created in 1989.

With the accumulation of significant experiences, indigenous peoples found themselves prepared for the unprecedented political opening provided by the advent of the Chávez government. Indigenous organizations participated with an extraordinary level of access in the construction of Venezuela's new constitution. Chávez's own declarations in support of the indigenous cause, along with his designation of three seats for indigenous peoples within the constituent assembly, brought an indisputable energy to the movement. By convoking a range of forums and internal consultations, CONIVE galvanized this movement and gathered the necessary force to push their proposals forward amidst opposition from the assembly's more conservative representatives.[5]

With the weight of an entire chapter committed to indigenous peoples, the Venezuelan Constitution significantly amplified their rights. The constitution set forth an ambitious agenda to grant an array of entitlements to indigenous peoples under their supervision, such as communal land titles and their own educational institutions. Chapter 8 of the Bolivarian Constitution recognizes and guarantees

the respect of indigenous culture, languages, customs, and traditional lands, while requiring that the government work with indigenous
communities to implement these rights.

The Guaicaipuro Mission was created in 2003 to bring these
promises to life by aiding indigenous communities with the processes
of self-demarcation and local development. In 2007, the government
created of the Ministry of Popular Power for Indigenous Peoples to
catalyze further energy in meeting the needs of Venezuela's indigenous peoples.

While indigenous peoples recognize that they have been provided with unprecedented opportunities, they also see many obstacles in the fulfillment of their new rights. Although the incorporation
of leaders from CONIVE into positions of power in the Venezuelan
government has brought indigenous representation within the state
to a new level, it has also brought criticisms from an indigenous base
that has sensed a loss in the organizations' autonomy and ability to
make stronger demands. And while significant territory has been
granted to some indigenous groups, a comprehensive response to
many communities' land claims remains elusive. The actual practice
of self-demarcation seems to be a far reality from what many in the
indigenous movement expected from the new constitution and the
many statements that have been made by President Chávez.[6]

The Indigenous University of Venezuela exists within this
challenging space between opportunity and obstacles and provides a
remarkable example of the aspirations of the indigenous movement.
Fortified by Article 121 of the Venezuelan Constitution, which gives
indigenous peoples the right to develop their own education, four
indigenous communities came together to create a space where their
youth can be educated as the defenders of their original ways; able
to resist the onslaught of the Western world upon their peoples.

Beginning with just a handful of students, seventy indigenous youth representing eight distinct ethnic groups now attend
the university: the Warao, Pemón, Kariña, Pumé, E'ñepa, Piaroa,
Sanema, and Ye'kuana. An autonomous project seeking recognition from the national government, the Indigenous University high-
lights the fragile and complicated relationship between Venezuelan
social movements and the state. While they draw strength from the
Bolivarian Constitution and the importance the Chávez government has placed on indigenous rights, they still find themselves
having to navigate independently and sometimes even defensively

within the world of Venezuelan politics. Nonetheless, it is through projects such as the Indigenous University of Venezuela and the battle in which it is engaged that Venezuela's constitution is being transformed into a reality.

Mecheduniya & Wadajaniyu

Personal Histories

Mecheduniya: My name is Mecheduniya and I am Ye'kuana, from the municipality of San Juan de Manapiare, specifically from the Cacurí community located in the Alto Ventuari sector of Amazonas State near the Brazilian border. I entered the Indigenous University of Venezuela as a student in 2003 and am now in the process of completing my thesis in order to graduate. I first heard about the university while I was studying in the city, in Puerto Ayacucho. Some students who were part of the first group at the university came to promote it. After deciding that I wanted to enter the university, I spoke with my family as well as my whole community about it. The community asked me many questions and we spoke about everything. It became clear to them that I was going to be able have a genuine education that would benefit my community.

When I first came to the university I asked myself who I was, where I was coming from, and finally where I was going. The university asked me these questions and with each one I had a new personal experience. Through this process I came to discover myself as an indigenous person, recognizing that I have a culture, a language, and an education. It became clearer to me how necessary it is to rescue the richness of my culture. My culture has been disappearing for a long time due to the arrival of Western education and the loss of our identity as indigenous peoples. Throughout all of this process at the university and the education I have received, I came to realize that I was outside of my community, outside of my culture, because I had already studied in a traditional school. This university is a place for young indigenous people to return to their community and their culture.

Wadajaniyu: My name is Wadajaniyu in Ye'kuana and Arturo Asiza in Spanish. I belong to the Ye'kuana tribe also from the municipality of San Juan de Manapiare in the Venezuelan state of Amazonas. I am on the council of academic rectors in the

University. I arrived here for the first time in 1997 when we first began the conversation about initiating this project, when we first spoke about what we needed to do in order to educate our children. About twenty elders from various parts of the country participated in that conversation, with support from Brother José María Korta, a Jesuit priest from the Basque country in Spain.[7] We spoke about the way we were losing our cultures and how traditional schools and universities were only exposing our youth to Western culture. We spent a month discussing this situation and came to an agreement to open the Indigenous University.

Origins of the University

Mecheduniya: The university was created with guidance from Brother José María Korta, who is now a nationalized Venezuelan citizen. He began his work here many years ago in the Caucarí community and came simply as an adviser without trying to impose his religion on the indigenous peoples. He helped them with the creation of three major projects in agricultural production, honey production, and cattle ranching. The community managed them and they became very successful.

In 2000, when the government recognized the rights of indigenous peoples in the new constitution, it also established our right to our own education. With the guidance from Brother Korta, representatives from four different tribes, the Ye'kuana, Pume, E'ñepa y Piaroa, were brought together for four months to discuss and develop the foundation of the university. This discussion was then taken to the indigenous communities to establish the nature of the university and determine what was necessary for its creation. We looked at the necessities of the communities involved and came to an agreement on the areas of study. We now have eight indigenous groups represented here.

Wadajaniyu: I always critiqued the traditional universities because I have two daughters who studied in them. They returned with their minds empty of their own culture, but full of Western culture. It was upsetting to see, to feel like I was losing my family. I now have two years working as a rector with the university. I have continued to come to the university because my people are here, and two of my sons are studying here. I am also here to learn from the other elders because I didn't have the opportunity to learn everything from my grandparents or my father who all died too young for me to take enough advantage of them. But, I still carry a lot of information in my memory as well as in written form because I learned to write in a traditional school.

The Effects of Evangelism

Wadajaniyu: Evangelists first came to the Amazonas region a long time ago. I was a young boy when they started arriving. The type of evangelism that they brought was extremely hard on our communities. It took our culture and religion away from us. They would tell us that our religion was that of the devil and that our culture had no value because it was unwritten. My father always defended our culture and our community, however. They attempted to evangelize him but he didn't allow this to happen. My father, along with others in the community, actually forced those evangelists out. I have that story written down in a book I have at home. That is a treasure for me. I always have this story in mind when we are fighting for our land because my father was a leader in defending his culture.

The Nuevas Tribus evangelist group that Chávez expulsed a few years ago took a lot of culture away from us.[8] They did great damage to us. For example, our peoples in the Alto Orinoco were left with nothing. When you ask them about their culture, they have nothing to tell you. All they can do is respond about Jesus Christ. Nuevas Tribus brainwashed them and poisoned them with their own beliefs. I see these brothers and sisters lost, dead without their culture.

This is why we want to show our youth how to maintain their culture firmly, in the way that their ancestors did. In the Ventuari region, we have been able to maintain our culture. Those in the Upper Caura have also maintained their culture firmly. But our elders are slowly being lost without having written the knowledge of our ancestors. This is why we decided that we had to accelerate the education of our youth. If that knowledge is lost, our youth are left with nothing, without a weapon to defend themselves.

Indigenous Education

Wadajaniyu: We are teaching in the jungle here. In the jungle we learn how to sing the traditional songs and to tell our stories. We use the materials from nature and put them to use in our communities. This is the case, for example, with the materials we use to make our drums and to make the *sebucán*, which we use to process our food.[9] We teach them about the traditional medicines and how to make the dugout canoes and paddles from the trees. This is why we care for nature, because it is from nature that we live, that we eat. This is what we teach the students here by showing them the plants and the trees, telling them their names and what they are used for.

Mecheduniya: When I was growing up, my father educated me in an indigenous way. I would accompany him while hunting and fishing and while making our traditional crafts. Every time we would enter the jungle he would tell me the names of the hills, the canyons, the animals, and the plants. That was the education that I received as a child that I have taken up again here at the university.

On a general level, here we all learn how to be responsible, disciplined, and to live in solidarity with one another. Academically, we have various subjects such as indigenous history, indigenous education, indigenous law, ethnology, ethnobotany, and agroecology. We learn how to use the modern technology available to us as well. We also analyze the situation in each of our communities and how we should be contributing to them as the Indigenous University because we are all a part of our communities, we were chosen by them to study here. We learn how to take what we have learned here back to our communities and to record that information.

My thesis is focused on studying the cosmovision of my people. I became aware how much of that knowledge and mythology remains unwritten. One of the ideas from the university is to have a written record of our history and our mythology, of who our creator was and our origins as a people. I see it as necessary to salvage that knowledge since many of our elders who have this information are disappearing. Our elders are like libraries, archives of our people. I still have a lot of work to do to complete my thesis. I have to sit with the elders and interview them, and then go about transcribing this in my native language with supervision from the elders. Afterwards, I have to return to the university to translate this into Spanish with the help of one of the tutors here.

Bringing the University to the Community

Mecheduniya: After finishing my time here I will return to my community because that is the responsibility we have. To continue this same kind of education, explaining the kind of work I have done here, collaborating with my community and the elders. I have a lot of work to do. I now have a vision. I have spoken with another Ye'kuana *compañero* here about creating another space like the university in our community, like a branch of the university, apart from the traditional school. This university is currently the only space indigenous peoples have to produce, strengthen, and consolidate our cultures. We still don't have this kind of space in our communities. We cannot continue to simply be in the hands of the Ministry of Education, which comes from outside of the community. The mentality of our youth is still to obtain money, which takes us to another world. But the communities have taken the students here very seriously, because we have demonstrated our ability to work.

Indigenous Peoples and State Politics

Mecheduniya: Today there is much talk about indigenous peoples in Venezuela since the national government has now recognized our rights. Because of that, indigenous peoples have been progressing little by little. Being recognized in the constitution is a tool that is laid out on paper, which has yet to be really placed into practice.

Wadajaniyu: Before we had no means to be able to defend ourselves. Now, under the Chávez government, we are mentioned in the constitution and we have the ability to organize ourselves. The constitution has given us the most strength where it mentions our right to our own form of education. That is what we are looking to create here. Indigenous groups have always organized here to try to figure out ways to support our communities. But we never had the value of maintaining our culture in the way that we wanted it. A lot of political factions would enter our communities and take our culture away little by little. I participated in an organization called the Regional Organization of the Indigenous Peoples of Amazonas State. We would always come together for meetings and make agreements, but we never achieved solutions. Those that led the organization were often indigenous politicians who had sold out to the world of politics.

Mecheduniya: When my community was founded, there was pure culture, indigenous organization, and our ancient knowledge was intact. Now we find ourselves in a much more complex situation, because the politics that exist throughout the whole world have entered our community which has meant the loss of our traditional forms of organization. These party politics have a way of imposing themselves on the community. Those that have involved themselves with this world have civilized themselves as *criollos* that don't think about returning to their communities and are not interested in their culture.

Support from the Government

Wadajaniyu: The truth is that we have received very little support from the government. We have received some funds from a few government institutions, such as Fundayacucho and Corporación Venezolana de Guayana, but the mayoral and state governments have given us almost no support.[10] We submitted a project to the city government of Maripa, where we are located, years ago during the last mayor's term, but to this day we have received no response. We have at least received some funds from the Amazonas State government as scholarship money for some of the students. Amazonas has also funded the travel expenses for the elders to the university since we have no resources to do this ourselves. But we have received very little.

Those who are involved in politics do not want to support us. We Ye'kuana have an indigenous representative in the government, Nicia Maldonado, whom we have invited various times to the university to speak with us. But we have received no response. Being our sister and having political power, she should be trying to support us.

Mecheduniya: We are in the process now of seeking recognition from the national government. President Chávez already verbally recognized the university and authorized the Ministry of Superior Education to recognize us. We have already organized ourselves into commissions and developed materials to prepare a meeting with the Minister of Superior Education. Twice now, the Ministry has committed to coming to the university and has cancelled at the last moment, claiming to have other work to attend to. Here we are, still waiting.

Here, in Venezuela, we have a situation in which many ministers, some of whom are indigenous themselves, are not responding to the needs of the people. This is the case with Nicia Maldonado, who directs the Ministry of Popular Power for Indigenous Peoples. In fact she wanted to impose herself on the university by renaming it the *Bolivarian* Indigenous University of Venezuela. We refused this however. Our rights to our own education are written in the constitution, as well as in Convention 169 of the International Labor Organization, which was ratified by Venezuela.[11] We are defending our university with these documents.

Of course, the situation for indigenous people has changed. Now we are recognized by this government. But there is still excessive bureaucracy. It worries us that this minister doesn't want to listen to us or support us. The indigenous representatives who are in government were not elected by their communities and have not gone to all of the communities to dialogue with the people there. This is why they don't understand us or respond to our needs.

Self-Demarcation

Mecheduniya: At one point, there was a lot of noise being made in this country about self-demarcation. Chávez talked about how indigenous people can now begin to demarcate their territory. But up to now, we have had no real results. There have been some areas granted, but we Ye'kuana don't have any large territories demarcated. This is one of the most important things for us, because an indigenous person with no land has no life or culture. This is a concern for us right now.

Wadajaniyu: The Ye'kuana continue struggling for the demarcation of our territories. We are fighting to organize ourselves and to have our territories legalized in three sectors in the Orinoco-Ventuari region. Individually, we cannot legalize our territories. If we unite we will gain more power so that we can be recognized. We have demarcated territory in the Upper Caura sector but it has not been recognized. Last year, we went through all of the steps of marking the borders of our territory but there is still much to do in order to have it recognized. Some people say that we are seeking to demarcate too large a territory. But the government cannot tell us that it is too large because we are not new here. We are native to this land.

The State-Sponsored Social Missions

Wadajaniyu: I have heard of people working with the Guaicaipuro Mission but we have not seen any results from those people. They have not really communicated with us about what they want or what they are seeking to do with the Mission. I have no idea how the Guaicaipuro Mission functions. In Amazonas State, there are some Ye'kuana working inside the Mission, but they have not arrived to the villages. They have not provided us with information.

We have seen the arrival of some of the other social missions to our communities. The Robinson and Ribas Missions have made it, as well as the Barrio Adentro Mission. This has been very positive. I had my eyes operated on through the Milagro Mission. I had cataracts on my eyes and was taken to Cuba to be operated on. Thanks to the mission, I am fine now. All of this was free. Many of us were sent, twenty from my community. I was actually the youngest of all of them! This is a good service that has been provided to the indigenous and other peoples.

The Struggle Then and Now

Wadajaniyu: When the Spanish arrived here, our peoples were dispersed. The Spanish arrived to recruit our men and women in order to enslave them, so our people fled. Those captured were tied up and forced to work on the Balatá tree plantations.[12] When they got sick, they were left to die like animals. Many Ye'kuana were killed. The elders tell us that we once had a much larger community. Many communities were abandoned. Our ancestors always sought to reunite our people again. To overcome these kinds of disasters we have to do the kind of work we are doing now. To recover from these problems we have to study. We have to study in order to recover what is rightfully ours.

We have ten years fighting for the university here, and we will continue demanding that the institutions and the government recognize it. We have made important advances and the students who have graduated from the university have become important human resources here. My hope is that we will receive recognition from the national government and that more people from our communities will come to the university. Since we are not recognized, the students are not able to receive an official degree. The parents of some of our students still believe that their children are wasting their time here because of this. They say the same things that are being said by those involved in politics that are opposed to the university. But, the youth want to be here because they don't need the same things that they need at a traditional university in order to fit in. They don't need to have money. Here they simply have to fill their minds with knowledge.

THIRTEEN

Jorge Montiel.

———

Jorge Montiel,
Maikivalasalii, Wayúu Community

(Sierra de Perijá, Zulia)

The early dawn sunlight barely begins to shine when the Wayúu women in colorful, long, loosely draping dresses emerge from their adobe mud homes to prepare the morning meal. Shirtless young boys wearing tattered pants and rubber boots fetch drinking water in plastic buckets from the crystal clear Socuy River twenty meters down the hill, while the older men sweat as they chop firewood in the already intense morning heat. The women make *arepas* and *chicha* using the water the boys bring.[1] The water from the Socuy River means everything here. It is what the Wayúu use for cooking, for bathing, and for cultivating their crops. The coal that lies so visible at the bottom of the Socuy creates a beautiful backdrop below the water, betraying the potential threat of its exploitation.

The Wayúu, living in the area known as the Sierra de Perijá in the northwestern region of the state of Zulia, have found themselves at the center of a paramount debate concerning nothing less than the fundamental direction of the development model within Venezuela. Resource nationalism — in which the state takes majority ownership over mining projects — has been one of the fundamental pillars of the Bolivarian Revolution. However, fewer steps have been taken towards creating an economy less dependent on the extraction of natural resources.

In 2004, Corpozulia, the Zulia State development corporation responsible for providing mining concessions and creating joint ventures with private multinational companies within the region, granted concessions to exploit coal within the areas surrounding the Socuy, Mache, and Cachirí rivers — all areas inhabited by Wayúu communities. Since the concessions were proposed, the Wayúu have been embroiled in a conflict that has brought them unlikely adversaries and the bitter reality that fighting against natural resource exploitation remains an uphill battle even in Venezuela.

Corpozulia now claims to be a socialist development organization, but many within the indigenous and environmental movements accuse it of essentially functioning in the way it has since its creation by the Venezuelan National Congress in 1970.[2] The region directly north of the Sierra de Perijá is already home to two coalmines responsible for displacing indigenous communities, both jointly owned by Corpozulia and multinational companies. Wary of having past experiences repeated, many of the Wayúu in the Sierra de Perijá now maintain a militantly defiant stance against further mining in their communities. While Corpozulia has used powerful media campaigns to argue that any new coal mining will be environmentally benign and will bring much needed jobs to the local economy, the Wayúu counter that the deforestation, pollution, and displacement caused by past coal mining operations is inevitable.

In response, the Wayúu living in areas targeted for coal mining have organized numerous rallies and meetings with government officials, bringing both national and international attention to their struggle. The complexity of the contemporary indigenous movement in Venezuela is revealed most starkly in the battles taking place in the Sierra de Perijá. The Wayúu struggle has been able to maintain a high profile through their alliances with environmental organizations such as *Sociedad Homo et Natura*, the autonomous and community media movement, and other indigenous groups in the region such as the Yukpa and Barí facing similar challenges to their traditional lands.[3] In contrast, their relationship to the leadership within the National Indigenous Council of Venezuela (CONIVE) and the Ministry of Popular Power for Indigenous Peoples has proven to be much less amiable, with each side calling into question the political integrity of the other. Yet the Wayúu have not gone without political support from the government. They have found support from Chávez, who famously stated in 2006, "If there is no method of assuring the respect of the forests and the mountains... in the Sierra de Perijá, where the coal is... this coal will remain below the ground."[4] Amidst further proclamations from Chávez opposing coal, the Ministry of the Environment also made repeated statements supporting the Wayúu position.

The Wayúu communities' location in the state of Zulia, which has been consistently dominated by opposition governors, has made their situation all the more complex. Former governor Manuel Rosales, a key leader in the opposition movement has frequently made provocative statements supporting the secession of the state of Zulia from the national government, a call also made by elite-led separatist movements in the resource rich regions of Bolivia and Ecuador.[5] Groups opposed to the Wayúu struggle, including other indigenous communities, have used this situation to accuse them of being influenced by the opposition movement. The Wayúu as a people have also been divided politically and culturally for some time. Many Wayúu who have now become part of Zulia's urban population see mining as an opportunity for further employment, vocalizing their antipathy to those Wayúu still living on their traditional lands. Corpozulia's many offers of employment and social investment in Wayúu communities have proven to be a significant tactic in intensifying this division.

The Wayúu conflict could be seen as a testing ground determining the orientation of the Bolivarian Revolution in regards to the exploitation of natural resources. The Wayúu and their environmentalist allies argue that at some point such damaging extractive industries must be challenged if indigenous peoples' territories and the environment are to be respected. This is of course no small critique in a country heavily reliant upon petroleum extraction, which has been unable to overcome its historical dependency on natural resource exploitation, like much of the Global South. Expectedly, multinational mining companies and their representative countries wield considerable pressure on the Venezuelan government to maintain their operations. While the threat of mining in their territory seems to be at a standstill for the moment, the Wayúu continue to demand that the concessions granted by Corpozulia be revoked. For the Wayúu, the Venezuelan constitution's enshrinement of indigenous rights will remain little more than words on paper until their demands are respected.

Jorge Montiel

The Wayúu Community

My name is Jorge Montiel and I am a member of the Wayúu community. I would not say that I am a principal member of the community since we are all principal members here. Here, we all have multiple functions, we must act as teachers, sometimes we have to travel, at times organize events; a little bit of everything. Of course, I may have more experience than some of the other *compañeros* here. But the idea is to always inject the experiences of everything we have learned back into those *compañeros*. It is the role of all of us to help with everything that is necessary for our community. Rather than talk about "I," we talk about "us." However, this is difficult because the habits of today have made us all more individualistic. So we are always learning how to share, how to be collective, and how to organize ourselves.

Our struggle has developed from defending our land, our water, the resources we have here, and our culture. We do this because we are afraid that if we don't defend our land, our culture will disappear and with the loss of our culture, we as indigenous people will disappear. What we want is to conserve our culture — to cultivate it, and to do this so that our grandchildren can also build upon it.

Building the Wayúu Movement

We currently have six Wayúu communities involved in this struggle, numbering around four hundred people. We have come together to form an organization by the name of *Maikivalasalii*, which means "Not For Sale" in our native language. We are always aspiring to have more communities join us. Our struggle is similar to the Zapatistas in this way. Our allies are the genuine social movements in this country, because we know that there are some social movements that exist only to make money. We know who these groups are because we ask them what their gains have been, as well as their failures. Only a movement that makes demands gets attacked. A conformist movement is not attacked.

From the beginning, we have had support from our environmentalist companions and the students. While they may not be indigenous, they have an indigenous ideology and they understand our indigenous thought. These *compañeros* have twenty-three years of struggle here in the Sierra de Perijá, fighting along side the Barí, the Yukpa, and us here in the north against the official government doctrine, which tells us that development happens through the promotion of industry.[6] We live here, immersed with this doctrine. But as a result of learning about the struggles of our Barí and Yukpa *compañeros*, we realized that this was not the type of development that we wanted. We realized that this was not strengthening our culture, but that it was actually exterminating it.

In 2003, our organization began to take shape and we organized marches in Caracas and in Maracaibo in 2004. We are clear about what we want and we declare our position in the face of anything. We are opposed to coal mining and we don't hide this fact. We confront, we declare, and we assume our responsibilities. This is why our struggle has experienced some critical moments — moments of happiness and moments of sadness.

We have also been the subject of accusations because we are opposed to projects of the government and the state of Zulia, which are considered sacred by government officials. When it is brought up that we do not support a development project, we are automatically accused of being anti-Chavista and counter-revolutionaries. It is as if they want us to shut off our pain, but we cannot shut off our pain. What we say we must say. We have to provide our opinions. The officials tell us that nobody can be opposed to the will and the rule of the state. We respond by asking, "Where is the mandate of the people? Where is the development project for the people? Where are the thoughts of the people?"

The government must learn how to govern by the word of the people, listening to the people. We cannot have a government immersed in its own political ambitions. We have suffered many accusations, but we have learned how to rise above all of that, weaving alliances with other movements inside Venezuela and in other countries because we understand that an isolated movement is a failed movement.

It has been necessary for us to distance ourselves a bit from the political parties, because we have seen that they have been one of the factors that have corrupted social organizations. Distancing ourselves means that our path is not that of gaining political positions. Our path is to contribute to the consolidation of our peoples and to the ideas of all of us within the organization, regardless of what groups some our *compañeros* participate in. Because we understand that some of these allies are activists in political parties, but we don't impose ourselves on them. We simply tell them that our organization will not lend itself to that. We don't accept political party propaganda or political posters in our areas. This is why we have survived, even without resources.

Wayúu Land & Culture

Our history and struggle as Wayúu stem from our origins in La Guajira, where we lived in a large territory and were able to develop our ways of life and our culture.[7] That is why we fear being displaced and forced to move into the *barrios*, because in the *barrios* we cannot develop our culture. Our culture and our development depend on the activity of agriculture. In the *barrios* we cannot cultivate. If we cannot cultivate, then we cannot develop culturally either. Having the space to cultivate, you can carry forth your cultural acts. How? By summoning your *compañeros* to participate in the harvest; having a meeting, and eating from that harvest; by performing our traditional dances, like the *Yonna*, and playing our drums. Without this kind of meal, we cannot convoke people in such a way. This is not possible in the *barrios*. This is why our land is so important to us.

We as Wayúu always had our own ways of doing things. For example, we always had our own traditional games and in the legal sense, our own laws. A lawyer out of a university doesn't solve our problems. Nor does a court, or a public prosecutor. It is the council of elders that makes the decision together in order to resolve conflicts. It is through consensus that we make decisions, not through an assembly with a majority or minority vote. It is something very different from the Western world. This is what we have defended because if we are not careful, all of that will disappear.

We do not have a religion; we have our healing form of spirituality unlike the kind of religion being spread throughout the whole country by evangelists, which attempts to instill fear. We were born without fear. For us god is *Mareiwa*, which we interpret as the combination of water and earth. *Ma* is earth and *reiwa* is water, the rain that impregnates the earth, and we are the children of this earth. Our god is not a person, as the Greco-Roman religions believe. The evangelists tell us that we cannot dream because that is a sin. They tell us that we cannot wear our traditional dress or play our drums because that is a sin. Sadly, this is what has been inculcated in some of our indigenous *compañeros*. We have maintained our own indigenous philosophy, our own way of thinking. This is why our struggle is so important. We are not just saying no to coal mining, we are also saying no to the death of our culture, no the death of our traditional medicines, no to the death of indigenous thought, and no to the death of our Mother Earth and the death of our Father Water. Because, of course, if there is no forest here then the water will stop to run.

We moved to the area where we are now from the Upper Guajira in search of water and life. We moved to where there is rain, following the animal herds. We have always functioned in this way. We indigenous peoples move to a place and set roots. We don't use this beautiful earth as merchandise. Rather, we leave it as an inheritance to our children. Before we arrived here, this was already the indigenous land of our ancestors. Here you can find pottery and the remains of our ancestors. When we arrived here, we realized that this is what has been robbed from us over many years, and this is our moment to rescue it and occupy what is ours by original right. This is why we organized ourselves in this way, because we knew that confronting a project of the state and the transnational companies is no small thing. They have power and money and we do not. But we do have something they do not. We have dignity. A social movement that has dignity is a movement that can be considered solid.

The Battle Against Coal & Corpozulia

We are demanding that the government annul all the coal concessions that they have already granted here in the Socuy, all 249,000 hectares which make up this whole mountain area. These are concessions that have already been made by Corpozulia, which is responsible for making concessions. Corpozulia is a corporation of the state of Zulia, and it receives its funds from the government. The president of Corpozulia is chosen by President Chávez. That is to say that President Chávez has the right to change the president of Corpozulia or to change the nature of the corporation, to say that this will now be an ecological corporation.

Corpozulia is promoting many projects that would destroy the Socuy. One of these is the Puerto Bolívar project, a deep-sea port, which depends on the outcome of our struggle. What do they want to deliver from that port? They want the coal that would be mined from the river basins here in the Socuy. If they open a mine here that would increase the annual output of coal from somewhere between 8 million to 36 million tons, or a potential increase of about 28 million tons. Currently they are producing 8 million tons from the Mina Norte and Mina Guasare. This is why they are also putting forth a railroad project, because they will no longer have the capacity to ship coal simply in trucks.

They tell us that in return we will receive more jobs, more schools, and more hospitals. Schools and hospitals for what and for whom? Who would inhabit this area if they begin to exploit coal? They can't fool us with that offer. To decrease illness you have to attack the root of the illness. If they open more mines, we will have more people suffering from pneumoconiosis, and then they would have to open a hundred more hospitals.[8] Because as they go about creating more open-pit mines, they continue contaminating and creating sickness. Their offer makes no sense. They tell us that there will be more freeways. Who is going to be driving down those freeways? The indigenous people? No, the containers filled with resources that they would take from this area.

The Constitution & Indigenous Rights

The new constitution is certainly an improvement to the prior constitution. But we also cannot say that it is perfect because in many ways it is a dead document. Many of the articles have been displaced by other articles, as in the case of the Organic Law of Indigenous Peoples and Communities.[9] There was an article that was proposed during the forming of the constitution that made us very happy when we read it. The article stated, "Under the previous consent of the community, the State can extract natural resources on indigenous land." Later that was changed to, "The State can begin to operate on indigenous land, after consultation with the community."[10] That is to say, if you consult me and I am opposed to the project, you can still enter my community. If we read the articles, article by article, we begin to see that there are many contradictions.

For example, when we begin to go through the process of self-demarcating our territory, which is stated as our inalienable right, and we go to the National Commission for Demarcation, they tell us what land is ours. This is what happened with the Barí. When the Barí went to demarcate their land, they demanded that various private properties be included within their territory. They were asked to sign a demarcation agreement that was false, that did not include the territory that was rightfully theirs. So where are those articles that supposedly protect indigenous peoples? In practice they are not executed. The Mining Law, for instance, is a law superior to all laws! Article 11 of that law even allows miners to enter sacred sites and ancient cemeteries of indigenous peoples.[11]

Allies & Enemies in the Government

President Chávez has said no to coal. Chávez told Corpozulia to stop coal mining, but they simply continue trying to make inroads into the community with their media campaigns. They make announcements in the newspapers and audiovisual media that Corpozulia wants development for the people. So we ask, "Who's in charge here? The indigenous people, Chávez, Corpozulia, or the transnationals?" Chávez says one thing but Corpozulia does another. General Carlos Eduardo Martínez Mendoza, the president of Corpozulia, has more power than Chávez, then? And most of the ministries are corrupted by Corpozulia.

We suspect that this is the case because of pressures on the government. There are embassies that place pressure on our government on behalf of transnationals. This is what has happened with the Brazilian Embassy, in the case of Vale Do Río Doce, which is a Brazilian company with 70 percent of its capital owned by North American investors. This is also the case with the British Embassy because the mining company Anglo American also functions here in the Mina Guasare. There is Peabody, which is a company from the United States. We also have Compañía Carbonífera Caño Seco, which is owned by Irish investors, whose embassy is also putting the pressure on.

And all of these have made links to the ministries and representatives in the National Assembly. Very few ministries have supported us. Chávez has supported us. The Minister of the Environment, Yubirí Ortega de Carrizales as well as the ex-Minister of the Environment, Jacqueline Faria, have said that they are opposed to coal and they would not grant the concessions for coal mining. However, there are other ministries such as the Ministry of Basic Industries and Mining as well as National Assembly representatives, like those in the Commission on Energy and Mines, that are with Corpozulia.

We had a meeting with the representatives from that commission during which they told us that there are laws that are superior to those laws for indigenous peoples. They told us that The Mining Law is superior. We told them that this couldn't be. We were here before everything, before the independence of Venezuela, before the State, before the corporations arrived. We had a long discussion with them in the National Assembly that went nowhere. We told them that the Mining Law must be revoked, that these laws are assassins of the people. They said that they would call us for more discussions. We were never called back.

There are many factors within this very government that are arming the real counter-revolution. There are so many interests involved. A calculation was done that opening a mine here would reap a profit of $350 billion dollars. A group of *indios* that is opposed to $350 billion dollars must be removed. That is too much money, too substantial an offer.

So what do we do? We keep ourselves in a rhythm of constant movement so that Chávez doesn't drop his guard. This all depends on pressure. If we maintain our pressure, then Chávez will maintain his position but if we stop placing pressure then Chávez will declare that coal is good. He will say, "Open up those mines!" Then the confrontation will be unleashed because we are willing to die for this land. We are willing to stay and burn the machines that are brought here. We have said this inside Miraflores and everywhere else.

But Chávez has said no to coal on many occasions as a result of the pressure that we have placed upon him. In 2005, we had an international campaign in which postcards addressed to Chávez demanding an end to coal mining were sent to Venezuelan embassies from movements in various countries, such as Mexico, Spain, and the United States. If we hadn't put that pressure there, there would already be a huge hole here.

The IIRSA: The Initiative for the Integration of Regional Infrastructure in South America

The origin of the funds to finance all of these projects, the ports, the gas pipelines, comes from the IIRSA.[12] In Venezuela, the government talks about three axes of development. We are located within the western axis. We have criticized the fact that the IIRSA is rarely talked about in Venezuela. Why is it that the government has only talked about the Free Trade Agreement of the Americas (FTAA), when the IIRSA is now the greatest monster?[13] When we talk about the dredging of the Río Catatumbo within Colombia in order to extract coal or the development of the Puerto Gabarrero de Encontrado for example, all of this falls within IIRSA. Why attack the branches without attacking the entire matrix?

When the IIRSA was in the process of being founded, there was a meeting amongst all the participating countries, during which Chávez spoke positively about the IIRSA. But why attack the Free Trade Agreement of the Americas and not the IIRSA? We have to attack the FTAA, Plan Colombia, as well as the IIRSA. We cannot let the IIRSA remain under a low profile. It has a number of projects located all over South America and many of those are major infrastructure projects. We have proposed that a center of investigations focused on the IIRSA be opened. Where are the resources for these projects? Where did they come from? Did they come from the World Bank or from the Andean Development Corporation?

CONIVE: The National Council of the Indigenous Peoples of Venezuela

CONIVE is a national council that is supposed to represent indigenous communities here in Venezuela. However, we don't recognize it as being an autonomous institution. CONIVE is a divided institution; there are now two CONIVEs. One is being led by Noelí Pocaterra, who is a deputy in the National Assembly. Nicia Maldonado, who is the minister for the Ministry of Popular Power for Indigenous Peoples, is leading the other CONIVE. When the leaders of an organization have political positions within the government, it is not autonomous. It is of the state; it obeys the lines of the government. This, for us, has not been a gain. For the leaders, it has brought personal gain because they have used it as an instrument of electoral politics. CONIVE has never pronounced its support for our struggle. On the contrary, Arcadio Montiel, who is a deputy in the National Assembly and a member of CONIVE, has come out against our struggle.[14]

The Ministry of Popular Power for Indigenous Peoples

Our relationship with the Ministry of Popular Power for Indigenous Peoples has also been terrible. The minister, Nicia Maldonado, said to us that we cannot talk about indigenous sovereignty. Sovereignty is only for the state, the government. It is a pity to hear an indigenous person speak in this way. Before she was minister, Nicia Maldonado accused us of being a subversive group — that we were armed, and that we wanted to separate the state of Zulia from Venezuela like the opposition has said they would do.

When I went to Mexico to participate in a Zapatista gathering and spoke of the Wayúu situation in Venezuela and our rights as indigenous people, it was broadcast on Venezuelan national television. The Ministry promoted an initiative in which some indigenous peoples were invited to attend a media and communications workshop. The government said that any organization that wants to participate can choose who they want to send, so the *compañeros* here chose me. When the Minister saw my name on the list, she ordered that I be removed, saying, "This is the one that travels to Mexico and sabotages our government!" We are not the only ones that have these criticisms; this disappointment is seen all over the place. Those that don't have these criticisms have likely never spoken up for themselves.

Resistance Against the Wayúu

Since we rose up in resistance, we have experienced many threats. Once we held an event here, a national gathering of indigenous peoples, and some people from Corpozulia attempted to enter and disrupt the meeting. There were blows between us and we had to physically force them out. We have had people from the mining companies enter to explore our territory and we have forced them out as well.

Corpozulia has tried to divide us by offering us machinery and resources from the government. They offered us equipment to make lagoons so that we can feed water to our cows here. We have told them that if anybody is going to offer us equipment it is going to be the government directly, not a company that is attempting to weaken and divide us. That is the responsibility that the government has towards its people. We understand that it is difficult to reject these offers when there is so much necessity. To others they have said, "if you work with us and separate yourselves from those crazy people, then we can offer you this and that."

We understand the necessities that we all have as mothers and fathers who have to work to maintain our families. But we are searching for ways to work together, to return to our customs that have been taken from us, such as the *Yanama*, which was the most significant aspect of Wayúu culture. *Yanama* signifies working together as a group without charging money from your *compañeros*. We are returning to that mode of work. Once we have fully consolidated ourselves in that way, we will be able to say that Corpozulia cannot divide us economically any more. We still have this weakness in which Corpozulia buys some of our people who lend themselves as leaders. However, it is not so easy to fool us anymore. This is why we are a threat to the corporations. Because when a group of people can no longer be corrupted, they know that they will not be able to get anything from them.

Our situation here in Venezuela is very complex. To truly understand our struggle, one has to be involved with it. When a person comes to Venezuela and asks the Ministries what is happening here, they will be told something else. But to really understand what is happening here, one has to go to the communities. That is the only way to have a deeper understanding. There are so many interests involved here, so much money involved. Those who truly feel like they are fighters, collaborators, and defenders must come to know the community and know the land.

FOURTEEN

Luis Perdomo & Freddy Blanco.

Luis Perdomo & Freddy Blanco, The Network of Afro-Venezuelan Organizations

(San José de Barlovento, Miranda)

O ne of the first things that you notice when arriving in the small community of San José is a gigantic statue of a cacao bean towering next to the highway. San José is located in Barlovento, a region covering six municipalities along the coastline east of Caracas. Long before petroleum was ever exploited in Venezuela, Barlovento was home to a booming cacao industry, dominated by a wealthy landowning elite and worked by thousands of enslaved Africans. To this day, Barlovento remains alive with Afro-Venezuelan culture that permeates its language, cooking, frequent festivals, and various religious traditions such as Palo Mayombe and the cult of María Lionza. All are the result of centuries of blending African traditions with New World realities.[1] Like much of Venezuela's countryside, the region was largely ignored by past governments; this exclusion is still present in physical form, embodied in the poor infrastructure of many of its cities. But a new political force has emerged over the past decade from this desolation, demanding inclusion in the politics of the central government and seeking to transform the cultural landscape of the entire country.

Like many organizations and movements in Venezuela, the Network of Afro-Venezuelan Organizations emerged in response to the creation of the 1999 Constitution, which stated the need to create a truly participatory and multi-cultural republic. Since then, the Network has sought to place a mirror in front of the Venezuelan people, pushing them to recognize their African heritage and overcome their legacy of institutional and internalized racism inherited from centuries of colonialism and exploitation. To speak of race in Venezuela is no simple task. The myth of racial harmony remains entrenched in Venezuelan culture. This belief holds that the Europeans, Africans, and indigenous peoples of the colonial era blended or co-existed to the extent of creating a new nation where all of these ethnic elements live together equally.[2] This belief is supported by the experience of many families in Venezuela in which one can find people with greatly varying ethnic features. According to many Venezuelans, there are no significant racial divisions amongst them, much less racism.

But the members of the many groups that make up the Network of Afro-Venezuelan Organizations insist that while racism may not seem obvious, it has certainly excluded Afro-Venezuelans from their country's history and politics. Working in their communities and through their government, they have sought to correct this with a variety of projects and proposals ranging from a National Law Against Racism and Discrimination to developing a regional television station called Afro TV. They sense that President Chávez, who has ceaselessly declared his Afro-Venezuelan and indigenous roots, provides them with a political opening unlike any other they have experienced before. Yet, they have still not achieved their primary demand, which is to be included in the Venezuelan constitution as a distinct ethnic group, similar to indigenous peoples, with the right to fully develop their own education and independent forms of organization with support from the government. Through countless forums, projects, and campaigns the Network of Afro-Venezuelan Organizations continues to place race on the political agenda, maintaining that a genuinely revolutionary process is impossible if the historical realities of racial exploitation are not confronted.

Luis Perdomo & Freddy Blanco

Introductions

Luis: My name is Luis Perdomo and I am a founding member of the Network of Afro-Venezuelan Organizations. I am coordinator of the San José de Barlovento Cumbe. A *cumbe* is an organizational structure within the Network. *Cumbe* is the name of the liberated spaces created by the *cimarrones*, or liberated slaves, here in Barlovento and in many Afro-Venezuelan areas. So we have adopted that name here to signify an organizational structure and a space for political education.

Freddy: My name is Freddy Blanco and I am a representative of the Afro-Venezuelan Youth Network working with Luis Perdomo within the San José de Barlovento Cumbe in the municipality of Andres Bello. We work within a very active *cumbe*, which day to day makes up part of the current political situation we are living within the country.

History of Afro-Venezuelan Resistance

Luis: To talk about the history of the Network of Afro-Venezuelan Organizations is to talk about our historical and cultural antecedents and about the contributions from our brothers and sisters brought here as slaves. To talk about the Network is to talk of the first uprisings by Africans here, such as was carried out by Miguel de Buria in Yaracuy in 1552 as well as the major revolt in Yaracuy in 1732.[3] And later, the uprising of the *cimarrones* here in Barlovento and the creation of the Mango de Ocoita Cumbe with the leadership of Guillermo Ribas between 1768 to 1771. Followed shortly afterwards by the uprising led by José Leonardo Chirinos in 1795 in Falcon State, in the Sierra de Falcon. We must also cite the contributions of Pedro Camejo, better known as Negro Primero, during the struggle for Venezuela's independence.[4]

But to talk about the Network is also to talk about another group of historical ancestors, beginning with the extermination of a significant population of indigenous peoples in the 16th century. With this extermination as a result of the colonial conquest, the Europeans were obliged to bring a workforce of enslaved Africans. This is the beginning of the Network. You could say that all the elements that currently make up the Network are a continuation of the historic and ideological struggles to combat racism and discrimination. Why combat racism and discrimination? Because these two sicknesses play a fundamental role today. Because to talk about racism and discrimination is to talk about exclusion — exclusion in the past and exclusion today. This is all our struggle, beginning with the uprising led by Miguel de Buria, but also taking into consideration the contribution of our indigenous brothers and sisters, who were always present.

Freddy: Here, in this area known as Boca de Paparo, is where the first slave ships bringing Africans to Venezuela arrived. Here the slaves were divided into groups of forty to be sold to the major landowners. These were the landowners who enslaved and exploited our ancestors for the cultivation of cacao. Those slaves who were able to escape would flee to places where they couldn't be reached by their masters. This is where we find the construction of the *cumbes*, such as the Mango de Ocoita Cumbe, founded by Guillermo Ribas who escaped from the plantation of Marcos Ribas, father of José Félix Ribas, one of our famous independence leaders.

Luis: Mango de Ocoita is a reference point for us, culturally, historically, as well as ecologically; here we have clean rivers and cacao. It has been elevated to a National Historical Heritage with support from the mayor of Acevedo, Juan Aponte, who recognizes himself as an afro-descendant. Keep in mind, to talk about cacao is to talk about the essence of Barlovento, of our African ancestors. The cacao culture — and we call it culture, because it should not be seen simply as the cultivation of a fruit—is what generated what we are now as *Barloventeños* and *Barloventeñas.*[5] You can sense this in our food, in our spirituality, in the spells spoken by our elders, and the faith that we have in our dead ones and ancestors. Even with our style of walking; you can see that it looks like people are dancing. Our whole way of life, our spirit, our values, our solidarity, all this was created by our relationship with cacao.

Beginning of the Network of Afro-Venezuelan Organizations

Luis: The Network of Afro-Venezuelan Organizations was born in 2000, practically at the same time as the birth of the new Bolivarian political process that we are currently living in the country. Beginning with some discussions already held between a few organizations, including the Association for the Cultural Development of the Andres Bello Municipality and Fundación Afroamerica, along with some other organizations, we convoked a national meeting here in San José de Barlovento.[6] It was not by chance that the Network was born here in Barlovento, because it is precisely in this region that we find the most afro-descendants in the country. From there, about thirty to forty organizations representing Afro-Venezuelans came to an agreement and decided to form the Network of Afro-Venezuelan Organizations. We saw that in order to continue our struggle it was necessary to form as a network from the thirteen communities that we represented at that time. This was done with the support of the *Consejo Nacional de la Cultura* (CONAC - National Council of Culture), which is now the Ministry of Popular Power of Culture.[7] All of the financial contributions with which the Network functioned, from the moment it was created up until three years ago, were provided by CONAC.

We took into account the new political opening provided by the election of President Hugo Chávez in 1998 and with the approval of the new constitution in 1999. The founders of the Network saw that the constitution of 1999 stated in its preamble that in order to build the country that we want, what is needed is an ethic of participation and protagonism, and of course the establishmet of a multi-ethnic and multicultural society.

Freddy: The Afro-Venezuelan Youth Network was formed in 2000 in the same way that the Network of Afro-Venezuelan Organizations was formed. If we take a look at our history, at our ancestral history of our brothers and sisters torn from Mother Africa, we see that the colonizers, the enslavers, would typically choose young African men and women to be their slaves. They did this because they believed that the younger Africans were stronger than the older ones. So that struggle of young Africans, who so strongly desired to be free to the point of breaking their chains of oppression, frames our current struggle to participate in developing the public policies of our country.

Building a Participatory and Multicultural Republic

Luis: Not until we arrive to the current moment, with the struggle being carried forth by our President Hugo Chávez Frías, do we see a political opening different from the other political processes we have seen in Venezuela, as well as throughout Latin America. In fact, we consider this new political process to be one of the most modern in the world. Chávez has called up everyone, as it is stated in the new constitution, to construct the revolution. What we are saying is that we cannot have the republic that we all dream of, that our brothers and sisters of the past dreamt of, if we the afro-descendants are not included. Because when you begin to look closely, for example, at Venezuelan cultural identity, you see that it is comprised of three fundamental ethnic components: indigenous, European, and African. This is why we say that this must be a cultural revolution, because it is from this understanding that changes must be made. If we are talking about structural changes, of profound changes, we say that this must be in essence a cultural revolution.

What is being said here is that each and every one of us must participate in order to fulfill what was dreamt by our ancestors, such as Miguel Geronimo Guacamaya and Guillermo Ribas from here in Barlovento, or Argelia Laya, also an afro-descendant from Barlovento, who participated in the guerrilla movement during the 1960s. Chávez, from the beginning, has said that power must be given to the people, so that we can build our own government, but with all those components that make up part of it: the indigenous, the Spanish, the African, and all those more recently arrived ethnicities. That is why we say that without taking into account the African ethnic factor, we cannot talk of building a revolution within this country.

Recognition of Afro-Venezuelans

Luis: We have been working to unite Afro-Venezuelans in each of our communities to learn how many we are, how we are doing, and of course where we are going. Here in Venezuela, for example, we don't have a census that has taken into consideration the variable of Afro-Venezuelan ethnicity in the way that has been done in Brazil or in the United States. We believe that is necessary in order to elaborate on the various plans and programs carried out by the Venezuelan state today. We find ourselves in a very different situation from our indigenous brothers and sisters who are already incorporated into the Bolivarian Constitution of Venezuela. Of course, because they are already included, they appear in the various organic laws that we have in our country.[8] That is in part what we are looking for.

This is not about asking or begging for something that is not ours, but rather we are demanding to be recognized for the various contributions made by our African sisters and brothers from the time of their arrival here as enslaved peoples. If you go and read Bolívar's speech at the Congress of Angostura as well as other speeches of his in which he advocates for the abolition of slavery, you will see that he recognizes the African contribution to Venezuelan culture.

From 1998 to 1999, when the constituent assembly was created to form the new Venezuelan constitution, two sister organizations that went on to become part of the Network made the proposal that afro-descendants be included in the constitution. These organizations were the Fundación Afroamerica, led by Jesús Chucho García, and the Union of Black Women, led by Nirva Camacho and Reina Arratia.[9] However, that proposal was not accepted by the constituent assembly, partially we believe because our proposal was not well understood by them, but also because there was an element of discrimination in their decision. Many of the people participating in the constituent assembly simply felt like it was not necessary to include afro-descendants in the constitution in the way that indigenous people were. Remember that the proposal to include indigenous peoples was pushed forward by Chávez himself, who understood the importance of this, and of course the indigenous peoples themselves were involved in supporting that.

When reforms to the constitution were being put forth by Chávez in 2007, we were one of the first groups to approach the National Assembly with a proposal for those reforms, which was to introduce a special chapter to include Afro-Venezuelans in the constitution.[10] Here as well, the representatives in the Assembly did not have a real understanding of our proposal and we were even ridiculed for it. After a long struggle to have an entire chapter placed in the reforms that provided various rights for afro-descendants such as the recognition of our ancestral lands, our proposal was reduced and included as Article 100, which was focused on the concept of cultural rights.[11] But, of course, the constitutional reforms went to a popular election and were not passed.

We also came out in support of the amendment in order to abolish term limits. This was not about the reelection of Chávez, this was about the reelection of the political process, because as Chávez himself stated: he is only a piece of this revolution. It's not that Chávez is going to reelect himself. No, it's the people that are going to reelect him. These are things that have to be said because of course the most recalcitrant and truly racist opposition groups of this country spread the propaganda that what Chávez wants is to stay in power forever. No, what we are talking about here is the most free, democratic process in the world in which the right of that same opposition to participate and have opinions continues to be respected. Before the elections, we convoked a meeting in Vargas State during which the Network was declared an electoral front in support of the amendment.[12] We brought together 5,000 people in the Vargas Sports Stadium. When you see an organization that can move 5,000 people in the country, that is something that has to be paid attention to politically because something is happening there.

Cultural Work and Interculturalism

Luis: We see cultural work as a necessary area within our struggles. From this we have branched out to various areas of organizing around health, education, sports, and communications with the ultimate objective of rescuing our culture and history. We want the political and social elements that make up Afro-Venezuelan culture in this country to translate into our inclusion in the public policies of the Venezuelan state and of its leader, President Hugo

Chávez. One of the fundamental cornerstones of our struggle is combating racism and discrimination — to talk about the racism that continues to persist in our society today and which takes the form of what we call institutional racism.

We believe that interculturalism is a tool for our struggle because interculturalism implies understanding between two, three, four, and more cultures that occurs with the recognition and respect for each of those cultures. We must take into consideration that in our schools we have children of African descent, indigenous descent, and European descent. When we teach about our history, our culture, about everything we are as afro-descendents, we are not saying that just those Afro-Venezuelan children should receive this class. We are saying that everyone should receive this class because we have to coexist. And that is what interculturalism is — coexistence, understanding, genuine communication. So when we talk about interculturalism, we are talking about breaking with the culture that has been imposed upon us by Europe. This is one of the most important processes within the country because we have seen real participation from the people.

Freddy: In 2008, a group of us within the Network came together to determine how we Afro-Venezuelans could be included within the new National Bolivarian Education Curriculum, which was being proposed by Chávez at that time. We wanted to expand the discussion about the cultural and political contributions made by Afro-Venezuelans throughout the history of this country. There was resistance from some people within the Ministry of Education when we insisted that our Afro-Venezuelan historical figures like José Leonardo Chirinos and Pedro Camejo be included as part of our national history. We had to explain to them that what we are doing here is re-founding the republic, which includes recognizing our heroes and heroines that have not been recognized. Finally, after a struggle, our proposal was included.

However, the President and the Minister of Education at the time, Adán Chávez, did not move forward with approving the National Bolivarian Curriculum due to protests from the opposition.[13] The opposition television station, Globovisión, came out and attacked the proposals to have afro-descendants included in the curriculum. We denounced this at the Office of the Defender of the People, demanding that Globovisión be cited for committing an act of racism.[14] The Office of the Defender of the People received us, listened to us and gave us coffee, but our demand didn't go anywhere. Since then, the proposal for a new curriculum has remained paralyzed.

Visibilizing Afro-Venezuelans

Luis: For us, it is important to include the ethnic variable within the National Census. The INE, the National Institute of Statistics, says that Afro-Venezuelans make up 10 percent of the population, but that remains to be seen.[15] For example, when you leave Barlovento, and you pass by Guatire and then Guarenas, you can see the vast majority of people are afro-descendants. When you get to Caracas, the largest population there is clearly afro-descendant and when you travel throughout the country, you will see that nearly all the states are dominated by Afro-Venezuelans. Of course this is racism — to hide, to continue hiding, the truth. Because to reveal how many Afro-Venezuelans we really are would represent a major force — a strength from the electoral point of view, from the point of making decisions and at the moment of creating policies.

I believe that we Afro-Venezuelans have a force here that government officials are not seeing, and that is why we have insisted on visibilizing who we are. How do we visibilize Afro-Venezuelans? With the various developments we've made through projects such as Afro TV; the Center for Integral Studies of Barlovento and the African Diaspora (CEIBA-DA); the Andresote Cultural Center; the creation of the Sub-commission of Afro-descendant Affairs within the National Assembly, led by the representative Modesto Ruiz, who is also an Afro-Venezuelan from here in San José de Barlovento; as well as the creation of the Presidential Commission for the Prevention and Elimination of Racism and Discrimination, which has sought to work through the Ministry of Education to confront racism in the educational sector.[16] We now also have the National Authority of Intercultural & Bilingual Education functioning within the Ministry of Education, which is playing a fundamental role in achieving everything the term interculturalism implies.[17]

The Center for Integral Studies of Barlovento and the African Diaspora has been conceived of as an integral community-based culture and research center. The majority of information about us in Barlovento has not been researched or compiled, so the idea is to catalog and expand this knowledge, in order to promote and spread information about who we are as *Barloventeños* and the connection we have with Africa and the African diaspora. This is also important for us to be able to provide the government with better proposals for our development in Barlovento.

Afro TV is conceived of as a culture and communications project. It is a response to the great deficiency in visibility of afro-descendants and our genuine history and culture on television. We have not been permitted to see ourselves on television as we really are. Traditionally, we have only been cast in roles as servants and criminals. Now, within this Bolivarian process, there is an opening for communities to organize themselves and develop their own alternative forms of media and we are taking advantage of this. Afro TV is a socialist television station designed to show our customs and culture in order to support the development of our peoples in Barlovento and strengthen our connections with all of the African diaspora. It will allow us to tell our own stories, present the way we conceive the world and the way we organize ourselves, and give the people in our communities the space to provide their opinions on the Bolivarian Process — all from their perspectives as afro-descendants.

Freddy: Currently, the Afro-Venezuelan Youth Network is engaged in the struggle to modify some articles in the National Law on Youth. In one of those articles, we studied the possibility of inserting a mandate to perform a study looking at why the vast majority of people occupying Venezuelan jails are afro-descendants. Because an adequate study has not been performed, we are not clear on how many Afro-Venezuelan youth are in jail and why. This year we are going to be pushing forward strongly in support of this article so that we can begin to answer these questions.

Institutional Racism

Luis: When we talk about institutional racism, we are referring to racism committed by whole institutions or state officials, but also racism that exists beyond simply those that are responsible for the institutions. For instance, when the schools in our communities do not teach our children their history and culture as afro-descendants, this is the perpetuation of exclusion and racism. This is why we responded with the creation of the Presidential Commission to Combat Racism and Discrimination.

We also find discrimination in the National Assembly — discrimination like there was in past republics; like there was during the time Bolívar was in the first Congress; such as when the

representatives from that period were in opposition to Bolívar because they did not agree with the abolition of slavery since they
were landowners and had slaves themselves. The two times that we
went to speak with representatives in the Assembly, they met with
us first in the front entrance of the National Assembly building and
the second time at the back entrance, while other groups, including
members of the opposition, have been received inside the National
Assembly hall. This is racism. When you go to a government building for a meeting and you are not allowed to enter, or you are looked
at strangely, this is racism — institutional racism in the midst of the
revolutionary process.

Last year, we proposed the creation of a National Law Against
Racism and Discrimination — a proposal that is still in process and
is in the hands of the Sub-commission of Afro-descendant Affairs.
The goal of the law is to penalize all acts of racism and discrimination, whether they be from government officials or from within
private enterprises.

Freddy: Any government ministry office that you go to, you
will see that most of the people working there have phenotypically
European features. Likewise, many of these people want us to look
at them as if they are superior because they have the privilege of
having a position in a ministry. They want us to believe that we are
inferior but they are the ones that need to recognize our ancestral
struggle.

Challenging the Bureaucracy

Luis: There are a lot of things that should still be revealed
here. We still see a lot of government officials fall into the same
consumerism as in the past, continuing to buy Hummer Jeeps for
example. One of Chávez's proposals was to change the name of
every ministry to now include The Ministry of Popular Power — for
example, the Ministry of Education is now The Ministry of Popular
Power of Education. However, in practice, this continues to be pro-
pagandistic since the people are not yet being attended to in the
way they deserve. Chávez himself said this angrily on February 15th
during the elections for the amendment to the constitution.

The government officials need to show that they are truly revolutionary. Being a revolutionary isn't determined by a document or
a law. Being a revolutionary is modeled by the attention given to the
people. There are many government officials who, when they are

named ministers or heads of a department of an institution, believe that they are the owners of that institution. They believe that it is theirs, but it isn't! Today they are there, but tomorrow they might not be. They have to see the other power. That is to say that they are there because of me, because of all of us. They are there because of the constituent power, the power of the people. So we are calling for these government officials to be re-educated on what it means to be a true revolutionary. We are not saying that we are the most revolutionary of all the people on the planet. We are just asking that they begin to exemplify what it is that we really want, because what we are seeing now contrasts with that and that makes us angry.

Many government officials still look at us like participants in a circus, and what they give us are crumbs — like the Roman Empire, offering its people bread and circuses. We don't want that, we don't want bread and circuses in this country. We don't want to be a deck of cards shuffled by someone else, like Ruben Blades sings; we want to shuffle the deck. We want to construct along with the president and the assembly representatives, and the ministers as well.

Freddy: Remember that in 1999 and 2000 during the time of the constituent assembly and the approval of the new constitution, countless social movements were created. One of those social movements that has maintained itself at the margin, that maintains its own discourse is the Network of Afro-Venezuelan Organizations because we don't just put on the red shirt in order to agree with everything that our government dictates. Social organizations must be taken into account in this process. It cannot just be the political parties that decide what needs to happen here. We cannot agree with everything until our struggle has achieved in giving us the kind of liberty that we want, until we obtain the kind of inclusion that we want. Our struggle will culminate when we are included in public policies and when the contributions made by our brothers and sisters descended from Africa are recognized.

Part VI:

THE STUDENT MOVEMENT

FIFTEEN

Cesar Carrero.

Cesar Carrero,
Socialist University Movement of Science Students,
University of the Andes

(Mérida)

The city of Mérida rests almost a mile high amidst the Venezuelan Andes. The colossal, green mountains encircle the city center, towering over its narrow streets. Unlike most Venezuelan cities, Mérida's history is still preserved in its colonial architecture.

"Welcome to Mérida... a university with a city inside it," reads a giant billboard on the way into the city. This is a university town. The 224-year-old *Universidad de Los Andes* (ULA - University of the Andes) is home to roughly 40,000 students and 6,000 teachers; that doesn't count the students from the city's other eight universities. The ULA is the second-oldest public university in the country and one of the most prestigious. With a budget larger than the entire Mérida state government, ULA is a powerhouse not just here, but across the country.

Naturally, Mérida has a long history as a hotbed for student activism. In the late 1960s, influenced by their counterparts in France and elsewhere, students across Venezuela launched the *Movimiento de Renovación Universitaria* (Movement for University Renewal). Organizing a flurry of campus building take-overs and student assemblies, they sought to increase student participation in the universities' governing councils and to promote education more committed to improving Venezuela's social conditions.[1] In 1970, President Rafael Caldera's administration cracked down on the movement by ordering a military raid of the Central University of Venezuela (UCV) in Caracas, which along with the ULA, was one of the bastions of student organizing from the 1960s through the 1980s.

Mérida is now once again home to a firestorm of campus politics. As in past student struggles, university autonomy continues to be at the heart of the conflict. Student demands for reform at Argentina's University of Cordoba in 1918 sparked movements throughout Latin America demanding the right to university autonomy — the idea that public universities should be allowed to manage their operations and budgets free of government intervention, including prohibiting police forces from entering campus grounds. After intense conflicts, Venezuela's universities won their right to autonomy, at least on paper if not always in practice, in article nine of the 1958 University Law.[2]

University autonomy would later be officially recognized in the 1999 Venezuelan Constitution, but it remains a contentious issue. Cesar Carrero, a founder of the *Movimiento Universitario Socialista de Estudiantes de Ciencias* (MUSEC - Socialist University Movement of Science Students) argues that the right has now been hijacked by the university administration, which "now uses the concept of university autonomy to maintain a state within a state." Echoing the Venezuelan student movement from the late 1960s, Cesar and his group believe that, "the university has its back turned to the country and is not fulfilling the roll that a university should, above all in the Department of Sciences."

President Chávez has lambasted the traditional public university administrations with similar charges, sympathizing with students that demand greater accountability and participation in managing campus affairs.[3] Meanwhile, many university rectors have become openly aligned with the opposition movement, responding that the Chávez administration is seeking to undermine university autonomy. Things heated up further in May 2009 when administrators flatly rejected a six percent budget cut applied to all government institutions, including universities, in response to the international plunge in oil prices. The university administrators protested despite having an overwhelming budget surplus the previous year. Cecilia García, rector of the UCV convoked a demonstration with opposition students. Violence, largely perpetrated by opposition student groups, rocked the UCV and ULA campuses for two months.[4]

The *Movimiento 13 de Marzo* (M-13 - March 13th Movement), an anti-Chávez student organization based at the ULA, has regularly taken to the streets with firearms and Molotov cocktails. Their actions have resulted in the death and injury of both students and police officers. Like others, Cesar believes that these groups use autonomy to protect themselves: "When there is someone that wants to burn someone's car, these people, these hooded right-wing movements hide inside the University."

Since 2007, Venezuela's right-wing student movements, under the name of the *Movimiento Estudiantil Venezolano* (Venezuelan Student Movement) have captured front pages around the world by leading many of the strongest protests against the Venezuelan government. Venezuela's political opposition has been intimately tied with this emerging movement, understanding the value of having young faces on their side. The mainstream media has presented this new opposition movement as representing the common voice of most students. However, pro-Chávez student movements say that the Movimiento Estudiantil Venezolano does't actually respond to genuine student needs and its members are little more than pawns of the opposition.

Despite this staunch resistance presented by opposition groups and university administrations, organizations like MUSEC attempt to maintain the tradition of past student movements through their goal of transcending the walls of the university and traditional education. MUSEC members seek to bring the university in line with the spirit of the Bolivarian Revolution. They want to open opportunities for higher education to the most marginalized sectors of society and use the science education they are receiving to solve problems in their local communities.

This may already be materializing with the passage of the new *Ley Orgánica de Educación* (LOE - Organic Law on Education) on August 14th, 2009, which stipulates that the Venezuelan government has the responsibility to provide all citizens with a free education from childhood through the undergraduate university level. The new law seeks to discard the aptitude entrance exam currently used in favor of a more holistic diagnostic test that would take into account the student's socio-economic conditions, as well as his or her academic history. Although the LOE continues to respect autonomy, it includes a variety of measures that seek to rectify issues of administration corruption by mandating the fair election of authorities by the entire university community as well as the creation of anti-corruption council.

However, in order for these changes to be implemented in the university system, a new National Law on Universities must first be approved. Many of the LOE's articles also remain open to interpretation. Nonetheless, student organizers like Cesar see this as a new opening for their cause and are already mobilizing to use it as a tool in transforming their universities.

Cesar Carrero

Personal History and History of the Organization

My name is Cesar Carrero. I am in my last year of study to receive a Bachelor's degree in physics from the Department of Sciences at the University of the Andes. I am a member of a student movement that up until now has only existed amongst students within the Department of Sciences, but which is now branching out to include students from other departments. We have taken the time to build a strong student organization within our department, which is called the Socialist University Movement of Science Students (MUSEC).

Our organization emerged as a response to the uneasiness that many students had who were participating in other student groups and saw that these organizations were getting off track. We decided to begin organizing amongst students who shared a similar ideological vision. We began to discuss the idea of starting a student organization within the Department of Sciences that would work to achieve our objectives, instead of being decided from above by people that didn't know the realities of the students inside the department. In 2006, eight or nine of us started to have meetings during which we would talk about how a student movement should be formed.

A tipping point took place when President Chávez called for the creation of the United Socialist Party of Venezuela (PSUV). We felt that the student movement also needed to transcend and break down all the barriers that separated us into small groups and movements on the left. We proposed the idea to the organization in which we were still involved at that time, to make a call to various groups to join together to form a single movement. The student leaders didn't understand us and simply ignored our proposal. Seeing the errors that this organization had committed in the past, we decided to move on and form our own organization.

We formed MUSEC with about ten active students and the support of many others who sympathized with our work. We made a lot of mistakes at first. We decided to run some of our members for the elections to our university's decision-making councils without having a foundation of doing work within the university. We didn't perform so poorly considering that they were our first elections, but we realized that we made an error in participating so early in those elections.

The creation of the organization went through various stages. After forming, we went through a process of internal discussion. With time, our organization grew and many of our sympathizers became more active. We decided that we needed to write a work plan based on our vision. We laid down some principles that responded to the socialist vision that is attempting to be created in our country.

We believe that the university should be opened to those people with fewer economic resources. We know that those who mainly have access to this university are the people who were raised in wealthier families or had the opportunity to go to an elementary or high school where they were provided with more benefits than other students because of where they lived. In other words, access is based on some variables that we believe must be transcended. The university should not evaluate someone based on an entrance exam for which a good grade can be bought with a few thousand *Bolívares* if you know the right person. I'm not going to name names, but we know people in the administration and pseudo-leaders in the right-wing student movement who sell test scores. These situations create a pre-determined set of results that continue to exclude the poor and those who live in the *barrios*. We understand that this is the reality of the university and our path is to change it.

Transforming the University

Our objective is clear. We want a university with a social vision that completely changes the way in which it operates. The university has its back turned to the country and is not fulfilling the roll that a university should, above all in the Department of Sciences. As scientists, we should be analyzing and solving problems in our communities. It's sad to see that in our department the scientists are more committed to discovering what properties are contained in the furthest star after Alpha Centauri, when we should be solving the problem of how to properly conserve our products here in Venezuela, for example. We barely produce our own antibiotics here! We don't even have enough technology to produce the plastics needed for syringes. The Department of Sciences does not focus on the problems we have in the country.

So what is the work of the organization? We are trying to break with this and develop consciousness about these issues. We cannot keep letting students just fall into the trap of doing thesis work for their professors that doesn't serve any purpose. We want to have students committed to doing thesis work that will solve the problems in the communities near us and in the country in general. For example, what can I do as a physicist? I can calculate how to make more efficient piping that will bring water from a river to a community that is located 500 meters up the Santa Maria Mountain. How many inches should the pipe be? How much pressure is needed? Whatever engineering or scientific methodology is necessary to resolve the basic problems that Venezuelans are confronting.

Working with the Community

In our early discussions, we recognized that we needed to make contact with the communal councils, in particular with those that were geographically closest to us. The Department of Sciences is located next to two communities; one that is called Santa Rosa and the other is San Pedro. We have developed relationships with their communal councils and are working on a few different projects together, such as a reforestation program. We are also collaborating with the Barrio Adentro module in their community by doing health censuses and acting as intermediaries between the communal councils and the government entities who can provide assistance and materials.

We know that what we are trying to do is very difficult. The ultimate goal is to change the way people think. The work that is being done in Venezuela, all the way from the President down to those of us who believe in this process, is to create a new mentality and a new Venezuelan. People must feel ownership of this country for this to happen. We have done simple things, like reforestation projects, where we invite people to plant trees. But while doing this, we talk to the students about what is happening with the environment, and how capitalism and consumerism have resulted in its destruction.

Through this experience, we are able to have a political discussion without talking to the students immediately about socialism, because people in the university don't fully understand what socialism is. People here tend to close down immediately when you start to talk to them about Chávez, because they have opposition viewpoints, but without knowing why. They might have these views because they come from a wealthy family and their parents are against Chávez or simply because of what they see on television.

Maybe their dad is a millionaire who's afraid that they are going to take away his five or six cars, so they don't really understand what's happening here. It's not that we are going to take someone's cars away from them, or their house. That's not it at all. This is about changing the way people think. This person can keep his six cars. This is about ensuring that the others, who don't have six cars, can at least have the right to transportation, the right the education, the right to healthcare, and all the basic necessities; and to ensure these basic necessities for all of the Venezuelans.

So we also do things like take students to a Barrio Adentro module so they can see what the Cubans are doing there and that they don't eat people! We explain to them that the Cubans are attending to people's health needs in the *barrios*, something that governments in the past never did.

The ULA Administration

We have pointed out consistently that the administrations at many of the public universities in Venezuela act as another political party, responding to their own interests rather than to the well-being of the students. There have been many instances in which the administration has come out making statements against the Chávez government during an electoral season or tense political moments. The most recent circumstance has been as a response to the economic crisis and the measures taken by the government to respond to it.

One of these measures was a 6 percent reduction to the budgets of all government entities, and included within that are the universities. But the reduction to the university budgets was made with the government demand that the cuts not affect the benefits for the students, such as the student cafeteria and student transportation. Rather, the university administrations were told that they needed to cut their private expenses, such as the purchasing of new automobiles or flights for the faculty. So the administrations came out protesting against the government, claiming that this was an attack on the university system. Meanwhile, last year, the ULA had a budget surplus — money that it did not use — of between 25-30 percent. We don't understand how the administration can protest a 6 percent budget cut when it had such a large surplus last year.

The ULA actually receives more money annually than the entire state government of Mérida. The [members of the] government responded to this uproar by asking the administration to show them the budget numbers so that they could determine what the problem was and how they could solve it. But the administration simply resisted, something that we don't see happen in other countries. This game that the administration is playing is the reason we say that the university has its backed turned to the country. Rather than attempting to resolve national problems, it is doing the complete opposite. It simply consumes, consumes, and consumes but doesn't contribute anything.

The Organic Law on Education

The new Organic Law on Education (LOE) is an attempt to overcome the contradictions that we have been fighting. If I'm not mistaken, the old LOE was created in the 1970s and it hadn't been updated to meet the interests of the community. It was a law created by those that controlled the National Assembly at that time, the bourgeoisie. It was a law created to maintain the status quo and to keep the children of workers from gaining an education.

The new law has come about to try to remedy all of those problems and to strengthen all of the social missions and policies that President Chávez has been creating. These programs have existed parallel to the old institutions, like the Ministry of Education, because these structures have been resistant to change. We know that the people that have maintained themselves in those structures were raised in a different time and that this is a cultural problem.

So what does the new LOE contain? From now on, the communal councils, the organized community, the communal government must be co-responsible for education, to make sure that a school is functioning well, that the teachers are doing their job, amongst other things. So that hurts a lot to those who are resistant to change. Why? Because the decisions that are taken in any school are going to be made by the grassroots, by the humble mothers and fathers who have their children in that school. The LOE also stresses, and with greater emphasis now, that education should be free.

The University Constituent Assembly

The *constituyente universitaria* (university constituent assembly) is an idea that has emerged as a response to the creation of the new LOE and the understanding that a series of special laws have to now be discussed, one of those being the National Law on Universities. We are calling for a university constituent assembly to discuss the National Law on Universities. We have already been meeting with some professors, students, and workers to propose changes to that law. The LOE talks about voting parity for electing the university administration, where the university community has been extended to include not just professors and students, but also workers.[5] And everyone's vote has the same power, that is to say that nobody's vote is more important than the other. Workers should be incorporated into the University Councils, and a greater number of students also, when decisions are being made.[6]

One example of the kind of issues that we want to confront with the new Law on Universities is the contracting of many workers at the universities. Last week, we had a demonstration where there was one university employee who has been working as a contractor for twenty-six years. All the basic benefits provided under the Labor Law, like social security, are denied to them. The university authorities say that this is the fault of the government because they now have a budget deficit, which is totally false. Something that we want implemented with the new law is a social auditing council, which will include students, workers, and teachers where we can demand to review the way the budget is being used.

University Autonomy & Historic Student Struggles

We know what happened during the student struggles that took place here in Venezuela during the 1970s and 1980s. Here, they fought for the student demands and for autonomy itself. But what is happening here now is that the opposition student movements and the administration are completely decontextualizing the previous struggles at the university. During the 1970s, the university was one of the trenches of the left. In other words, it was where the student movements fought against the right-wing governments of that period in order to demand the rights that students should have in society. Students responded to the needs of the country. They were fighting to solve problems in society at that time — violations against true autonomy that were being committed.

For instance, here in Mérida, various students were assassinated. They were killed in violation of autonomy and human rights. The government sent in tanks and the National Guard marched into the university with rifles and killed those students and shut down the universities, just like that. The university's freedom of autonomy means the freedom of education, the freedom of the professors and the administration, but there should always be accountability.

The administration now uses the concept of university autonomy to maintain a state within a state. [Its members] understand university autonomy as the ability to handle finances without government oversight. But we know that this money goes to political campaigns in support of the opposition during elections. In other words, this government is financing campaigns that are opposed to it. We are clear that university autonomy should be maintained, but not in the way that it exists now. The administration is allowed to arbitrarily spend university funds, while science students don't have the basic instruments and chemicals needed for their laboratory. There is no accountability. No transparency. We want all the students and the workers to be able to have a say in how those funds are managed.

The Opposition Student Movement

Sociologists or foreigners come here and try to study Venezuela's student movements and they go crazy because the situation is so complex. It's a mistake to say that all of these right-wing "student movements" exist, because they don't represent many students and they don't struggle. Yes, the organizations themselves exist as a group of students who answer to certain economic sectors without knowing it. It's sad. They answer to the bourgeoisie and the university administration. We can't say that everyone who belongs to these movements are millionaires, but the leaders — although they don't necessarily come from money — are bought buy it. Let me explain. There is a certain movement, and its four or five leaders are directed by the university administrators, and by the mainstream media, and the political parties on the national level, and they are against the Bolivarian process. So these four or five people completely manipulate a larger number of students who join their ranks. It is easy for people from the upper class to feel threatened by what is happening. They shouldn't feel threatened, but it is normal that they do. And another portion of these students enter into these student movements because they are completely dissociated, or because they are manipulated by the mainstream media. And on top of that, they have a large amount of economic resources at their disposal with which to buy students over.

Now, thanks to the university administration, the transportation system and the student cafeterias are in a deplorable state and it's sad to know that the student movements don't respond to the need of the students. That's why I say in quotes, "student movements," because at no point do they confront these types of problems, because these issues challenge the university administration.

During the first years of the Chávez government, the student movements responded to what was happening in the country and supported the government. At that time, there were student leaders who were well prepared, and had clear ideology and knew where they were going. But these students graduated and didn't leave well-pollinated seeds in their movements. When the right-wing administrators, professors, and political parties saw that there was beginning to be a lack of student leaders with a clear ideological vision, that's when this phenomenon began, which I explained just now, in which they saw that they could buy off these student leaders and their movements, which had originally begun with mass student support in defense of student demands.

Beginning of the March 13 Movement

That's how the famous March 13 Movement began. It was on that day, March 13th, 1987, that the university student, Luis Carvallo Cantor, was killed, and it is one of the saddest dates in Mérida, because it led to protests that practically destroyed the center of Mérida. And from then, there were numerous discussions in which the government — which at that time was right-wing — had to be accountable to the university. There is a professor who says that at this university there were fifteen days of continual protests in response to death of this student. According to government statistics from that period, they spent more on tear gas during those fifteen days, than they had spent in the entire country in normal protests in ten years. They spent the reserves for the next ten years of protests. Imagine the amount of people that protested at the time because they were demanding respect for the students.

It was an assassination, but more than that, it was the impunity that occurred afterwards. The killing was done by someone who was in the government. I don't remember the position that this person held but someone who belonged to the government murdered this student and because he belonged to the government, he was completely let off the hook. In fact, the government got this person out of the country, and that's why the students responded with these fifteen days of protests, demanding justice.

Working with the Government

What were the options for left-wing movements before, when the government was right-wing, and didn't listen to any of the demands that the people made? Well, the option was to go to the street and protest. Some people went out hooded. Students were killed.

Now what happens? When there are right-wing protests from the university, the members of the National Guard are hurt more than the students. They are shot, killed in fact; there are attempts at raping female police. It is completely astounding. So, us left-wing students who are in the university believe that we have to work together with the government, because right now the government is not an enemy.

We know the government is going to listen to us. We know the government is going to lend us a hand. When there are protests, we know the government is going to resolve the issue. So we understand that it is not necessary to be hooded. We know it's not necessary to protest, we know that the struggle is not in the streets confronting the power of the police. But, rather, the struggle is ideological. The struggle is the discussion. Because we know that the government is not like it was before. Now the government responds to the demands. It is a government that fulfills its promises.

Working with the PSUV

MUSEC and various organizations that work out of the University of the Andes also belong to the United Socialist Party of Venezuela (PSUV). We are very clear that within the university, we have a particular role, which is to try to organize the people and carry the true message. But the relationship with the national government is to go to the communities and help to organize the people, and organize us with them. I mean, I'm an active member of this organization within the university, but at the same time I belong to a Socialist Battalion, which is the basic cell of the Socialist Party of Venezuela.

So what we try to do is to create, within the same party, tactical policies and strategies to develop inside and outside the university, always within the national objective. That's why we speak about opening the university, breaking the barriers that the administration and some students have built; and for the university to go hand in hand with society and the people in solving problems.

Making Criticisms

More than Chavista, we consider ourselves revolutionary. We are clear that in this process, although Chávez continues to be the leader, this goes much further than him. Tomorrow, Chávez's plane could crash, or something could happen to him, he could die, he could get sick, he can make mistakes, anything can happen, but we understand that this process is already larger than Chávez. We are very clear that you have to begin to point out mistakes also.

Until now, Chávez has made mistakes, but he has always been willing to correct them. He has already corrected the most problematic ones. Our job in the party has also been to point out mistakes that people have made — [people] who have been in positions of power at the time, and we have pointed them out.

We have a lot of criticisms, but we feel we have the moral base to make these criticisms, not like other sectors that aren't participating in what is happening in the country, but rather focus on criticizing without offering a solution. We know there are mistakes, but we are trying to correct them so we can continue to build this ever more perfect road.

We have identified some student movements in the university that act like the right-wing within the university, but when necessary, like when they are outside of the university, they say that they are left-wing in order to be recognized within the party as a movement. I mean, they call themselves leftists, but the work they do is completely on the right. They don't do ideological work; they don't defend the work being done on a national level. They often end up working in the government because of their discourse, and they fall into the same game of buying people's votes with a beer or a t-shirt. They do well in the student government elections, so they end up as figureheads within the Federation of Student Unions. After they are elected, the media help them to become well known and they end up receiving high posts in the Chávez government somewhere. That's why we point out that there are mistakes in the government, and our hope is that little by little they will be getting rid of these people. And we have been pointing this out from our tiny corner here.

Government Repression Against Student Movements?

Repression doesn't exist. The government has followed all of the laws to a T. There are laws that say how to put down a demonstration that is being violent. You can't repress with bullets, but there are special gases that exist for this, which exist all over the planet. The government has used these. The right-wing students have committed heinous crimes from burning automobiles to blocking traffic, damage to private property — which they defend so strongly but in the end they are the first ones to violate it. So when they commit all of these crimes, including physical aggression, the government has had to respond. But it has not gone beyond the use of gases.

There are accusations against some of the police, but we know that the police here in the state of Mérida are infiltrated. You have to point out that there are police who don't respond to the interests of the people; who take bribes; who violate the laws; who respond to the interests of those that were previously in government. But there is a struggle happening within the government to purify these police in order to create a type of control. And in general, it's a police force that is completely different from what existed before.

When I mention the police, I'm also talking about the National Guard, and the government in general, who aren't playing the sad roll of previous authorities, which in right-wing governments attacked with everything they had against the students, causing three or four student deaths in each student protest, hunting students down in the university. But in general now, the police have been humane, fulfilling all of the laws, while the student demonstrations have been completely violent. Now the protests come first without a context or a reason to be protesting, and often having nothing to do with student demands. But regardless the state has not overstepped its laws, fulfilling all of the laws when confronting a protest.

Media Manipulation Around Student Movements

The media manipulation is tremendous. You see it from the newspaper you buy at the corner, to the largest mass media, like television and even the Internet. The manipulation here in the state of Mérida comes above all from the newspapers here. The owners are all people with money. They are full of it. They are people that have a lot at stake, economically speaking. So they utilize the students to make it appear as though the government was acting illegally, which it is not. They manipulate, and paint up baseless protests over nothing, to appear justifiable. They make completely violent protests appear to be peaceful. When someone from the police force ends up hurt, they hide the information completely.

And what we can say is that we are being victimized here in the state of Mérida and throughout the country by this famous "War of the Fourth Generation." They are attacking us with the media, saying things that aren't true. The right-wing students are part of this manipulation. They take the mainstream media and use it to manipulate the people.

Current Moment

The country is truly passing through a stage of social progress, but there are still many groups of people that resist it. It's natural that they would. They are responding to economic interests and resisting these changes that benefit the majority. Unfortunately, a large part of this minority are in this university. As I have had the opportunity to be benefited by studying here, I try to offer another vision to what the administration wants. I try to demand true rights. My organization demands that the government and the university administration provide to us what should be ours, and at the same time we fulfill our responsibilities as university students by giving back to the country. That is our job, and that's the word we are trying to spread.

SIXTEEN

Margarita Silva.

**Gabriela Granados & Margarita Silva,
Bolivarian University**

(Caracas)

The statue of the oil derrick standing outside of the entrance to the Caracas campus of the *Universidad Bolivariana de Venezuela* (UBV - Bolivarian University of Venezuela) may seem out of place, yet it is a salient reminder of the history of this institution and Venezuela's challenging political process. The campus once served as offices for the state-owned oil company, PDVSA, before its management and most of its workers walked out and shut down the company in December 2002. When the Venezuelan government fired the upper management and 18,000 employees involved with the shutdown, it was left with numerous office buildings throughout the country that had apparently been under-utilized for years.[1]

Assuming greater control over the company, which once seemed to act completely outside of the state's authority, the Chávez government now committed to put its profits and resources towards social development. On July 18th, 2003, President Chávez celebrated the opening of the first Bolivarian University of Venezuela at the former PDVSA offices in Caracas.

On almost any day of the week, the ten-storied grey and blue building is bustling with activity. The main hallway is covered with posters and signs announcing an endless number of campus activities, forums and events. Thousands of students now study a wide variety of degrees on the Caracas campus, with full access to radio, audiovisual and computer labs, a free cafeteria and a Barrio Adentro specialized health clinic.[2] All of this is provided free of cost with profits generated by PDVSA.

The UBV was launched by President Chávez to open the doors to a growing population of Venezuelans unable to afford a private university education or to compete for the rigorous entrance exams at traditional public universities. Following the creation of the UBV, Chávez launched the Sucre Mission in September of the same year.[3] The Sucre Misson was created to make university education widely available throughout the country by developing smaller *"Aldeas Universitarias"* (University Villages) in municipalities that lacked opportunities for higher education. By 2008, the Sucre Mission had created 1,915 University Villages, reaching all of Venezuela's 335 municipalities.[4]

The UBV and the Sucre Mission are the latest programs in the government's robust educational policy. Through the creation of the UBV and the Robinson, Ribas, and Sucre Missions, hundreds of thousands of adults have finally received their elementary, high school and college degrees.[5] With the help of the UBV and the Sucre Mission, student enrollment in higher education has seen an increase of over 200 percent in the last ten years.[6]

This is a far cry from access to education under previous administrations. Between 1984 and 1998, admissions to public universities dropped 40 percent for students from working class families, as the government decreased public spending for education amidst a rapidly growing population.[7]

Students at the Bolivarian University such as Gabriela Granados and Margarita Silva see the UBV and the Sucre Mission as fundamental aspects of the process of transformation taking place in Venezuela. "Here, we are building the university that we want, the university that this process needs in order to consolidate," Gabriela explains. Rather than simple receptors of information, students at the UBV are expected to be protagonists in developing their own education. The UBV programs emphasize student participation in community projects meant to confront social problems.

Though grateful for this new space that has been opened to them, Gabriela and Margarita affirm that not everything is perfect in Venezuela's new education system. While seeking to address the issues at the UBV, they have had to confront the university administration and launch a nation-wide student debate on the future of Venezuela's higher education. In 2007, President Chávez created the *Comisión Presidencial para la Organización Estudiantil* (Presidential Commission for Student Organization) to promote the creation of a Bolivarian student movement and to provide university activists with the opportunity to participate in national discussions on Venezuela's educational policies. But through their experiences of organizing in the UBV, Gabriela and Margarita have come to believe that an autonomous united student organization is necessary for students to be genuine protagonists in creating the kind of universities that Venezuela needs.

Gabriela Granados and Margarita Silva

Background

Gabriela: My name is Gabriela Granados and I am studying Political Sciences at the UBV. I started studying here in 2004, the first year the university was opened. I'm now in my seventh semester and I'll be graduating with a Bachelor's degree soon. I was born in Valencia, in the state of Carabobo. I would say that I come from a revolutionary family. They were never active in any particular political party, but they were always *anti-Puntofijismo* — they were opposed to the *adecos* and *copeyanos*.

I studied engineering at a traditional public university, the Antonio José de Sucre National Experimental Polytechnic University in Barquisimeto, before coming to the UBV. This is where I began my life as a student activist. At that time, I was involved with a Cuba solidarity group. There is a really rough environment at these kinds of universities for student activists, particularly for those that identify with the revolutionary process in Venezuela. When the professors at these universities realize that you support this process, they try to put stumbling blocks in your way. They tell you that your beliefs are wrong and that you should stay away from political activity.

Just being accepted into the traditional public universities is very difficult. People who want to attend the universities have to pass an exam during which you are tested in mathematics, science, and language. But the majority of people in Venezuela have never received a quality education because they attended public schools that never received support from past governments. So, of course, only people who attended private schools are prepared for this kind of exam. The *Consejo Nacional de Universidades* (CNU - National Council of Universities) also requests all kinds of information from students when they are applying, including information on their socio-economic status. Students who come from families that are able to pay for their education are privileged over those that can't. The majority of students enrolled at these traditional public universities come from the upper and middle classes, even though the universities are paid for by everybody.

Margarita: My name is Margarita Silva. I arrived in Venezuela from Chile in 2004. I am from outside of the capital, Santiago de Chile. It is very common in Chile for people who grew up during the dictatorship to have revelations later in life about all the problems that our country has due to that experience. In Chile, I had never participated in politics, but even if you are not involved in politics, you are marked by that history. I began to learn about politics because my older sister's boyfriend had participated in the *Frente Patriótico Manuel Rodríguez* (FPMR - Manuel Rodríguez Patriotic Front), an armed movement that was active during the time of the Pinochet dictatorship. He would talk to me about Chilean history and the *Unidad Popular* (Popular Unity) movement that brought Salvador Allende into power. When I left Chile, I had the feeling that the country was not the way that I wanted it to be. Chile is still a very classist and racist society and the inequality is incredible. There are places in the center of Santiago where the poor can't go without being harassed by the police. I knew that I didn't like to see those things, even though I didn't understand why at that time. This was why I left Chile with my sister when I was eighteen years old.

We traveled around South America and lived in Argentina for a little while. Having more political consciousness by that time, we felt the need to do something more than just live a nomadic life, and instead establish ourselves somewhere with a purpose. We came to Venezuela seeing that there was an important political process taking place here and we wanted to support it. This is a process that a lot of people compare to what happened in Chile because of the way that Chávez came to power via the electoral route like Salvador Allende. The way in which the Venezuelan opposition has attacked this government is also the same way that the Chilean opposition attacked Allende's government.

We arrived just before the 2004 recall referendum. This was a very tense and beautiful moment when everybody was completely committed and out in the streets organizing with the famous electoral battalions. After a few years of being here, I made the decision to enroll in the UBV to study political science, because obviously that's what my interest had been for some time.

The Francisco Miranda Front

Gabriela: In 2003, I participated in the Francisco Miranda Front, which was an initiative put forth by the government. At that moment, there was a need for more people to be trained to perform the community work that the government was beginning to promote. I was studying at the university and was already frustrated with my experience there when the government convoked students to receive a political education that was in line with the new national project that was being created with the new constitution, and with our Bolivarian ideals. So I was chosen to participate in a delegation that went to Cuba for nearly three months where we studied our new constitution in depth, reading the entire thing up and down, and about how to put it into practice. I participated in the fourth brigade to Cuba. There are now eleven brigades that have gone.

We studied social work with the Cuban teachers there, like how to do a community assessment, how to properly enter a community that you are not from to perform social work. We didn't have a strong culture of social work or volunteer work in Venezuela at that time. The Front was created to train young people who were open to confronting the various issues we have in Venezuela and who could staff the social missions the government was initiating. Mission Identity was just getting started then, created to provide people with legal documentation so that they could vote. Most people in this country are supportive of Chávez and many were not able to participate in our electoral processes because they didn't have documentation, an identity — they were not full citizens. Mission Identity was a way of providing these people with an identity and a way of dignifying them. So, through the Francisco Miranda Front, many of us became involved with the documentation campaigns to get people into the electoral registry.

Afterwards, I got involved with the Barrio Adentro Mission, and we worked with the Cuban doctors to do health assessments of the community, to find out how many people lived in the communities — how many elderly people lived there, for example. We did this work hand-in-hand with the Health Committees and Urban Land Committees. After all this I decided that I didn't want to study engineering any more. I felt like I had found my vocation. I wanted to either study social work more profoundly, or political sciences.

That was when President Chávez announced that they were going to establish the UBV. He offered the Miraflores Presidential Palace as a campus at first but that wasn't possible. So eventually it opened at the old PDVSA offices. I had to move from Barquisimeto to Caracas to attend, which my father wasn't very happy about. But I did it anyways, was able to find a job, and have been living here ever since.

Transforming the University

Gabriela: At the traditional universities, the professors are considered to be the only ones with the knowledge, and they are simply supposed to deposit that knowledge into the heads of the students — what Paulo Freire refers to as the banking style of education. The traditional university administrations want students that can be easily molded to fit into the capitalist system that we have today. They want to produce people who are willing to sell their labor to transnational corporations, people who have no vision for their country. These universities have their backs completely turned to the development of our national project, and even to the constitution.

Here, we are building the university that we want, the university that this process needs in order to consolidate. We want to create students with dignity; students with a class consciousness; students who want to work for their country, who don't just exploit themselves and sell their labor to the highest bidder, but rather work to support our national project. We are in a time of transition and I am here to deepen this process. This country needs to replace those so-called "professionals" that still dominate the government's institutions with their bureaucratic vision, with people that are working under a new paradigm.

Education in the Bolivarian University

Margarita: The Bolivarian University has been questioned a lot because it was created with a presidential decree. Often, people in the opposition try to devalue what our experience is here, saying that our education is controlled and we are only learning about Karl Marx. But that's not the case. There has been a strong effort to provide a quality education here. The Bolivarian University talks about education as an exchange of knowledge between students and professors. The professors are not considered to be the only ones with all the knowledge, rather they are thought of as guides. They don't just come here to provide lectures and then give you an exam the following week. They try to provide us with a more humanistic education. You can see that the professors here are very committed to what they are doing.

The idea at the UBV is to produce graduates who are capable of changing society, of working with communities. For example, instead of completing a thesis in order to graduate, students doing an academic degree have to do a project that covers their four years of education here. By the time you graduate, the project should be implemented within a community. The idea of the project is to bring the university to the community. I am doing my project with other students in the political science department. We are looking at the problem of student organizing within the Bolivarian University. We conceive of the university as a community consisting of students, professors, and workers. We took up this theme feeling that what we needed within the Bolivarian University is a strong student organization, recognizing that this is not something that we have had here up until now.

The Presidential Commission for Student Organization

Margarita: There have been attempts by the administration within the university as well as the government to create a student organization within the UBV. In 2007, President Chávez created a *Comisión Presidencial para la Organización Estudiantil* (Presidential Commission for Student Organization) to energize the Bolivarian student movement in Venezuela, which led to the creation of the *Consejos del Poder Popular Estudiantil* (Councils of Student Popular Power). These councils are supposed to be like the equivalent to communal councils for the universities. The idea is that each university has a council. There were some student representatives chosen from a variety of universities to lead these councils. But, they were simply appointed undemocratically by the authorities within the commission, such as the Rector and Vice-Rector of the UBV. Although there were a few students from the UCV that were chosen that I know do good work there, those chosen from the Bolivarian University were never really recognized as leaders here.

These representatives traveled around the country to the various UBV campuses to collect ideas from the students about the way they should organize themselves in order to form the councils at their university. Councils have been created at some UBV campuses in other parts of the country, and there have been attempts at forming a council here at the Caracas campus but to this day we don't have one. I know a lot of students who have tried to support the creation of a council here, but haven't had any success. Some of the councils have functioned, but the majority have not. None of the council representatives really tried to work at the grassroots level and organize the students there.

What we have heard from a lot of students is that they did not feel like the Councils of Student Popular Power provided the type of setting in which they could participate. In Venezuela, people want to participate, they want to be protagonists like it says in the constitution. People don't just want representatives like they had in the Fourth Republic. They want to be able to participate in the decision-making process. We think that a lot of the frustration that we see amongst the students at the UBV when we talk to them about student organizing comes from this experience. They don't know if they can trust people who are talking about student organizations, because they are worried that the same thing might happen again — three or four people are chosen to be student representatives and they show up on television making declarations, but no actual work gets done at the university.

Gabriela: The creation of the Presidential Commission for Student Organization was a response to the opposition, which began to hold up student activists as the new poster-children for their cause. The opposition became so illegitimate in the eyes of the public that they needed something new to mobilize people, to get people out into the streets; and they found this in the students coming out against the government, who claimed to be the vanguard in the defense of democracy in Venezuela. They claimed that RCTV was closed down, when in reality its concession had expired and was not renewed by the government, which is the legal right of the state.

So in response, these opposition students asked for the right to address the National Assembly, which was provided to them. But rather than simply be allowed to address the National Assembly, they were asked to participate in a televised debate against students who support the revolutionary process. So seven students from different campuses were called upon to participate in that debate. While all of them spoke, the opposition students decided to only have two students speak for them, who read from a script the whole time. Afterwards it was revealed that the script they were reading from was created by ARS Publicity, which is a company owned by Globovisión![8] They were left fully unmasked — they were just new faces with the same old ideas being manipulated by the old defenders of *puntofijismo*. The debate made it clear that they had no proposals for a national project or even for the universities.

President Chávez saw the clarity and consciousness that the students who support the process spoke with, and wanted to find a way to harness that in order to create a larger student movement. So he decided to create the Presidential Commission for Student Organization. But that was an error on the part of the President — a movement cannot be created from above. He got excited with the idea that the students who spoke represented large collectives, but that wasn't the case. We were just dispersed groups who were confronting opposition students whenever it was necessary, but who didn't have the capacity to develop a united plan of struggle.

I actually traveled around the country to various states with Osly Hernández, a law student from the UCV who is on the Presidential Commission, to generate discussion about the situation with our universities — what kind of universities we have now, what kind of university we need, and what we have to do to generate the conditions that we want. All of these discussions and proposals were then compiled into a single document and plan of action at a national meeting with all of the student representatives on the commission. But it didn't go any further; it ended up just being sensationalist. People began to question who had elected these students to be on the commission and the truth was that there was no electoral process. It was all very circumstantial. They were just chosen to respond to the opposition in the National Assembly; we didn't know that this was going to become a presidential commission and that they were going to have that level of responsibilities.

Moving Beyond Elections

Gabriela: Eventually the elections for the reform to the constitution came along and everyone's attention was diverted towards that. In Venezuela, we have a strong culture of being excessively focused on major political events like elections during which our agenda is constantly being set by the next electoral process or by having to respond to the opposition. Electoral politics aren't bad; we are in a democracy and we have to play that game. But it can't simply be about mobilizing to guarantee that we get ten million votes to support Chávez. We have still not been able to break with that paradigm.

This is why we are in such an important political moment right now, because we don't have any elections until 2010 for the National Assembly, and our political agenda won't be dominated by that. So we are taking advantage of this opening to develop a real student movement and fight for the kind of universities that we need. Things are not perfect even here at the UBV. We have had serious issues with rectors here in the past, that have had their backs completely turned to the students, that didn't even want to meet with us. We have also had to confront many structural issues within the UBV relating to our policies.

Debating the UBV Internal Policy

Margarita: When the current UBV Rector, Yadira Córdova, was appointed she sensed that the university was in institutional disorder. There was a lack of communication and coordination between the different departments and she saw the need to better organize the UBV. So she began a process of popular consultations and assemblies within the university called UBV 21, as in 21st Century, with the intention of creating a new *Reglamento Interno* (Internal Policy). The Internal Policy is like the constitution for the university that establishes the political and bureaucratic structure and principles of the UBV.

When the final document that resulted from the UBV 21 process was released, there were complaints from some students who didn't agree with all of its content. For example, one of the structures defined in the Internal Policy was the University Council, which is considered to be the main decision-making body at a university. The new Internal Policy establishes that the Council would consist of the Rector, Vice-Rector, the Secretary, a General Coordinator from each campus, the deans from each department, one representative for the workers, one for alumni, and one person to represent the entire UBV student body. We don't feel like this is a just representation of students on the University Council. In fact, the National Law on Universities that was passed back in 1970 under intense pressure from the student movement at that time, states that University Councils should have three student representatives. For example, the University Council at the UCV has three student representatives. So the UBV Internal Policy is not even complying with this law that we consider to be essentially expired since it is based on the old 1961 constitution and does not fit within the current Venezuelan reality. One of the other problems that we disagree with is that professors are allowed to receive private donations. What we've seen happen at other universities is that private companies provide money for research and thus guide the direction of the university. We want to make sure that research done at the UBV stays oriented towards solving problems in our communities.

Challenging the University Administration

Margarita: An initiative from the students within the Political Sciences department was put forth to have a new series of forums and debates about the Internal Policy. Then, only a week after the administration submitted the Internal Policy to the students to review, an official announcement was released stating that it had been approved by the Minister of Superior Education. There had only been one conversation about the Internal Policy held when the announcement came out. We didn't even have the chance to have a second public forum that we were planning! That created a major conflict within the University.

Some students began to get organized and have more open debates about the nature of the Internal Policy and the way it was approved. As more students got involved, a number of us called for an open assembly with the Rector. A group of about ten of us actually broke into a meeting that the Rector was having with the UBV administration. We sat and waited until the meeting was over. At the end, we asked her to attend a public assembly with the UBV students and she agreed. So we began a campaign to inform the students about the content of the Internal Regulation so that they would be prepared to discuss it at the assembly. We did this all independently without resources from the university. We made the flyers ourselves and went around classrooms asking students for money to pay for copies.

The assembly was very different from other assemblies that the Rector had convoked in the past where very few people attended. We had over 300 people in the auditorium, which was a very unusual thing to see at the UBV. The Quiriquire Auditorium, where it was held, normally only holds 200 people. This was one of the most interesting situations that I had experienced at the UBV, because it was an assembly called for and organized by the students during which we had the space to actually debate with the Rector. I should emphasize that this also showed the distinction between the UBV and traditional universities, where students may call for an assembly with their Rector but just get ignored. While it took some work, it was still possible to have this kind of dialogue with the Rector.

A lot of students brought forth issues that they had talked about for a long time but had been unable to voice to the administration. The assembly opened up a very important space at the

UBV. We expressed to the Rector that the Internal Policy should be considered null since there was not sufficient consultation from the students. The debate around the Internal Policy has allowed for a lot of other issues to get discussed now.

The Battle over the UBV Budget

Margarita: The students inside the UBV are now having discussions about the university budget. Just recently, the national budget for all the universities in Venezuela, including the UBV, was dropped by 6 percent for the 2009 school year as a way to combat the effects of the global economic crisis. The public universities, like the UCV, received a budget increase of 55 percent for the 2008 school year. But the Bolivarian University System had only received a budget increase of 14 percent for 2008. So that has left us with a major deficit. The entire UBV system only receives 2.84 percent of the national budget that the government provides to the whole university system, while the UCV alone receives 15 percent of that budget. In fact, studies have been done showing that the UCV receives more money than some state governments in Venezuela.

The annual budget for the UBV system actually only takes into account those students enrolled in the five campuses located throughout the country, which in total is about 10,300 students. But in reality, the Bolivarian University System attends to over 325,000 students, most of whom are studying in the municipalized universities through the Sucre Mission. The idea of the municipalized universities is to provide a university education to people in the interior of the country who are unable to move from their communities to study at one of the campuses. Meanwhile, the UCV only has a student population of about 58,000 students. The UBV provides many of the professors and coordinators for the municipalized universities and is the institution that submits the diplomas to graduates of the Sucre mission. Currently the Sucre Mission is funded as a state foundation, which receives contributions from the government. But we want the people who are studying in Sucre Mission to be considered a part of the UBV budget because in reality they are dependent on its resources. The current budget is way too small to meet the needs of all these students. If the government genuinely believes in the Bolivarian University system and the project of producing new kinds of students that will work to change society, then it should provide the minimum budget to make it function properly.

We now have a situation in which the administration and opposition students at the UCV have come out protesting their budget cuts. From our point of view, their protests are unjust considering the major discrepancies between the UCV and UBV budgets. The opposition students always take advantage of these political moments to get media attention, and of course this situation hasn't been an exception. We are not trying to do the same thing as the opposition students, who are just protesting and burning tires in the street. We want to participate in creating proposals. We think that there should be a reduction in costs amongst the faculty and administration, who are known for using the budget to buy new cars for themselves, for example. The administration at the UCV responded to these budget cuts not by reducing their own personal costs, but by stating that they were not going to be able to receive more students for next year. But the UBV, with all the limitations we already have in our budget, has received 1,700 new students for the new school year.

We are trying to spread this knowledge throughout the country to the people studying at the municipalized universities, because we know that this information isn't reaching them. We did a tour over the last month talking to the students about these issues. They need a response for why the UBV coordinators and professors may be unable to attend to their classes.

The National Law on Universities

Gabriela: Through the discussions about the Internal Policy and the budget, we realized that all of these issues really have their origin in the 1970 National Law on Universities, which still remains contrary to the process that Venezuela is undertaking. This law ignores the changes in our new constitution, which states that we now have a participatory democracy — not just a representative democracy — in which the State guarantees inclusiveness for all people in the public universities, free of charge and without making distinctions based on class or race. The current government has created policies of inclusion. The UBV, the Sucre Mission, the opening up of the UNEFA and the other technical institutes are all examples of this.[9] But what has been created is a parallel university system without touching the old institutions.

We still have laws from the Fourth Republic that continue reproducing the same system of classism. We think that the President has been waiting for the students, along with the workers and the entire university community, to mobilize around this because he talks a lot about popular power. But we are in a moment of transition and people are still afraid of assuming that power. Popular power isn't just about some leader talking out his ass. Popular power demands organization and unity. Right now is the moment to change the Law on Universities, which has been getting discussed in the National Assembly. But it was going to be discussed behind closed doors. So we have responded by saying that the law should be discussed with our participation. We have been living the realities of the current university laws in practice; we know what the flaws and needs are, and we have proposals and criticisms.

The University Constituent Assembly

Gabriela: Our strategy is to change the entire university structure, and the tactic that we are proposing to achieve this is a nation-wide *constituyente universitaria* (university constituent assembly). We have formed a group called *Colectivo Foro Proponente*, which is a united front of student collectives. We realized that we needed to transcend this discussion about our local issues at the UBV, and point out that this is a national issue and a structural problem. Through this collective, we organized a march to the National Assembly called "The National March for the Necessary University" that brought students from all over the country — from the various UBV campuses and municipalized universities as well as from the traditional public universities.

It was a very exciting experience and I think historic, because the student movement over the last ten years has been dispersed; we never had a common project. We now have a reason to organize and we are using the university constituent assembly to unite forces. This will organically create a student movement that will be able to respond to the demands of the students and continue making criticisms and proposals to change our educational system.

Part VII:

COMMUNITY ORGANIZING

SEVENTEEN

23 de Enero.

Golon & Coco,
Coordinadora Simón Bolívar & Che Guevara Collective

(23 de Enero, Caracas)

t's sunny and already hot. The *Guaraira-Repano* sits majestically over the city and the slight morning smog.[1] Gardel-style 1930s music echoes from some hidden sound system across the street in a mass of block homes, staircases, and satellite dishes. The sound of nearby hammering floats on the cool breeze. Aging cars belch fumes into the air as they drive up the hill deep into the western Caracas *barrio* of 23 de Enero.

Tall fading blue-grey apartment buildings loom overhead. Clothes hang from the barred windows. Nestled beneath them, makeshift cinder block homes built one on top of the next — typical of Venezuela's poor *barrios* — are lodged in to the hillsides.

The apartment blocks stretch on for miles, constructed originally for military housing during the Marcos Pérez Jiménez dictatorship of the late 1950s. When an insurrection on January 23, 1958 ousted Pérez Jiménez, thousands of poor Caracas residents from the surrounding hillsides moved into occupy the buildings. Most of their families are still here. The neighborhood took on the name of 23 de Enero, the day of the uprising, overthrow, and occupation.

It was the dramatic beginning to what has become one of Venezuela's most politically radical and emblematic neighborhoods. During the forty years of what Chávez supporters call the "pseudo-democracy" before President Chávez came to power, it was here that the police would come to seek retaliation on poor residents for supposed "subversive" activities against the state.

On February 27, 1989, President Carlos Andrés Pérez launched an IMF-prescribed package of neoliberal shock policies, which privatized state businesses and cut social services. Gas prices doubled and public transportation prices rose by 30 percent. Venezuelans responded by taking to the streets in a spontaneous uprising that would later be known as the *Caracazo* or *Sacudón*. The metropolitan police responded in 23 de Enero in a bloody reactionary witch-hunt, which residents say killed and disappeared more than 3,000. Bullet marks still riddle the sides of some fifteen-story apartment blocks. The police repression was enough to convince the collectives of 23 de Enero that they needed some sort of legal organization. They created the *Coordinadora Simón Bolívar* (The Simón Bolívar Coordinator) to unite the then fourteen grassroots collectives in 23 de Enero.

Today, there are more than three-dozen radical collectives organized throughout 23 de Enero, each responsible for their apartment block or region. Names are spray-painted on the top of apartment buildings, highlighting the collective responsible for the block or region, such as "Alexis Vive" or "Pensamos."

After years of police repression and abuse, 23 de Enero, with the help of the local city government, finally succeeded in kicking the police force out the neighborhood in 2004. The collectives now coordinate security among each other. Chosen residents act as liaisons between the collectives and the police force outside of the *barrio*.

"The collective that is there is usually the one that attacks the problem, and attacking the problem means talking and conversing… You don't solve insecurity by killing, but by studying, educating," says Henry Gamboa, or "Golon" as everyone calls him. He was born and raised in the La Cañada sector of 23 de Enero. Golon has been doing community work here for more than two decades, and is one of the founders of the Coordinadora Simón Bolívar.

The Coordinadora headquarters in La Cañada is the former police station taken over by the group in 2004. In 2006, they moved from their tiny two-room office across the parking lot into the new headquarters, and launched a community radio station, and an *Infocentro*, which provides free computer access to the public.

The *barrio* winds further up towards the southwest and into the hills, past countless red cinder block homes and apartment blocks, with spray painted revolutionary murals; past the giant mural of Jesus Christ toting a machine-gun painted by the La Piedrita Collective — one of the region's more militant collectives. It is so radical that in early 2009, its members were lambasted by both the opposition and President Chávez, who went so far as to call them "counter-revolutionary agents" for their violent stance against figures of the opposition.

In La Cañada, just beneath the Coordinadora and in front of apartment block 17, is the first Bolivarian school set up in Caracas in the year 1999. Inside, they're having a school assembly. The elementary school kids are studying sex education and acting out an amusing play about gonorrhea.

Outside, across the brightly painted *Plaza de Juventud,* a pair mingles in front of the state-run Che Guevara emergency medical health clinic. The corridor is lined with giant murals of Che and Venezuela's independence heroes. Across the hallway is the headquarters of the Che Guevara Collective, which coordinates activities around apartment block 17.

Gidilfredo Solzano, or "Coco", is inside. He is a member of the collective, but was in diapers when his family moved into the neighborhood on January 23 more than fifty years ago. He's been an important community activist ever since he was a teenager in the mid-1970s. When he was eighteen and studying Civil Engineering at the Luis Caballeros Mejia Technical School in Caracas, he was one of the founders of the Tupamaro Revolutionary Front, an armed leftist organization that named themselves after Uruguay's well-known Tupamaro urban guerilla insurgency from earlier that decade. After the rupture of Venezuela's Tupamaros, Coco helped to form the two-decade old *Remadel,* one of the oldest collectives in 23 de Enero, and the only one which unites all of the *barrio* for cultural activities surrounding Three Kings Day every December.

After the failed Chávez-led coup on February 4, 1992, Coco spent six months in hiding, as the community was raided by the police, the National Guard, and the Venezuelan security forces known as the DISIP.[2] Hundreds of activists were jailed.

23 de Enero is one of the hotbeds of support for President Chávez and the Bolivarian process. In fact, Chávez is a member of a PSUV battalion here, and he votes in the "Manuel Palacio Fajardo" technical school, located in 23 de Enero. Despite this, 23 de Enero tends to be one of the least understood sectors within the Bolivarian process. Mainstream media portrays the *barrio* as a lawless zone and the collectives as violent drug running gangs who fight against one another for each other's turf. Coco shakes his head in disbelief "These are people that have never in their life entered 23 de Enero," he says.

Much has changed in 23 de Enero over the last five decades, but the community commitment of the collectives has not. Then, community work some times meant demanding water at gunpoint. Now, for many, it means promoting the local missions and building basketball courts. But it's all part of the same process of organizing amongst the community and improving conditions for all.

Golon & Coco

Personal Histories

Golon: My mom came here to live in this part of 23 de Enero, in the sector of la Cañada in 1968. My mom tells me that in 1967 we lived in another part of 23 de Enero, in the area of El Mirador. From El Mirador, we came here to the sector of La Cañada. I'm thirty-nine years old, and my thirty-nine years have been dedicated to this *barrio* to improve the quality of life for the people that live here, including sports, and to say, "No to drugs; No to delinquency; No to insecurity; Yes to security." I've worked together with various *compañeros* who have dedicated themselves to this struggle. In my case, I began to struggle in the year 1987, but *compañeros* of mine in this organization have struggled much longer than I, because they were born before me. We knew that we ran a risk of death, because in a country such as this in the Fourth Republic we were considered "subversives," and the community looked to us to deal with the delinquency. The government looked to the criminals for them to kill us or scare us, but they didn't frighten us. On the contrary, we became even stronger through this struggle against delinquency and fighting for a better quality of life in the *barrio*.

Coco: Yeah, I remember when we got here. This was really beautiful. There were public areas. There weren't any problems, and there were no slums. I remember that right there across the street was just forest. There were tons of mangos, guava, and all types of fruit, and you could head in there and grab one of those giant squashes. They were huge. Here we call them *auyamas*. They were all over this *barrio*.

I remember there was never this maliciousness like now, that everyone has to put bars on their windows and things. I remember that you saw open doors and you walked down the staircases without a problem, and the people were charitable and very united. I remember those things.

I have always liked to read. I always read about things that were going on. I was always with older folks, who belonged to a left-wing party, and we always had conversations, and they took an interest in everything that we asked them, and that's how we began to get involved. At that point we founded the Tupamaro Revolutionary Front, because the Tupamaros had a really important history, and at that time they were already much older than we were, and in fact some have now passed away or were disappeared.[3] And that's when we began with this project to do community work. Out of this community work, over time, various collectives formed in the Parish. Later, the Tupamaro Revolutionary Front decided to split, because many collectives were formed here in 23 de Enero, like *La Piedrita, La Coordinadora, Acampa, el Muro de la Dignidad*, as well as our collective. And all of these collectives are working in 23 de Enero. Of course we have always respected each other, each one working in its area.

Fighting Against the Delinquency

Golon: In more or less 1979, under the government of Carlos Andrés Pérez, the problem of delinquency got worse. 23 de Enero was totally subversive. It seemed like anyone would throw a rock at the police, because really they were just fighting for a better quality of life.

So Carlos Andrés Pérez, then President of the Republic, realized that 23 de Enero was organizing, and preparing to demand their rights, and once he said, "If we need to insert drugs in 23 de Enero, we're going to put them there." And that's what he did. They grabbed people that were already mixed in with the delinquency and our *compañeros* that were throwing rocks, and brainwashed them. The government gave them drugs, so they could sell them and we would have this enemy next door: the neighbor, *el pana*, the friend, or the brother. They converted us into enemies, because with drugs you could make some money, and you could support your whole family.

But this brought death. It brought death between gangs. It brought greater instability to the country because the Fourth Republic said this, "The more absorbed they are, the more we can walk all over them." But as it turns out, we were preparing and learning to say no to this Fourth Republic, which was repressive and non-participatory.

Coco: We fought against people who caused trouble in our community. I remember, at that time, that we hooded ourselves and got involved because it got to the point where 23 de Enero was getting really ugly and intense, with the drugs and *el hampa*.[4] There were centers here where you could find labs where they made drugs. So we decided unanimously that we needed to hood ourselves and go to the streets to begin to put a stop to all of this. We made a sign and hung it outside the buildings, or in the elevators, or the stair well saying, "Tom, Dick and Harry live in this building and it is known that you are selling drugs, you have twenty-four hours to leave this building." And they would leave. But it was really hard work. It wasn't the work of one or two days, but eight or ten months, and in the end we were successful.

Fighting for Public Services

Coco: There were a lot of issues here during the Fourth Republic. We suffered a lot from the lack of basic public services, including the lack of water and trash pickup. At one point we made the decision to make them understand that we are human beings and wanted to live as anyone would. We began to send letters to the public services. I remember that the first was because of the water problem. We sent letters to the company offices in charge of the water, which at the time was Hidrocapital and such. When it became clear that they weren't going to pay any attention to the issue, we opted to hijack their trucks and put pressure on them to resolve the problem. We went all across 23 de Enero, and found the water and trash trucks, and we took them with us. How did we take them? Well, we were armed and we told the drivers, "get out or…" We took the trucks, put them in the parking lots down behind the apartment blocks and put the pressure on.

Immediately, the situation was resolved. It was intense because we were just days from Christmas and we had been without water for fifteen days. I remember that December, the people saw us in a new light, because when you resolve an issue the people say, "At least these guys took care of the problem." At this time we had these trucks for two days and the following day a group of people came with the police, but we were ready for anything. So they arrived, and we talked and looked for an agreement, and I told them, if we don't have an answer in a half hour, we're going to see what we're going to do. So they turned the water on. I remember that we had water all December, January, and February. So, it wasn't a problem with the water system. Because at that time they alleged that it was a problem with the system. So what was it?

Late 1980s – Forming the Collectives

Coco: After the rupture of the Tupamaro movement, various collectives began. Among the oldest, they founded *Remadel,* and the community organized here in block 17. Afterwards they formed the *Coordinadora, la Piedrita, Acampa, Milicia 0*, el *Frente Nuevo Vitrine.* We were persecuted. We always had problems with the police.

February 27, 1989 – The Caracazo

Coco: It was intense because there was a really strong confrontation with the government forces. It was an intense confrontation that lasted for days. At that time, the police were shooting to kill. The list of assassinations from the Caracazo totaled more than 3,000 people. I remember that the police went up there above Apartment Block 22, and shoved the cadavers in plastic bags, threw them below, picked them up with a truck and bam, that was that. And the same thing happened with the bodies on the road. They put them in plastic bags and threw them in a truck. It was intense. It was a hard battle.

Yeah, and a lot of people were jailed, and in fact all of us — all of the old group of us — appeared on a list of the DISIP with photos and everything. And among our comrades, we have various disappeared who were never found, not even their cadavers, nor did we ever know where they were taken.

Well, after something like fifteen days later, here in 23 de Enero, things started to calm down, and the state bodies started to intervene — the repressive ones as well as representatives from the Ministry of Education. I remember that they started to repair the schools, repair the buildings, because all of those buildings up there were machine-gunned. It was terrible. It's a shame that we had to dispose of all of the photos and film we took of this as evidence, because this place was raided more than three times. You know, the Coordinadora Simón Bolívar didn't have their new office yet, but they were in one just like this up there. That was also raided. The police came here ten times — five times they entered the premises. So we had to get rid of everything, all of the movies, photos, and anything that incriminated us, because they came here, and destroyed these ceilings looking for things.

La Coordinadora Simón Bolívar

Golon: The Sacudón was a social explosion. It wasn't planned. It wasn't organized by anyone, but rather the *barrios* descended because of an economic package that Carlos Andrés Pérez had launched in his second term, and this economic package was going to hit the pockets of those that had the least, which was us. The people went to the streets and what the political police, the DISIP, did, was repress social groups all over Caracas. They locked us up for sixteen days in the jail cells of the DISIP and the DIN, saying that the Sacudón had been organized by the social groups and the Tupamaros and 23 de Enero.[5] That was simply false, because it was a social uprising.

So we said, "We want to create a legal organization." And we put it under the Coordinadora Simón Bolívar, because in 23 de Enero there were various groups that were doing political work, and we needed to unify. So we came together to make up this Coordinadora Simón Bolívar. All of us coordinated to do our work in our area in each sector, with one end in mind: to resist what the Fourth Republic was doing —invading us with drugs — and work with each other to repair our elevators, our roofs, and our infrastructure.

That's why we formed the Coordinadora, on December 17, 1993, to have a legal framework and demand as the Coordinadora Simón Bolívar that the Fourth Republic government resolve our problems. We could march together with a National Assembly Representative, but alone each of us couldn't. Alone, they would see us as weak, but organized as the Coordinadora, there was a structure, there was an organization.

Now President Chávez has come to power. He has been in power for ten years. The police don't attack us, nor are they with us. But we have had ten years of rest, of not running, of them not repressing us as they repressed us before. And organized as the Coordinadora, we've done really well. We already have our projects, like setting up a radio. And our project is to work and fight for the President's policies.

Kicking the Police Out

Coco: We had already held various meetings at various times with the mayor, because the police here were very corrupt, and involved in the sale of liquor, drugs, and illegal gambling.[6] They were really corrupt, and we demanded a change. So, we made the decision among nearly all of the collectives to kick the police out of 23 de Enero. There are no police here now, and the police and the government respect the autonomy of these spaces.

Golon: The police are the neighborhood. The neighbors are those who have to be in charge of security, because they know us.

They know our friends, our delinquents, our neighbors, our brothers and sisters, and we know how to deal with delinquency. All the police did was repress us and the delinquency got much worse.

So that's what we do, and when things get out of hand, our *jefe civil* arrives, "well, I'm the *jefe civil*." [7] He'll send a card for you to visit him, or [say] "look, if you are going to continue doing this, you leave us with no other choice but for us to confront you." In this case, the Coordinadora would follow through. But it could be the Ché Guevara Collective or whatever collective depending on the sector where the people are located. The collective that is there is usually the one that attacks the problem, and attacking the problem means talking and conversing: "Look, this isn't the way. We aren't going to allow this in our community." And like that, we speak until the person understands, and stops involving himself in the delinquency.

This gets to the person, and he stops doing it, because there is respect for us and our organizations, because we are serious organizations that work for the good of the community, so people can improve their lives. You don't solve insecurity by killing, but by studying and educating, by grabbing these kids and putting them on a soccer field, taking these kids and giving them classes.

Coco: We want nothing of guns. None of that. This has gone to another level. The weapons we have here are books, culture, sports.

You ask your friends at CNN how many deaths there have been in 23 de Enero over the last two years, and how many there were in the eastern side of the city. They should do this comparison so they can see what is happening in 23 de Enero. It's been a long time since 23 de Enero was on the front page of the newspapers: "John Doe was assassinated in 23 de Enero." That time is over here.

You notice the difference immediately. In yesterday's front page there were two people dead next to Sambil.[8] "John Doe dead on the East highway." So you tell me what has been reported about 23 de Enero which isn't positive for the Parish? The misinformation is really intense.

On Chávez's Response to La Piedrita?

Coco: Well, I respect the opinion of Hugo Chávez about La Piedrita, but I don't share it, because this collective has been a collective that has done really intense work within the sector up there above the *Observatorio*. That's like lawless land and the members of this collective were able to guide the people in this community. So I think that our commander in chief, either he was misinformed, or they misinformed him about the collective, because all of us here in 23 de Enero know that the work that this collective has done has been profoundly important for the community. They have done things that the police haven't — intense work and overwhelmingly important. And these people in the region are very appreciative for everything that this collective has done. So I don't understand the reaction from the president against this collective.

Misrepresentations of 23 de Enero

Coco: Well, I would say that the media is even more misinformed than our president, because, to begin with, these are people who never in their lives have entered 23 de Enero. They don't know what type of work is done here, because when they had the opportunity to show the world the realities of 23 de Enero, they didn't do it. Either they were paid by the state, or were with the opposition, or still believe they own Venezuela. They never showed the realities, and right now, they can't have the luxury of showing this type of news, because they can't come here to 23 de Enero. Not because we wouldn't want them to, but rather that they won't come here, because they don't want to show how things have improved in 23 de Enero, since these Fourth Republic governments were in charge.

Changes in 23 de Enero under Chávez

Coco: And how have things improved? In every way. Look, public services, transportation, the roadways, electricity, water service, and running water have all improved. We've consistently had them all for a while. We aren't going to say we've had only an improvement, but rather an *enormous* improvement, that's very notable.

Before, we had none of this. Today we have emergency health clinics, the cultural mission, Barrio Adentro and any number of missions, each one having to do with a different objective: health, sports, culture. Today there are various collectives that are working on the issue of information. They are going to do things for film and recordings, community radios, which you never saw even one of before. Can you believe it? So now, do you think things have improved?

Ten Years of the Process

Golon: I think that after ten years of the process, this is still very young. We have a long way to go. There are *compañeros* in the government who don't know what revolution is, they don't know what socialism is, but rather they are there to simply have a political position and have a good place to accommodate their personal life. After they're up there as ministers, they forget the people. They don't come down here and they don't see what is happening with the people, in the communities. They don't approach us, but rather send someone.

That is what this government is missing. It needs to work more with the people. This relationship of the government to the people, and the people to the government, still hasn't been reached. And this is what has made this process, over its ten years, go slowly.

But yes, we have advanced. I think that the president has advanced in education. He formed the missions and here we are. We are no longer a country of illiteracy. We have a very low level of illiteracy. People are studying in the Ribas and Robinson Missions, and the Sucre Mission, which is the university. They have opened the university to the people. And that's why I believe that socialism is for all. There is equality amongst everyone. Education is for everyone. Before, in the Fourth Republic, education was for those who had money. Those of us who really needed school couldn't study because they denied us access for the simple fact that we lived in 23 de Enero.

I think that's what the president is doing that the Fourth Republic never did, which is to educate the people, to make them wake up, to give the people the opportunity to decide, to participate, to organize for a better quality of life. Meanwhile, in the Fourth Republic they said, "Don't let the people organize, don't study, so we can walk all over them." It's the contrary now, it's the opposite.

The Collectives & Community Organizing

Coco: Precisely as a result of this rupture of the Tupamaros into all of these separate collectives in all of these sectors, each group in its sector keeps an eye on its region. And there have never been hard feelings among us. What happened is that everyone opted to occupy their space, which in my opinion is really important, because I don't have to go up there to La Piedrita, when only the people who live there will know the problems of La Piedrita.

And the job of the collectives is to continue to work with the communities, because the fact that we already have everything does not imply that the struggle is over, or that we are not going to continue to work. Now is when the work is the hardest, because now you have to teach the people the value of these things, the value of the cultural mission, the sports missions, the Barrio Adentro Mission, the emergency health clinics, and this series of things that we have achieved as a result of the government of President Hugo Chávez.

And yes, there is more participation than before. Right now, almost everyone depends on a collective. Because a collective is an organized group of people and that's where the communal councils come from. Of course, someone else who lives in the community and wants to participate in the communal council is more than welcome. We already have a commune.[9] The Panal Commune up there that was organized by our friends in the Alexis Vive collective. This is a process that takes work. It takes time, but we're getting there.

EIGHTEEN

María Vicenta Dávila.

María Vicenta Dávila,
Mixteque Communal Council

(Mucuchíes, Mérida)

The lofty mountains loom overhead. Thick white clouds slowly glide through the valley as potato growers traverse the mountainside, picking their crops. Beneath them, multi-colored homes bask in the chilly morning sun. The land is green and fertile. An aging farmer, dressed in thick wool, encourages his ox ahead of him as he manually directs his plow across his field. Beyond him, past the swiftly moving crystal blue Chama River, is the small town of Mucuchíes.

The road into this community is paved, but only recently. A thick stone wall follows it up along the fields, past the pastel-colored community center, and into the community.

This is a far cry from the bustling streets of the country's capital, Caracas. Here, in Rangel Municipality, the small farming community of Mixteque lies nestled in the hillside of the Andean mountains, a few hours up from Mérida, the state capital.

A network of irrigation pipes covers the hillside, one of the latest achievements of Mixteque's communal council.

"Rangel Municipality is one of the showcase municipalities of Venezuela, in terms of community development. There are ninety-two communal councils here, of which some are working on their third project, and we in this community are going for our fourth," says María Vicenta Dávila. She steps out from behind a long waist-high concrete tub where she's been watering worms for her women's composting cooperative.

María Vicenta starcs out over the valley. She is middle-aged, but quick and nimble. She has to be. She is one of the movers and shakers in the community; one of the co-founders of the decade-old thirteen-person cooperative; and one of the prominent members of the communal council formed even before the Communal Councils Law was passed in April 2006.

Since the passage of the 49 Laws Decrees in 2001, communities had already been organizing into local committees, based around issues important to the community, such as water, health, urban land, culture and sports. In 2002, the Venezuelan government created the *Consejos Locales de Planificación Pública* (CLPP - Local

Public Planning Councils) with the goal of electing community representatives to work hand in hand with government officials to agree on municipal budgets. But with political cronyism and without real community participation, the CLPPs quickly ran aground.[1]

Meanwhile, in the communities, there was often little coordination between diverse committees and they often found themselves fighting individually for government resources. This changed in 2006 with the passage of the Communal Councils Law, which laid the groundwork for the creation of communal councils, thereby bringing the various committees under one roof.

Communal councils are now the new bodies of local democratic governance in Venezuela. Any community can form its own communal council.[2] They are organized by the community, composed of a representative of each of a neighborhood's organizing committees, and democratically elected by community assemblies of 200-400 families. The communal councils have three separate branches of at least five people each: the executive branch (which coordinates), the financial branch (which oversees the finances, and the communal bank or cooperative) and the social controller branch (which audits the other branches). The elected spokespersons of the communal council belong to one of these branches, in which they can elaborate projects. Ultimate power, however, lies in the general assembly of all community members over fifteen years of age, which must approve projects and fund allocations.[3]

Over 30,000 such councils have been formed over the last three years, and billions of dollars have been passed directly down to the banks of these communal councils by the Venezuelan national government for infrastructure and socio-economic projects.[4]

While communal councils have been organized across the country, some of the most successful experiences are in the rural Andean hillsides of Mérida state.

María Vicenta Dávila

Personal History

My name is María Vicenta Dávila, and I've lived here in this community my whole life. Well, I'll tell you about my name. I was born on July 24, the same day that Simón Bolívar was born, and so the doctor and my mother, who is also very revolutionary, said that they had to name me by combining the names of the parents of Simón Bolívar. That's why they named me María, for his mother, María Concepción Palacios, and Vicente for Simón Bolívar's father, Juan Vicente Bolívar, and Dávila because I'm the daughter of a single mother, so I have just one last name.

Community History

In the beginning, the community grew wheat and *papita negra*, but after the "green revolution," when the industrial revolution came with the pesticides, the people began to plant other types of potatoes, garlic, and other crops.[5] But at first they planted wheat, and well before that it was corn, because that is the main staple of our diet. Right now we are in the process of reviving our *papa negra*, our original potato, native here, from the *Páramo*.

According to a document I have now, they divided up these lands in 1836. An *aguacil* came from Spain — that's what the document says — and they divided up the lands to the native people.[6] And they numbered them like animals, to put it one way. For instance, my family is number 213. They gave you a number and said, "OK, you're owner of this area here."

This was also a community with a lot of legends. The homes here had dirt floors and the roofs were made of straw. You find the *mintoyes*, places where our indigenous people were said to have hidden from the Conquistadores, to save their food and to protect them. You find a lot of lands that have their legends. This is a Catholic community, there are cultural groups, and our principle income comes from agriculture.

Community Work

How did I begin to do community work? Well, first, I have roots. My mom was a fighter and she used to work trading produce between here and the community of El Carrizal. They took potatoes from here to trade. So really those were my roots on my mom's side. My uncle is a *murero*, a wall builder in the community. Another uncle worked on the Andean roads here, and during the dictatorship, he was in the military. So I think it's in my roots, and I began to formally work with the Popular Education Centers, based on the literacy methodology of Paolo Freire, in 1974. The national literacy campaign here in Venezuela was a proposal that also came from the pedagogy of Paolo Freire and his work on popular education.

We started these Popular Education Centers in 1974 in each of the communities, and then we joined together in one larger group. Now there still exists one popular education center called the Popular Education Center for Integral Development of the Family. And we've carried out various projects in the community: the *lumbricultura;* the *tejido,* as a revival of our raw wool; the training center in Gavidia; transportation; and one of the most important things is the popular education human resource training.[7] We consider ourselves popular educators. I, for example, am a popular educator.

In the communities, these popular education centers worked until 1994, and then came the boom of the neighborhood associations. So they formed these associations in the communities, and in this government the communal councils came along, so the others no longer exist.

The Mixteque Communal Council

The communal council is more aligned with the structure of the popular education centers. We set our council up with this style of structure in 2005, and then we brought it up to code when they passed the Communal Councils Law.[8]

How did we set up the communal council? We did a census. We went from house to house, speaking with everyone in the community. We figured out how many voters we had, and each family said who they would like to be members of the communal council. Then we elected them. We called an assembly and we said, "OK, these are the candidates." We elected the electoral council, and they prepared everything for the vote according to the law — because there was already a law proposal, although there wasn't a law yet. And then they held elections and everyone voted according to his or her choice.

In the community of Mixteque there are eighty-eight families, so multiplied by five, that's about 300 or 400 people, who make up the communal council. That's the entire general assembly, the whole community. But there are about twenty-five people who are active and participate, because people are still adapting to the process, which they have to internalize. But more or less seventy people go to the assembly. And when we have elections, it is mandatory for everyone in the community over twelve years old to vote, because there are also interests for the children, and the idea is that they also have a say. So, we really take it seriously. We have the voting booth, the inscription, and these people go and vote, and the people that don't vote have to present a note justifying their excuse why they couldn't vote — for instance if they were sick or traveling or something. But yes, everyone in the community has to vote. It's mandatory. And the assembly elects the projects, and then they are prioritized within the assembly. So it's not an individual but the assembly that prioritizes the projects.

We say that a vote needs to be more than 50 percent. The majority has to approve it. If at least half the people don't come, the assembly is suspended, because they aren't going to go blaming things on everyone else or say that we are managing things alone.

Right now we are still adjusting, because we've had the communal council for a while, three years, and we formed the council before they wrote the law.

The projects have all been finished, and now we're about to start the next project, which is going to be the *casa comunal.*[9] We are close to electing the new communal council that will guide things for the next couple of years. We have elections every two years, but you can make adjustments each year if necessary.

Venezuela's Showcase Municipality

In terms of community development, Rangel Municipality is one of Venezuela's showcase municipalities. There are ninety-two communal councils here and some of them are on their third project, and we are going for our fourth. First, the communal council has a structure that is totally horizontal, which people have a hard time seeing because they are so used to the vertical type: a president, a secretary, a treasurer. No, right now there's a completely horizontal structure, where instead there are only committees. So, we're also in a learning process.

Right now we're working, well let's say, at about 50 percent, because to say 100 percent would be an exaggeration, and we're not going to say that. The idea of working at 100 percent, in which all of the committees are working, would be a success and that's where we need to get to. But for that to happen, people need to have more or less a clear vision about what we are after; we need to guide and inspire others.

In my case, I'm part of the social controller branch of the communal council. The rest of the group and I have to keep an eye on how the money is being managed; if the others are managing it as they should; if the committees are working.

The structure of the communal councils is very beautiful. For me, it is a structure that we had been speaking about for many years, with the Popular Education Centers. It's a flower, right? A flower where you have this team, and each petal makes up a different committee. There are five people in the social controller branch. There are also five people in the cooperative. So I think that we are all in this process of learning and adaptation.

One of the most important things is that we ourselves are administering the money. Before, you had to go to the mayor's office. And not all the funds got to the mayor's office, and then you had to go… but not now. Right now all of the funds come directly to the communal councils, and we administer the money and it goes further.

For example in Gavidia, in one of the communities, they asked for funds to improve an agricultural road and we made the comparison. I don't know how many thousands of *Bolívares Fuertes* (Bs.F) a company normally spends to pave 400 meters, but the 30,000 Bs.F that they gave to us paved more meters than the company ever would.[10] So you can compare it.

I think that the proposal of the communal council is excellent, but there is also another side to it. The communal councils have to be constantly educating and training themselves ideologically. What do we want with the communal council? Why does the government want to pass funds to the people? So, it's not simply that we are working with the economics, which would convert the communal councils into only project-based councils. No, the idea is that they become councils, which originate in a true integral development, in endogenous development.

What is endogenous development? Well, for us, endogenous development comes from below, from the grassroots. Not exogenous development, which comes from above. That's what it was like before. So it's endogenous development, because we're working with things from the grassroots. We discuss things in the assembly, we approve it or we don't. Projects aren't imposed from above. They are projects that come out of necessity.

Projects

The first project that was set up, here in our community, was to improve the irrigation system, and the second was to improve part of the Chama River Valley with a containment wall. The other project we are contemplating is for the *casa comunal*. We already have a communal center, but we want one with enough space to do workshops; for youth, adults, and children. Our center has just one room and there are various groups meeting, and this one isn't big enough. So we want that to be the next project.

The housing project is also something that we've consolidated this year. We received some 300,000 Bs.F approved for this community for ten new homes and nine home restorations.[11]

But there was a change in ministers. I hoped that would end the bureaucracy. Unfortunately, it seems to have grown even more. So we're going to meet, so we can plan what to do in each of the areas.

Communal Councils & the Bolivarian Revolution

Across the country I feel like there are a lot of communities that really aren't interested in the communal councils. Because there is paternalism, I-ism, egoism, and really there's a lot of apathy, that the government is simply supposed to give, and especially in the *barrios*. That's the hardest part — to change the mentality of the *barrios*. For me, I'd say that, through the communal councils, the government has to really train leaders of their own communities so that they have the ideological capacity to create, and continue with these projects. So that it isn't just *ad honoren*, but that they give these people an incentive to deepen the ideological development in the communities, and also to exchange. For example, bring another community to ours, and from there continue to exchange.

In our case, we have made exchanges. Our friend, James Suggett, has brought the Wayúu people. They were impressed, and we're going to go there. The people from the Guajira came here, also people from Palmarito and Zea. Women came to see what we were doing, because they were impressed that we were working with trash, which is dirty work.

Changing Times

Let me tell you. This is not the same community it was before. I mean, Rangel Municipality has changed so much in five years. It's amazing. There are three taxi lines, there are two communities that already have their own transportation, and a few days ago I was in the plaza, and when was the last time you saw children roller skating and the people on the corner dancing to the music?

A lot of people came from Valencia to experience the tranquility and they say, "Wow, Venezuela has changed a lot. And Mucuchíes has changed a lot." The people that left with the petroleum boom are returning and many of these folks are sorry that they sold their property and left. They left for Caracas and now they are returning. And the other part that I have also seen in my community is the Colombian immigration. There's an incredible amount of Colombian immigration.

Changes Under Chávez

The difference is that now, the resources go directly to the people. Now you can go speak with your mayor. Before you had to schedule one or two months out, and you couldn't speak because you felt embarrassed. And when there were elections, to win your vote, they said, "well, I'll give you some cinder blocks, I'll give you some tin for these shacks." There was no growth. Now, you're not embarrassed to speak with a governor. I have spoken with Chávez, with the President. What's more, he recited a poem to me by José Marti when they were launching the Science Mission in Aló President, #247, and I told him about all of these projects that we're doing.

We've been in international meetings in Caracas. When did you ever see this before? Us? Never. The people couldn't go. You might find it naïve, but many times we heard about the Hilton hotel and we asked ourselves what it was like inside. We've also been to the Teresa Carreño Theater.[12] So now, the people are taken into account, but one of the things that we need to really focus on is the ideological part, because we make mistakes; we're human beings.

But in comparison, under the Fourth Republic, they built housing here. All of it was the same — on the coast, in the lowlands, in the mountains. And they made them with asbestos, a roof of asbestos, which now the doctors tell us is carcinogenic. And in my house, beneath the asbestos it is black, all black, and my child is sick. The doctor has told me that it's because of problems with this, and so now you see. Compare the housing from before and housing now; dignified housing, really pretty, with a tile roof, made of wood, dignified for us Venezuelan men and women. So really things are changing.

Relationship with Chávez

I'll tell you something. Not everyone who wears a red hat and a red shirt is... I wouldn't say *Chavista*, I'd say they are not all socialists. They don't want change. Not everyone wants changes. Everything is disguised. For instance I've only been to one Chávez march. And like me, there are a lot of people that are really making the change that we want, and what we really want is to educate and train the communities in ideological principles.

I think that the most beautiful thing is this, collective work — that we respect each other, and we join together and change. We have to change. The world can't stay the same as it was 50 or even 500 years ago. I think that this is what is being created here in Venezuela. With or without Chávez, Venezuela is no longer the same, and this is Chávez' great challenge, to change the mentality of the people.

And wow, how the mentality of the people is changing. To be speaking and planning in our meetings. To see a young girl like Marlin thinking differently.[13] That she dares to measure the PH in the humus. That she dares to go to a meeting and debate. I think that things are really changing. Even more so, I'm studying now. I'm getting my high school degree with the Ribas Mission. I'm going to study Physics.

Communal Councils, Just for Chávez Supporters?

I completely disagree. The communal councils aren't just for Chávez supporters, because the whole community makes up part of the communal council, and there are some people that are with the process and others that aren't, but they still benefit from the projects. For example the whole community benefits from our irrigation system, not just the chosen agricultural producers. Right? So, I believe that this education or socio-political training has content, and in one way or the other we need to maintain this and we need to work within this process. We have to have education on the community level, the communal council. We have to have socio-political education, so that they aren't just band-aids, so that there is a true process of education and training.[14]

And you are not going to understand this process overnight, which is a process of change from the grassroots. I think that speaking of ourselves on the global level... a few days ago a few adolescents from the United States came to visit us and that's what we told them, we believe that each generation is going to have new ideas, and that we need to allow ourselves to have them.

Neighborhood Associations vs. Communal Councils

The neighborhood associations were politicized. Not now, because now we have a collectivity, where you have to have an assembly in order to approve things. It's not individualized. Before it was more representative than participatory. And now there is a tremendous increase in participation. Wow, yes. Because it offers the space for participation, that's why I say that you have to educate well, because you can't short change the ideology that we want to implement, which is socialism, and which is still in construction. And yes, people are empowered.

For example, now they say, "We are useful." Before we felt worthless because they didn't take us into account. They covered our mouths with a little handout, a little cement, a few concrete blocks, but you didn't know where the resources really went. There were so many resources because Venezuela was even richer before. And well, now, despite everything, look what we've achieved. The economic crisis isn't affecting us, thank god. We have our chicken here at the *Mercal*.[15] We have meat and rice. We have everything.

So yes, now you really feel that Venezuela is making this shift from representative to participatory democracy. What is participatory democracy? For me, participatory democracy is giving power to the people. Give power to the people in a good sense. Power to the people, as I was saying, for the people to administer their own resources.

But there also has to be follow up. We need one part audit and transparency, and one part follow up. For me, that is participatory democracy, where you can speak of your rights and your duties, where the freedom to protest exists, where there is no marginality, where there is no poverty. For me, this is participatory democracy, and I feel that we at this moment, in this municipality — I'm going to speak for the municipality — we are practicing participatory democracy.

But you have to know that it's hard to understand this in the *barrios*. When you are in a community like ours, it's easy to see things, because we have more space. We don't have this concrete trapping us. The natural environment enables us to have space to think and analyze things. But in the largest cities the poor children and the poor youth don't have any alternative space, so they dedicate themselves to watching TV, and it's burning their brains.

International

The mainstream media is terrible. It has to change. The media needs to educate people. It needs to open spaces of participation in the community. They shouldn't be closed spaces. They should be open. I think of the youth. The youth have to sit down to discuss their future, because I'll tell you, a few days ago, I don't know if it's true or not, but I heard that the United States Constitution is more than 200 years old and it hasn't been reformulated even once. For me it's a constitution, which is like an old Bible, which you are never going to be able to change.

I think that the generations are changing, and I'll tell you, my mother who is seventy-eight years old, doesn't have the same beliefs that I have today. When she was my age, she didn't believe what I believe today. There should be some respect, that passing generations should respect the new generation, and that this new generation has to come together as a collective and elaborate its own ideas. And these ideas should be written and respected by the collective, because with a 200-year-old constitution, what is the new generation supposed to do? Youth like these fifteen-year-old boys who believe in something else? They are going to be ignored by the elite, who are the ones in control.

I was shocked when they told me that war is convenient to the United States, because there is a war industry which wants there to be war in order to sell its weapons. Please! For me, this cannot be because we are killing other brothers and sisters who we should be supporting.

Endnotes

Prologue

1   For more detailed accounts of this transition, see, for example, William I. Robinson, *Latin America and Global Capitalism* (Baltimore: Johns Hopkins University Press, 2009), 1-50 and Robert Brenner, *The Boom and the Bubble* (London: Verso Books, 2002), 16-93.

2   The International Monetary Fund (IMF) did this by requiring borrowers to implement so-called "structural adjustment programs," which meant privatizing state-owned enterprises, cutting back on social spending, eliminating environmental and workplace regulations, and opening their economies to "free trade" by reducing tariffs and subsidies. The IMF represented a "creditor's cartel" because private banks would not lend to governments unless they had already signed an agreement with the IMF.

3   World Bank, World Development Report 2000/2001, 51.

4   Mark Weisbrot and David Rosnick, "Another Lost Decade? Latin America's Growth Failure Continues into the Twenty-First Century" (Center for Economic and Policy Research, Washington, DC, 2003), http://www.cepr.net/index.php/publications/reports/another-lost-decade-latin-americas-growth-failure-continues-into-the-21st-century/.

5   For a review of these social movements in Latin America, see Richard Stahler-Sholk, Harry E. Vanden, and Glen David Kuecker, *Latin American Social Movements in the Twenty-first Century: Resistance, Power, and Democracy* (New York: Rowman & Littlefield Publishers, 2008).

6   Patronage-clientelism refers to the ages-old practice where politicians use government resources such as jobs or material benefits to favor their own supporters against political opponents. Personalism refers to the tendency among citizens and political leaders to place greater importance on loyalty to individual politicians instead of loyalty to a particular political program. For a discussion of these and other problems, see Gregory Wilpert, *Changing Venezuela by Taking Power: The History and Policies of the Chávez Government* (London: Verso Books, 2007).

Introduction

1 Marta Harnecker has contributed greatly to developing the theoretical concepts of participatory democracy and popular power. Marta Harnecker, trans. Coral Wynter and Federico Fuentes, "Popular Power in Latin America – Inventing In Order to Not Make Errors"(Closing lecture given at the XXVI Gallega Week of Philosophy, Pontevedra, April 17, 2009), *Links: International Journal of Socialist Renewal,* July 2009, http://links.org.au/node/1136.

2 Vijay Prashad, *The Darker Nations: A People's History of the Third World* (New York: New Press, 2007).

Introductory History

1 Early Spanish conquistadores were drawn there by the grandiose tales of the golden treasures of El Dorado hidden deep in the Venezuelan Amazon. In the 20th century, reports of vast oil deposits around the Lake Maracaibo enticed a new generation of treasure hunters. The quadrupling of the price of oil in 1973 provoked what came to be known as the oil shock in the industrialized countries of the North. While this produced fears of economic downfall for those countries, in Venezuela it created what has been referred to as a "petroleum euphoria." In that same year, Carlos Andrés Pérez won the presidential elections with a large margin, campaigning as *el hombre con energía* (the man with energy), promising that he could now magically bring Venezuela into the future with oil. Fernando Coronil, *The Magical State: Nature, Money, and Modernity in Venezuela* (Chicago: University Of Chicago Press 1997), 237-238.

2 Simón Bolívar was born on July 24th, 1783.

3 As of late 2006, slightly more than 2 percent of the Venezuelan population of 26 million was indigenous. "There are some 28 different indigenous groups in Venezuela, but only four of those groups, the Wayúu, Warao, Pemón, and Añu, have populations in excess of 10,000 people." Statistics, University of Maryland, Minorities at Risk (MAR) Assessment for Indigenous Peoples in Venezuela, December 31, 2006. http://www.cidcm.umd.edu/mar/assessment.asp?groupId=10102.

4 "Cumbe is the name of the liberated spaces created by the *cimarrones,* or liberated slaves," Luis Perdomo, Chapter 11.

5 John Lynch, *Simón Bolívar: A Life* (New Haven: Yale University Press, 2006), 76.

6 Gregory Wilpert, *Changing Venezuela by Taking Power* (London: Verso Books, 2007),10.

7 As in two other highly US-influenced Caribbean countries, Puerto Rico and Cuba, the national sport in Venezuela is baseball, not soccer. Even Hugo Chávez jokes about how he tried out for the New York Yankees as a young man, but didn't make the cut.

8 The first democratic transfer of power from one party to another in

Venezuelan history didn't take place until 1968, and even then it was under the *Acción Democrática- Copei* power-sharing Punto Fijo pact.

9 Wilpert,10.

10 There have been five republics in Venezuelan history. Venezuela's Fourth Republic began shortly after the dissolution of Gran Colombia in 1831 and lasted until President Chávez came to power in 1999. President Chávez' political party, which helped him to win the 1998 presidential elections, was called *Movimiento Quinta República* (MVR - Movement for the Fifth Republic). Despite the fact that the Fourth Republic lasted for more than 150 years, when most Chávez supporters now use the term "Fourth Republic," they are generally referring to the forty-year period immediately preceding Chávez' rise to power beginning with the Punto Fijo Pact.

11 Terry Lynn Karl, *The Paradox of Plenty* (Berkeley: University of California Press, 1997), 234.

12 Wilpert,11.

13 Wilpert,13.

14 Ibid.

15 Chapter 15.

16 *Caracazo* - Caracas + azo, the ending "azo" in Spanish means beating or hit. Venezuelans typically name their uprisings like this, i.e. Barcelonazo, Carupanazo, Porteñazo. Sacudón means "the big riot" or "the big loot."

17 Venezuela's has an indigenous population of roughly 500,000. Chesa Boudin, Gabriel González, and Wilmer Rumbos, *Venezuelan Revolution: 100 Questions —100 Answers* (New York, NY: Thunder Mountain Press, 2006), 74.

18 This power was granted to two presidents before Chávez. And the National Assembly granted it again to Chávez for eighteen months beginning in January 2007, during which time he decreed twenty-six laws.

19 Pedro Carmona - the President of the Venezuelan Chamber of Commerce, Fedecameras, who assumed the Venezuelan presidency during Chávez' absence. President Chávez calls him, Pedro "the brief."

20 Venezuela produces between 3- 3.5 million barrels of petroleum per day, roughly half of which is sold to the United States. Production during the lockout was next to nothing.

21 Venezuela's social missions are almost all named after Venezuelan "founding fathers" or important moments, events, or people in Venezuela's revolutionary history.

22 As of January 2009, there were 3,105 Barrio Adentro I basic medical centers functioning throughout the country, and a total of 476 Central Diagnostic Centers (CDI), where more in-depth diagnosis and treatment is conducted. Tamara Pearson, "Venezuela Launches 732 New Public Health Works For 2009," *Venezuelanalysis*, January 28, 2009, http://www.venezuelanalysis.com/news/4150. Colin Burgon, "10 Years of Progress in Venezuela," *Venezuelanalysis*, February 6, 2009, http://www.venezuelanalysis.

com/analysis/4181.

23 *No Es Poca Cosa: 10 años de logros del Gobierno Bolivariano*, pamphlet based on Chávez' speech, February 2, 2008, 10-11.

24 Ibid.,18-24.

25 Bolivarian bourgeoisie - new bureaucracy.

26 Certain "pro-Chávez" governors showed little interest in supporting the reforms that would drastically limit their powers, passing them up to Chávez and down to the Venezuelan people through the communal councils. In fact, on the eve of the 2007 referendum, many basic public services — such as trash pickup — simply stopped functioning, cluttering Caracas streets with debris, even more so than usual.

27 In 2008, the Bolivian states of Pando, Beni, Santa Cruz, and Tarija in the country's rich lowlands (known for the half-moon shape made by the states on a map) held referenda and asked their residents if they supported autonomy from the Bolivian government. The majority of the population of this region is of European decent, while the majority of Bolivian population is indigenous. The votes came on the heels of the election to power of Bolivia's first indigenous president, Evo Morales, who took steps to use the profit from nation's energy production for the good of the poor majority, rather than the middle-upper class sectors that had traditionally received preferential treatment.

28 Manuel Rosales is a leading figure of the Venezuelan opposition, the former Zulia state governor, and the former presidential candidate who ran against Chávez in 2006.

Chapter I

1 *Barrio* - slum or shantytown. In Venezuela, the word *barrio* is synonymous with the Brazilian term *favela*.

2 *Favela* - Portuguese, meaning shantytown or slum.

Paróquia - parish. Venezuelan term for a small county. Many parishes make up a municipality.

3 In the 2005 census, Venezuela's urban population rose over the previous five years from 89 percent of the population to 92.3 percent. This numbers puts Venezuelan urbanization slightly above Uruguay (half of whose population of 3.5 million people live in the capital, Montevideo) but below some Caribbean island-nations such as Martinique with an urban percentage of 97.9 percent of the population. Population Division of the Department of Economic and Social Affairs of the United Nations Secretariat, World Population Prospects: The 2006 Revision and World Urbanization Prospects: The 2007 Revision, http://esa.un.org/unup.

4 Most of the land is actually owned by someone or some entity. In large part, the land is owned by the state (municipality, national), state institutions such as the National Housing Institute (INAVI), or private entities (individuals or companies such as Pepsi-Cola).

5 Comité de Tierras Urbanas, Prensa CTU's, "Comités de Tierra

Urbana convocan a marcha para el 23 de septiembre", *Aporrea*, September 17, 2009, www.aporrea.org/actualidad/n142387.html

According to University of Nottingham, PhD Candidate Jennifer Martinez, who is writing her doctoral thesis on the CTU, "some states haven't received a single land title. Almost half the land is private, which essentially isn't covered by the law. And I would guess (although the numbers are really fuzzy) that of the publicly-owned land that have CTUs on them (and not all do) only about half of those have titles. And the process has been getting slower the more time moves on."

6 *Movimento Sem Terra* (MST) - Brazilian Landless Worker's Movement, which has garnered international recognition for acquiring millions of acres for its members through land-occupations. The Pioneer Camp tactics are actually more closely related to that of Brazil's urban landless movement, the *Movimento dos Trabalhadores Sem Teto* (Roofless Worker's Movement – MTST), of whom they are in contact. The major difference being however, that both of the Brazilian organizations do actual occupations, executed with hundreds and thousands of families. The Pioneers in Venezuela do 'symbolic' occupations. Their primary mode of acquiring land is through negotiations with the state.

7 According to Iraida in late 2009, there are a dozen Pioneer Camps across the country, half of them in Caracas. This is up from only four active Caracas Camps in 2008.

8 The Metropolitan District of Caracas is divided in to five different municipalities: Libertador (the Capital District), Chacao, Baruta, Sucre, and El Hatillo. Each Municipality has it's own local mayor. There is also a mayor for the overall Metropolitan District of Caracas. The Liberatador Municipality is currently the only Caracas Municipality in the hands of a Chávez supporter. Jorge Rodríguez (PSUV) was elected Mayor in the fall 2008 regional and local elections. As mayor of the Libertador Municipality, he has launched the *Plan Caracas Socialista* (the Socialist Caracas Plan) and has brought numerous members of Venezuelan social movements (including the CTU and the Pioneer Camps) into his local government.

9 *Marcos Pérez Jiménez* - Washington-backed Venezuelan dictator from 1952 to 1958.

10 *Partido Bandera Roja* - Red Flag party, a Venezuelan radical and at times armed Left-wing group. It was formed in 1971 by anti-revisionist members of the Movement of the Revolutionary Left (MIR). After the electoral victory of Hugo Chávez in 1998, the party started aligning itself with the right-wing and social democratic opponents of Chávez. This led to desertions from the party, as many members joined the Chávez camp instead.

11 *Copeyanos* is a term used to describe members of the Christian Democratic Party, COPEI.

12 Pioneer Camps have weekly assemblies to discuss the organization and issues in the community. Decisions are made democratically.

13 The pioneer camps have a team of architects that help them to

elaborate projects, decipher laws and look for land, which they call their technical support team. The CTU are very clear that, while these people may have this technical understanding, they are there to support the work of the CTU, and not impose their opinions or do it for them.

14 José Vicente Rangel Ávalos, of Chávez's former MVR party, was the mayor of the Municipality of Sucre from 2000-2008. He is the son of the journalist José Vicente Rangel, who served as Vice-President under Chávez from 2002-2007.

15 EPS is a term designated to certain local businesses in Venezuela which are considered to be rooted in equality and the social good and either state or collective property. The designation falls under the Venezuelan Ministry of Basic Industry and helps local businesses to received contracts through the Venezuelan government. http://www.cvg.com/espanol/portal_eps/index.php

16 Most of the land titles acquired through Decree 1666 were on state land.

17 In the Land Bank a commission of urban soil does an inventory of all of the unused land in the region. They investigate if it is private or if it belongs to the state, and after this inventory they organize groups to which to transfer this land.

18 Libertador Municipality Mayor, Jorge Rodríguez approved the *Decreto de Uso de Tierras Urbanas* (Decree on the Use of Urban Land) on May 8, 2009.

19 The concept of the new socialist communities came out of the failed 2007 Reform Referendum. The Pioneers consider them to be roughly synonymous with the communities to be formed through their housing policy (such as in El Junquito), which are rooted in the community, have collective property, and make decisions democratically.

20 President Chávez announced the construction of the first socialist city outside of Caracas in July 2007. According to Chávez, the "socialist cities" would be made up of small productive communes designed around family life, and not "at the service of capitalism." The communities would be made up with people from the poor sectors that lack adequate housing. Communities would have universities, cultural and medical centers, among other social structures. Chris Carlson, "President Chávez Announces "Socialist Cities" and Constitutional Reforms" *Venezuelanalysis*, July 23, 2007, http://www.venezuelanalysis.com/news/2513

21 The Liberatador Municipality Mayor Jorge Rodríguez served as Vice-President under Chávez in 2007 (immediately following Rangel), during which time his office acted as mediator in the dialogue between the Pioneer Camps and then Sucre Mayor, José Vicente Rangel Ávalos.

22 According to Iraida, roughly 80 percent of the Pioneers are women.

23 The new pro-Chávez *Partido Socialista Unido de Venezuela* (PSUV) was

formed in 2007 out of a variety of pro-Chávez parties, including his Fifth Republic Movement (MVR) party, through which Chávez was elected in 1998. The PSUV is said to be the most democratically-elected party in Venezuelan history with local battalions (committees of neighborhood PSUV members) electing representatives to local, region, state and national commissions. Electoral candidates are elected in primaries. Over six million people are said to be registered as PSUV members. As of October 2009, according to PSUV statistics, 74 percent of Venezuelan state governors, 79 percent of mayor's offices, and 84 percent of National Assembly Legislatures are PSUV members. www.psuv.org.ve

24 The Battalion was the smallest grassroots unit of the United Socialist Party of Venezuela, until the Community Patrols were formed in mid-2009.

25 *Junta*: Junta del Barrio - neighborhood council, similar to the board of directors of the community.

26 *Bicho* - literally, bug or animal
Nefasto - evil, unlucky, ill-fated.

27 *Carajos* - fools, jokers.

28 ALBA - The Bolivarian Alternative for the Americas is a trade agreement between Venezuela, Cuba, Nicaragua and Bolivia in which decisions are said to be made in cooperation not competition with the needs of the member countries. Under ALBA, trade may occur through a direct bartering of goods. The most popular example of ALBA is the Venezuelan exchange of petroleum for thousands of Cuban community medical professionals who work in Venezuela's poorest *barrios*. ALBA was first proposed by President Chávez earlier this decade as an alternative to the US-backed Free Trade Area of the Americas (FTAA). The FTAA proposes a neoliberal agenda of eliminating trade barriers, which has resulted in a huge cost to small farmers, local markets, businesses, and communities. Michael Fox, "Defining the Bolivarian Alternative for the Americas – ALBA," *Venezuelanalysis*, August 4, 2006.

Chapter 2

1 *Cachama* - Black Pacu fish, common to Venezuela and South America.

2 One of the pillars of the cooperative and the FNCEZ is food security. Their goal is to also support the surrounding communities with affordable fresh food and produce.

3 *Campesino* - small farmer.
1227 Hectares = 3030 Acres (1 hectare = 2.47 acres).

4 *Llanos* - Venezuelan planes.

5 *Joropo* - llanero music played traditionally with a harp, cuatro, and maracas. Women raised in the Venezuelan llanos confirm the saying that the key to their heart is through the Joropo. Among the most famous Joropo singers are Jorge Guerrero, Armando Martinez, and Reinaldo Armas.

6 The four-year-old campesino organizations, *Frente Campesino*

Revolucionario Simón Bolívar (FCRSB - The Simón Bolívar Revolutionary Campesino Front) and the *Frente Campesino Revolucionario Ezequiel Zamora* (FCREZ - The Ezequiel Zamora Revolutionary Campesino Front) joined forces. For full history of the FNCEZ, www.FNCEZ.net.ve.

7   On November 13, 2001, Chávez made Decree n° 1.546, the Land Law and Agrarian Development Law. "Ley de Tierras y Desarrollo Agrario," *Agencia Bolivariana de Noticias*, http://www.abn.info.ve/go_news_especiales3. php?articulo=24.

8   Greg Wilpert, *Changing Venezuela by Taking Power* (London: Verso, 2007), 112.

9   Julia Buxton, *Venezuelan Politics in the Chávez Era: Class, Polarization and Conflict* (Boulder: Lynne Rienner Publishers, 2004), 129.

10 Greg Wilpert, "Land For People, Not for Profit in Venezuela," *Promised Land: Competing Visions of Agrarian Reform* (Oakland: Food First Books, 2006), 251.

11 According to the FNCEZ, 217 Venezuela campesinos have been assassinated since the passage of the 2001 Land Law.

12 As of September 2009, sixty-seven students were currently studying at the IALA from Brazil, Uruguay, Paraguay, Colombia, Haiti and Venezuela. *Friends of Vive TV*, http://www.larevolucionvive.org.ve/spip.php?article189.

Olga E. Domené P., "El Instituto Agroecológico Latinoamericano "Paulo Freire" de estudios campesinos, indígenas y afrodescendiente (IALA)," *Aporrea*, November 8, 2006, http://www.aporrea.org/actualidad/a26985. html.

13 According to the Venezuelan Ministry of Communes, the Simón Bolívar Communal City has been formed over the last two years. Currently, 1,600 families, and 8,000 nearby residents participate in the project, through 8 communes and 39 communal councils. Maria Victoria Rojas, "Comunidades del Alto Apure ya hablan de Ciudad Comunal," *Prensa MPCyPS*, August 20, 2009, http://www.mpcomunas.gob.ve/noticias_detalle.php?id=3063.

14 Coordinadora Agraria Nacional, "Ezequiel Zamora," "Historia de CANEZ," December 14, 2005, *Cordinadora Latioamericana de Organizaciones del Campo*, http://www.movimientos.org/cloc/show_text.php3?key=6041.

15 In Barinas, *campesino* land occupations are known as cooperatives. In Apure, they call them *asentamientos* (settlements), like their friends from the MST.

16 *Latifundio* - large plantation.

17 *Andina* - Part of the Andean Mountains.

18 Among the more than 100,000 hectares handed over to Barinas cooperatives. On *Aló Presidente*, February 6, 2003, President Chávez handed over 1400 hectares of land to the 99 families of the Jacoa cooperative, or "Jacoa" Zamorano Fund, as it is known.

19 Pablo Neruda, excerpt from poem, *Un Canto Para Bolívar*: "Yo conocí a Bolívar, Una mañana larga, En Madrid, En la Boca del Quinto Regimiento.

Padre, le dije, ¿Eres o no eres o quién eres? Y mirando al Cuartel de la Montaña, Dijo: Despierto cada cien años, Cuando despierta el pueblo."

20 The first term of Venezuelan President Carlos Andrés Pérez ran from 1974-1979. He was reelected a decade later and served from 1989-1993.

21 *Monte y culebra* - forest and snake.

22 *Mano peluda* - underhanded.

23 SASA - *El Servicio de Sanidad Agropecuaria* (Agricultural Health Service).

INSAI - *Instituto Nacional de Salud Agrícola Integral* (National Institute of Integral Agricultural Health). With Decree 6129, and the passage of the Law on Integral Agricultural Health, President Chávez created the INSAI on July 31st, 2008. The new institution substituted the sixteen-year-old SASA, with the goal of "strengthening the construction of participatory democracy" within agricultural policies in the countryside. The organization is charged with "Contributing to the Food Defense, Security, and Sovereignty of the country, through the execution and development of actions of prevention, control and eradication of diseases and plagues that affect agricultural and animal products." According to Virigay, the INSAI has broken with the previous SASA bureaucracy, and is actively working in conjunction with local communal councils and social organizations. "I believe that the INSAI is one of the best steps that we have take at the institutional level, and that it is truly an institution of popular power," says Virigay.

24 *Sur de Lago* - in Venezuela's Zulia state, South of the Lake. This has been an area of numerous campesino assassinations in recent years.

Chapter 3

1 Article 88 of the Bolivarian Constitution of Venezuela states, "The State guarantees the equality and equitable treatment of men and women in the exercise of the right to work. The state recognizes work at home as an economic activity that creates added value and produces social welfare and wealth. Homemakers are entitled to Social Security in accordance with law."

2 Such as "*el Presidente o Presidenta.*"

3 Prensa Web RNV/Prensa Banmujer, "Banmujer celebró octavo aniversario," *Radio Nacional de Venezuela*, September 3, 2009, http://www.rnv.gov.ve/noticias/index.php?act=ST&f=4&t=107018&hl=banmujer&s=8bacdb2b 817d2abc9993bf6ca4e313ce. For more information about BANMUJER, visit http://www.banmujer.gob.ve. See also Kristen Walker, "Venezuela's Women's Development Bank — Creating a Caring Economy," *Council of Hemispheric Affairs*, July 15, 2008, http://www.coha.org/2008/07/the-women%E2%80%99s-development-bank-in-venezuela-creating-a-caring-economy.

4 The full name of the program is *Fundación Misión Madres del Barrio "Josefa Joaquina Sánchez."*

5 For a detailed history of the women's movement in Venezuela, see

Elisabeth J. Friedman, *Unfinished Transitions: Women and Gendered Development of Democracy in Venezuela, 1936-1996* (Pennsylvania: Penn State Press, 2000). For a more recent analysis of women's grassroots organizing emerging from Venezuela's *barrios* in the Chávez era see Sujatha Fernandes, "Barrio Women and Popular Politics in Chávez's Venezuela," *Latin American Politics & Society* 49, no. 3 (Fall 2007): 97-127.

6   Woman's House of Maracaibo - *Casa de la Mujer de Maracaibo.* A number of *Casas de la Mujer* continue to exist throughout Venezuela. They are non-governmental organizations that provide information and resources for women. Some do receive funding from the government.

7   For an extensive World Bank study containing statistics on inequality in Latin America see David de Ferranti, Guillermo E. Perry and Francisco Ferreira, *Inequality in Latin America: Breaking with History? World Bank Latin American and Caribbean Studies. Viewpoints* (World Bank Publications, 2004).

8   María del Mar Álvarez de Lovera is a lawyer and went on to serve as the *Defensora Nacional de los Derechos de la Mujeres de Venezuela* (The National Defender for the Rights of Venezuelan Women).

9   UNAIDS/ The Global Coalition on Women and AIDS, *Keeping the Promise: An Agenda for Action on Women and AID*, 2006.

10 Venezuela currently has an adolescent fertility rate of 91 births per 1,000 women aged 15-19. World Health Organization, *World Health Statistics 2009.*

11 For more information about women's participation in *Misión Madres del Barrio* you can visit their website at http://www.misionmadresdelbarrio.gob.ve.

12 Prensa Web YVKE/ABN, "Ley Orgánica para la Equidad e Igualdad de Mujeres y Hombres Será Aprobada Próximamente," *YVKE Mundial*, October 9, 2008, http://www.radiomundial.com.ve/yvke/noticia.php?13130.

13 James Suggett, "Gender in the Venezuelan Elections," *Venezuelanalysis.com*, December 15th 2008, http://www.venezuelanalysis.com/analysis/4041. See also, ABN, "Se Incrementa la Presencia Femenina Para Cargos de Elección en Venezuela," *Agencia Bolivariana de Noticias*, January 16, 2009, http://www.abn.info.ve/reportaje_detalle.php?articulo=983.

14 Prensa Web RNV/Prensa Presidencial, "PSUV es el Mejor Fruto de la Revolucion Bolivariana," *Radio Nacional de Venezuela*, March 2, 2008, http://www.rnv.gov.ve/noticias/index.php?act=ST&f=2&t=61938.

15 This statement is a quote taken from Louise W. Kneeland, a socialist feminist from the United States and member of the Socialist Party of America in the early 20th century. Louise W. Kneeland, "Feminism and Socialism," *New Review* 2 (August 1914): 442. For an article with Chávez's statements, see Prensa Presidencial/Rafael Márquez, "Presidente Insta a Mujeres a Organizar Empresas Socialistas," *Direccion General de Prensa Presidencial*, October 25, 2008, http://www.minci.gob.ve/noticias_-_prensa/28/185189/presidente_insta_a.html.

16 The full title is the Organic Law on the Right of Women to a Life Free of Violence *(Ley Orgánica sobre el Derecho de las Mujeres a una Vida Libre de Violencia)* Specifically, 29 courts focused on gender-based violence have been created since the beginning of 2009. Tamara Pearson, "Venezuela Expands Outlets for Denunciations of Violence Against Women," *Venezuelanalysis.com,* April 23, 2009, http://www.venezuelanalysis.com/news/4389.

Chapter 4

1   *Buhoneros* - Street vendors.

2   Sujatha Fernandes, "Barrio Women and Popular Politics in Chávez's Venezuela," *Latin American Politics & Society* 49, no. 3 (Fall 2007): 97-127.

3   Natalie Obiko, "Venezuelans on the Cutting Edge of Beauty," *LA Times*, January 1, 2006, http://www.articles.latimes.com/2006/jan/01/news/adfg-beauty1.

4   MIR was a leftist political party whose founders split from the Acción Democrática (AD) Party in 1960 and participated in the guerilla movement.

5   *Maquiladoras* are factories, predominant in northern Mexico, where the materials are imported from a foreign country, like the United States, without import tariffs, and the finished product is then exported back into that same foreign country. Women are known for being the dominant workforce in maquiladoras and the term has become synonymous with sweatshops due to their reputation for exploitative labor conditions.

6   UNESR is a national public university with campuses located throughout the country.

7   *Fundación Gran Mariscal de Ayacucho* (Fundayacucho) is a government foundation under the Ministry of Popular Power for Superior Education created in 1975. Since 1999, it has focused on providing scholarships to organized communities supporting popular education projects as well as to low-income students to be able access higher education.

8   The *Bolívar Fuerte* (Strong Bolivar) is the new currency of Venezuela since January 1, 2008. It replaced the *Bolívar* at the rate of Bs.F 1 = Bs.1000. The fixed exchange rate to the U.S. dollar is 2.15 Bs.F to one US dollar. 100,000 Bs.F = $46,511 US dollars.

Chapter 5

1   Michael Fox, "6th Annual Gay and Lesbian Pride Celebrated in Venezuela," *Venezuelanalysis,* July 3, 2006, available at http://www.venezuelanalysis.com/news/1816.

2   *Caraqueña* – A woman from Caracas.

3   Formed in 1980, *Movimiento Ambiente* was one of the first gay rights organizations in Venezuela. Federico Fuentes and Kiraz Janicke, "Struggling for Gay and Lesbian Rights in Venezuela," *Green Left Weekly*, December 5, 2005.

4   Marianela graduated from the Central Venezuelan University of Venezuela (UCV).

5   Both Navarrete and Gutiérrez were and still are professors at the UCV.

6   *Grupo S* - "S" as in "sex."

7   Venezuela's Constitutional Reform Referendum was defeated in a popular vote on December 2nd, 2007, 50.7 percent to 49.3 percent, with 44.1 percent abstention. Chávez had proposed thirty-three changes to the constitution while the National Assembly proposed an additional thirty-six changes, for a total of sixty-nine changes. The reform proposed lowering the work week to thirty-six hours, creating a social security fund for the self-employed, and would have passed more power down to Venezuela's communal councils and up to President Hugo Chávez. Consejo Nacional Electoral de Venezuela (CNE), *Statistics*, December 2, 2007, http://www.cne.gob.ve/divulgacion_referendo_reforma/.

8   Juan Barreto served as Metropolitan Mayor of Caracas, 2004-2008.

9   Opposition leader, Antonio Ledezma is now the Metropolitan Mayor of Caracas. He won the seat against PSUV candidate, Aristóbulo Iztúriz, 52.45 percent to 44.92 percent in the November 23, 2008 local elections. Previously, Ledezma served as the mayor of the Caracas municipality of Libertador, from 1996-2000. CNE, "65,45% de Participación en Elecciones Regionales," November 24, 2008, http://www.cne.gob.ve/noticiaDetallada.php?id=4662.

10   *Chavista* - a Chávez supporter.

11   *Chavismo* - Chavism

12   The 4th World Conference on Women was held in Beijing in 1995. Building off of previous conferences it laid out a "Platform for Action" as an "agenda for women's empowerment." It highlighted "Critical Areas of Concern" and "Strategic Objectives and Actions" for the future under twelve major themes such as Women and Poverty, Women and Health and Violence against Women. The Fifteen-year review of the Beijing Platform for Action will take place in New York in March 2010. UN Division for the Advancement of Women, "Beijing and its Follow-Up," http://www.un.org/womenwatch/daw/beijing/.

13   *Aló Presidente* - Chávez' weekly talk show.

14   *La Hojilla* - a pro-Chávez media talk show on the state TV channel, *Venezolana de Televisión*. http://www.vtv.gov.ve/programas-videos/la-hojilla.

Chapter 6

1   Steve Ellner, "The Labor Movement and the Challenge of Chavismo," *Venezuelan Politics in the Chávez Era: Class, Polarization and Conflict* (Boulder: Lynne Rienner Publishers, 2004), 161-178.

2   Steve Ellner, *Rethinking Venezuelan Politics: Class, Conflict, and the Chávez*

Phenomenon (Boulder: Lynne Rienner Publishers, 2008), 155-158.

3 Labor tendencies are also often referred to as labor currents (In Spanish, *corrientes sindicales*).

4 The FSBT was formerly called the *Fuerza Bolivariana de Trabajadores* (FBT - Bolivarian Worker's Front).

5 *Hallacas* - A Venezuelan food typically eaten during the Christmas season.

6 SINGETRAM - *Sindicato Nueva Generacion de Trabajadores de Mitsubishi*.

7 The Italian worker-based model for occupational safety and health (sometimes referred to simply as the Italian Worker Model) is a participatory research methodology for occupational health prioritizing the role that workers play in identifying workplace hazards and health issues. Francisco J. Mercado-Martínez, "Qualitative Research in Latin America: Critical Perspectives on Health," *International Journal of Qualitative Methods* 1, no. 1 (Winter, 2002): http://www.ualberta.ca/~iiqm/backissues/1_1final/html/mercadoeng.htm.

8 The fixed exchange rate to the U.S. dollar is 2.15 Bs.F to one dollar. 46 Bs.F = $21.40 US and 26 Bs.F = $12.09 US.

9 Article 91 of the Constitution of the Bolivarian Republic of Venezuela states, "The payment of equal salary for equal work is guaranteed, and the share of the profits of a business enterprise to which workers are entitled shall be determined."

10 For more detailed articles of the Mitsubishi motor plant occupation and updates on the SINGETRAM struggle, see http://www.marxist.com/venezuela.

11 Article 77 of the Organic Labor Law states that contracted work is permitted for a determined period of time only under certain circumstances that are further detailed in the law. *Ley Organica del Trabajo*, Gaceta Oficial Nº 5.152 de fecha 19 de junio de 1997.

12 SIDOR (*Siderúrgica del Orinoco "Alfredo Maneiro"*) is a steel plant located in the Guayana region that was re-nationalized in April, 2009 following a brutal sixteen-month conflict between the company and its workforce, more than 70 percent of which had been pushed into non-unionized contract labor. James Suggett, "Venezuela and Ternium Reach Final Compensation Agreement for SIDOR Steel Plant," *Venezuelanalysis.com*, May 8th 2009, http://www.venezuelanalysis.com/news/4432.

13 Shigeru Sato and Alex Emery, "Japan, Venezuela Sign Orinoco Oil Cooperation Deal," *Bloomberg.com*, http://www.bloomberg.com/apps/news?p id=20601086&sid=ax33EbHc4AoQ&.

14 CUTV - *Central Unitaria de Trabajadores de Venezuela*. A left-wing labor federation that was formed after a split with the CTV in 1963.

Chapter 7

1 Maisanta began as an army general under the Cipriano Castro

regime towards the end of the 19th Century and was appointed to rule over the Sabaneta region where Chávez was later born. After Juan Vicente Gómez overthrew Castro, Maisanta joined forces with the peasants of the *llanos* region to form a guerilla movement against the Gómez dictatorship. Years later, Chávez would invoke the legend of Maisanta by naming the electoral headquarters for his "No" Campaign in the 2004 recall referendum after him. Richard Gott, *In the Shadow of the Liberator: Hugo Chávez and The Transformation of Venezuela* (London: Verso, 2000), 36-37.

2 Venepal - *Venezolana de la Pulpa y Papel* (Venezuelan Pulp & Paper Company). CNV - *Constructora Nacional de Válvulas* (National Valve Manufacturer).

3 Invepal - *Industria Venezolana Endógena del Papel* (Venezuelan Endogenous Paper Industry). Inveval - *Indústria Venezolana Endógena de Válvulas* (Venezuelan Endogenous Valve Industry).

4 Federico Fuentes, "Venezuela: Class Struggle Heats Up over Battle for Workers' Control," *MRZine*, July 28, 2009, http://www.monthlyreview.org/mrzine/fuentes280709.html.

5 PDVAL: *Producción y Distribución Venezolana de Alimentos*. PDVAL is a subsidiary of national oil company, PDVSA, and was launched in January 2008 to confront the hoarding of nationally produced food products, such as milk, by having the government distribute these products directly. James Suggett, "Venezuelan Government's Strategies for Confronting Food Supply Shortages," *Venezuelanalysis.com*, February 7, 2008, http://www.venezuelanalysis.com/analysis/3129.

6 INDECU was changed into INDEPABIS after the passing of the Law for the Defense of People's Access to Goods and Services in July 2008 in order to strengthen citizen engagement and legal protections against food hoarding. Clara Nunez, *Venezuela Agricultural Situation Consumer Defense Law 2008*, *GAIN Report Number: VE8089*, USDA Foreign Agricultural Service, November 6, 2008.

7 Socialist enterprises are often mixed enterprises. In Venezuela, mixed enterprises (*empresas mixtas*) usually refers to joint ventures between the Venezuelan government, which typically holds the majority stake, and a secondary group, which can be a private enterprise, a worker cooperative, or a foreign government.

Chapter 8

1 INCE, el *Instituto Nacional de Capacitación y Educación*. INCE was founded in 1960, and is now under the direction of the Ministry of Communal Economy. INCE has been the major training institute for the government-supported cooperatives, weather under the Vuelvan Caras or Che Guevara Missions.

2 *Vuelvan Caras* - About Face.

3 286,687 students had graduated, forming 7,917 cooperatives. "Logros del MINEP 2006" End of year report. *MINEP*, Ministerio de Poder

Popular para la Economía Popular (Popular Power Ministry for Popular Economy).

In 2007, the Vuelvan Caras Mission was transformed into the Che Guevara Mission. The major difference being that "the Che Guevara cooperatives are already set up according to specific needs in the communities. When they did create Vuelvan Caras, they did it on the run and formed all types of cooperatives. Now, they are specifically set up according to the concrete needs in the area. For example, if we need a concrete block company here, we'll create a Che Guevara cooperative here to make concrete blocks. These cooperatives are the same as the Vuelvan Caras cooperatives. Perhaps a little better, better planned and prepared to receive the government investment, but with the same problem, because they are setting up cooperatives, without *cooperativistas*," says Olivo.

4   According to the director of the National Superintendent of Cooperatives (SUNACOOP), Juan Carlos Baute, through 2008, 262,000 cooperatives were officially registered in Venezuela. SUNACOOP news, January 16, 2009, www.sunacoop.gob.ve/noticias_detalle.php?id=1361

Alfonos Olivo says that the actual number could even been much higher. There were officially 762 cooperatives in the country before President Chávez' election. Interview,

Carlos Molina, SUNACOOP Superintendent, March, 2006, Caracas.

5   In January 2009, SUNACOOP director Juan Carlos Baute, said that roughly 60,000 of the 262,000 registered cooperatives were "active". SUNACOOP news, January 16, 2009, www.sunacoop.gob.ve/noticias_detalle.php?id=1361

According to the Cooperative 2006 Census, only a third of the registered cooperatives were functioning. Alfonso Olivo and others believe these statistics have stayed roughly the same. Olivo also says that while a third of the cooperatives may be functioning, only fifteen percent are actually producing. In Lara State, they are nearly 9,000 registered cooperatives. But according to Alfonso, only 2,200 cooperatives are actually working. The majority of these functioning Lara state cooperatives participate in the Lara state coop councils.

6   Cooperatives in Lara were promoted extensively in the 1960s by Jesuit Priests and the U.S. Alliance for Progress, who was looking to undermine growing support for Cuban-inspired guerrillas who had set up in the mountainous region.

7   CECONAVE, *el Central Cooperativas Nacional de Venezuela*, the National Cooperatives Union of Venezuela. The majority of Venezuela's traditional cooperatives are grouped in to a network of 18 regional Cooperative Centrals (CECOs) across the country. Since 1975, these CECOs have been organized under a "third-level" cooperative, the National Cooperative Central of Venezuela, CECONAVE, which according to former CECONAVE President,

Olga de Amoroso, had roughly 400,000 associated families in 2006.

    8   *Cuarta República* - Fourth Republic.

    9   *Cooperativista* - a cooperative member.

    10 CECOSESOLA is one of the eighteen regional Cooperatives underneath the umbrella of CECONAVE. The majority of the traditional cooperatives are service or banking oriented, while most of the new "Bolivarian" cooperatives (coops formed since President Chávez took office) are worker cooperatives.

    11 *Contraloría social* - social comptroller or social auditing.

    12 The most recent project of the Lara State Coop Councils is the creation of a Lara State Cooperative Bank, which they have called, *Sistema Económico Solidario Cooperativo* (Solidarity Cooperative Economic System). "We're bringing together all of the experiences of our coops, and we are systemizing them, so we can put them into practice and make this work like a bank, to support the cooperatives," says Olivo. They hope to have the bank up and running by 2011.

    13 Old or new, traditional or Bolivarian.

    14 *Adeco-Copeyano* government – Under the Punto Fijo pact, the *Acción Democrática* (*Adeco*) party and the Christian Democrat (*Copeyano*) party agreed to alternate power in government. The minority *Unión Republicana Democrática* (URD-the Democratic Republican Union) party also participated in the pact, although never reached the presidency. The pact lasted until the 1990s.

    15 All presidents under the Punto Fijo Pact:

        Rómulo Betancourt (President, 1945-1948 & 1959-1964, *Acción Democrática* Party),

        Carlos Andrés Pérez (President, 1974-1979 & 1989-1993, *Acción Democrática* Party),

        Rafael Caldera (President, 1969-1974, 1994-1999, *COPEI* & *Convergencia Nacional* Party).

    16 *Buhoneros* - street vendors.

Chapter 9

    1   Efraín Valenzuela, "El Cuartel San Carlos," *Aporrea*, February 17, 2007, http://www.aporrea.org/actualidad/a30844.html.

    2   Leonard V. Dalton, *Venezuela* (Whitefish, MT: Kessinger Publishing, 2008), 77.

    3   Portal ALBA (*Alianza Bolivariana para los Pueblos de Nuestra América*),"Venezuelan History," http://www.alternativabolivariana.org/.

    4   The prison was home to the anti-Castro Cuban terrorists, Orlando Bosch and Luis Posada Carriles, who were held for the bombing of a Cuban airliner in October 1976 in which seventy-three passengers were killed. Posada Carriles escaped in 1985. Both he and Bosch are still wanted by Venezuela and Cuba for terrorist activities. They now live in Miami.

    5   *Cuartel* - barracks.

6 NUDE - *Núcleo de Desarrollo Endógeno* (Endogenous Development Nucleus). The Venezuelan government launched the first pilot Fabricio Ojeda NUDE in the Caracas region of Catia in 2004. Over the last few years, dozens of NUDEs have been formed across Venezuela bringing together local cooperatives, community committees, communal councils and government social programs all in one area.

7 José Ñañez says that during his thirteen years in prison here at the San Carlos barracks, the three hundred or so political prisoners held twenty hunger strikes. He was in jail during both of the famed San Carlos barracks prison escapes. The first escape occurred in early 1967 when three leaders of the communist party crawled out of a tunnel they had been digging for a year and a half. Among them was Teodoro Petkoff, ex-guerrilla, now a leading member of the Venezuela opposition, founder of the opposition newspaper, *Tal Cual*, and an outspoken critic of President Chávez. The second took place close to midnight on January 18, 1975, when 23 political prisoners crawled out of the prison through a 150 foot-long tunnel into a neighboring home.

Pedro Reyes Millán, "1975: la fuga del Cuartel San Carlos," *Soberanía*, January 16, 2004.

8 Carlos Delgado Chalbaud, (1909-1950). Member of the juntas that carried out both the 1945 and 1948 coups. He was a presidential candidate when assassinated on November 13, 1950.

9 *Roja rojita* - another name for Chavistas or Chávez supporters. The phrase literally means red, little red, for the color of the Bolivarian process. The term came into use during Chávez's 2006 presidential reelection.

10 Jorge Rodríguez - founder of the Socialist League, tortured and assassinated in the basement of the DISIP on July 25, 1976 under the first government of Carlos Andrés Pérez. He was the father of Chávez's former Vice-President, Jorge Rodríguez, who since late 2008 has been the Mayor of Caracas' Libertador Municipality, where his team has been working to develop the *Plan Caracas Socialista*. www.jorgerodriguez.psuv.org.ve.

11 *Lanceros* – the name for the graduates from the Vuelvan Caras job and coop training Mission. Lanceros graduate from the mission and form their own cooperatives, which are often contracted for government services.

12 Iván Nolasco Padilla Bravo - the current Venezuelan Vice-Minister of Culture. According to accounts, the Venezuelan police picked up Padilla and David Nieves in 1976 for the kidnapping of the United States businessman, William Niehaus, director of the multinational Owens-Illinois. Nieves resisted the torture, but Padilla succumbed, pointing the finger at both Nieves and Jorge Rodríguez. The DISIP quickly picked Rodríguez up and he was tortured and murdered. Ramón Freites, "Memoria histórica para no olvidar ni al traidor ni al héroe," *Aporrea*, April 7, 2008, http://www.aporrea.org/ddhh/a54620.html.

13 *Cuartel San Carlos Libre* - The San Carlos Free Barracks.

14 *Viejitos* – old men.

Chapter 10

1   Liz Migliorelli, "Community Media: The Thriving Voice of the Venezuelan People," *Venezuelananalysis*, July 31, 2009, http://www.venezuelanalysis.com/analysis/4678.

2   Several mainstream private channels encouraged opposition protests and then fabricated news to make it appear as though Chávez supporters were firing on the marches. Rebelling military officials used this as an impetus to remove Chávez from power and instill the de facto government led by Pedro Carmona, FEDECAMERAS President. Naomi Klein, "Venezuela's Media Coup," *The Nation*, February 13, 2003, http://www.naomiklein.org/articles/2003/02/venezuelas-media-coup.

See also *Puente Llaguno: Claves de una Masacre* (Panafilms, 2004, VZ).

3   Gregory Wilpert, "RCTV and Freedom of Speech in Venezuela," *Venezuelanalysis*,   June   2,   2007,   http://www.venezuelanalysis.com/analysis/2425.

4   However, this realty could change quickly. In August 2009, Venezuela's National Assembly began to debate controversial reforms to the Telecommunication Law, with the goal of breaking up the "media latifundios" by limiting ownership of radio or television stations to three per private owner. At the time, according to Diosdado Cabello, Infrastructure Minister and the head of Venezuela's telecommunications agency, CONATEL, nearly 30 families controlled a third of the Venezuelan television and radio waves. The same week Cabello announced the closure of 34 additional privately owned Venezuelan radio and television stations, whose broadcast licenses had expired or were violating regulations. The minister said many of the stations were operating illegally and had failed to register or pay fees to CONATEL. He added that their recuperated licenses would be handed over to community media. The reaction internationally and with Venezuela's opposition was similar to the closing of RCTV. Community media celebrated the decision. Andrew Kennis, "What is the Venezuelan News Media Actually Like?" *Media Accuracy on Latin America*, *NACLA*, July 15, 2008, http://www.mediaaccuracy.org/node/62. Tamara Pearson, "Venezuelan National Assembly Discusses Combating Media Terrorism," *Venezuelanalysis*, August 6, 2009. Kiraz Janicke, "Venezuela to Transfer Private Media Concessions to Community Media," *Venezuelanalysis*, August 3, 2009.

5   *Movimiento Político Rutptura* was the legal front organization linked to the Partido de la Revolución Venezolana (PRV). *Comités de Luchas Estudiantiles Revolucionarias* (CLER -Committees of Revolutionary Student Struggles) was a student organization linked to *Bandera Roja* active in many high school and universities in Caracas in the 1980s.

6   Constantin Stanislavski was an innovative Russian actor and theatre director. Bertolt Brecht was a German poet, playwright, and theatre director

critical to the development of political theater.

7 *Movimiento Revolucionario de los Trabajadores* (MRT - Revolutionary Worker's Movement).

8 Blanca Eckhout was a co-founder and president of Catia Tve. She went on to serve as the president of Vive TV, a government television station, and in April 2009 was appointed the head of the *Ministerio del Poder Popular para la Comunicación e Información* (MINCI - Ministry of Popular Power for Communication and Information).

9 *Jefatura civil* – Office of Civil Affairs and *Junta parroquial* - The Neighborhood Council.

10 *Jefe civiles* – The head of the *junta parroquial.*

11 *Cineclub* – Film Club.

12 CONAC was in charge of managing the government's cultural programs and policies since 1975. This responsibility was taken over by the Ministry of Culture, created in 2005. CONAC was subsequently dissolved in 2007.

13 The Vargas tragedy occurred in December 1999, and was the result of torrential rains that caused massive mudslides in the coastal Vargas State. Thousands of people living in the *barrios* along the mountain sides were killed or displaced.

14 A *radio parlante* is a radio that is only broadcast through a speaker system, rather than over the airwaves.

15 The *Fondo Único Social* is a government agency that funds projects in line with the government's policies.

16 CONATEL regulates the telecommunications sector in Venezuela. It is the equivalent to the Federal Communications Commission in the United States.

17 One of the first acts of the de-facto government of Pedro Carmona, which came to power during the two-day 2002 coup, was to shut down the state television station, VTV, channel 8. Members of Venezuela's community media helped to get the station online again and reporting.

18 Since these interviews, Argentina's Senate overwhelmingly approved a new media law that opened the door for Argentine community media, and did away with dictatorship-era rules that allowed a few companies to dominate the Argentine airwaves. The new law preserves two-thirds of the radio and TV spectrum to noncommercial media and requires increased national programming. Mayra Pertossi, "Argentine Senate Overwhelmingly Approves Media Law," *AP*, October 10, 2009.

Chapter II

1 *Convenio Cuba-Venezuela* - Cuba-Venezuela Agreement. Signed in late 2000, in which Cuba agreed to provide support or expertise to Venezuela in ten areas, ranging from agriculture to tourism, education to health. In exchange, at the time, Venezuela would send upwards of 50,000 barrels of oil a

day. As of 2006, well over 10,000 sick low-income Venezuelans had traveled to Cuba to be treated under the health portion of the *Convenio*. The agreement is now just a small piece of cooperation between the two countries, and encompassed under the framework of the Bolivarian Alternative for the Americas (ALBA). Michael Fox, "Felix's Miracle and the Convenio Cuba-Venezuela," *Venezuelanalysis*, August 24, 2006, http://www.venezuelanalysis.com/analysis/1907.

2　As of July 2009, according to the National Telecommunications Commission (Conatel) and Nelson Belfort, the President of the *Cámara Venezolana de la Radiodifusión* (Venezuelan Chamber of Radiodifusion), there were 243 legally operating community radios in Venezuela. But Luis Peña, Secretary of the Venezuela Network of Community Media says there are at least 600 more that aren't licensed to operate. Many of them are broadcasting anyway. Daniel Uzcátegui and Soniberth Jiménez, "La Radio No Es Comunitaria," *El Universal*, July 26, 2009.

3　Of the twenty-three community radios in Trujillo, six are members of ANMCLA. The ANMCLA network is much stronger in Caracas and other areas.

4　In 2006, the groups launched a nation-wide campaign entitled "For all of our Struggles," during which they held numerous marches in Caracas and around the country. ANMCLA has recently been actively building international ties with grassroots movements across Latin America. ANMCLA's correspondents in Bolivia, Palestine, Lebanon (during the 2006 Israeli invasion), and Honduras under the de facto government of Roberto Micheletti, have been instrumental in reporting the on-the-ground un-told stories for community media outlets across Venezuela and the region. For more information, see http://www.medioscomunitarios.org.

5　Some program producers, or hosts, do receive community support for their programs, a portion of which they pass to Radio Libertad to help pay their three sound engineers.

6　*Pueblos* – small towns. The term, *el pueblo*, also means "the people."

7　*Comisión Nacional de Telecomunicaciones* (CONATEL), established in 1991, is Venezuela's national telecom regulator. It is an independent body with the responsibility of issuing new mobile concessions, setting equipment standards, monitoring quality of service, and developing telecommunications policy.

8　MINCI – *Ministerio del Poder Popular para la Comunicación y la Información*.

9　ANMCLA was formed in June 2002, although "community media have functioned in Venezuela for many years; experiences like Radio Convite, TV Michelena, among others, began the road over 10 years ago; Radio Morrocoy, later transformed into Radio Catia Libre 93.5 FM, would be the pioneer of the radios in Caracas, on air since 1995; Radio Alternativa, Radio Perola, Radio Activa de La Vega, followed, and as such many other experiences arose in the '90s throughout the country." ANMCLA Website background: *Somos expresión de la multitud,* http://www.medioscomunitarios. org/pag/index.php?id=48.

10 *Guarimberos* – counterrevolutionary rioters.

11 *Golpe Larense* - Traditional music from the state of Lara.

llanera music – music from the Llanos, the planes of Venezuela, such as Barinas and Apure.

Chapter 12

1 Donna Lee Van Cott, *From Movements to Parties in Latin America: The Evolution of Ethnic Politics* (Cambridge: Cambridge University Press, 2005), 183.

2 Tobias Haller, Annja Blöchlinger, Markus John, Esther Marthaler, Sabine Ziegler, *Fossil Fuels, Oil Companies and Indigenous Peoples: Strategies of Multinational Oil Companies, States and Ethnic Minorities* (Berlin: LIT Verlag Berlin-Hamburg-Münster, 2007), 235-280.

3 Minority Rights Group International, *World Directory of Minorities and Indigenous Peoples - Venezuela: Overview,* 2007, http://www.unhcr.org/refworld/docid/4954ce6821.html.

4 Donna Lee Van Cott, "Andean Indigenous Movements and Constitutional Transformation: Venezuela in Comparative Perspective," *Latin American Perspectives* 30, no. 1 (January 2003): 49-69.

5 Ibid.

6 Kathrrin Wessendorf, *The Indigenous World 2009* (Copenhagen: IWGIA, 2009), 135-146.

7 For a detailed story of the life and work of Brother José María Korta, see the documentary film *Ajïshama the White Ibis,* produced and directed by John Dickinson (Documentary Educational Resources, 2003).

8 Humberto Márquez, "Venezuela expulsa a las Nuevas Tribus," Inter Press Service, October 12, 2005, http://ipsnoticias.net/nota.asp?idnews=35437.

9 The *sebucán* is a tube-shaped pressure strainer woven from palm leaves used to make casabe bread from the cassava root.

10 *Fundación Gran Mariscal de Ayacucho* (Fundayacucho) is a government foundation under the Ministry of Popular Power for Superior Education created in 1975. Since 1999, it has focused on providing scholarships to organized communities supporting popular education projects as well as to low-income students to be able access higher education. Corporación Venezolana de Guayana (CVG) is a government development corporation with the stated mission of promoting the humanistic and sustainable development of the Guayana region of Venezuela.

11 Convention 169 recognizes the rights of indigenous peoples to their traditional lands as well as their social and cultural rights, and obliges signatory governments to work and consult with indigenous peoples to implement these

rights. It was adopted on June 27, 1989 by the General Conference of the ILO at its 76th session and was ratified by the Venezuelan government in 2002. The full text is available at www.ilo.org.

12 Balatá trees were cultivated along the banks of the Amazon River throughout South America for their natural latex.

Chapter 13

1 *Arepas* – A traditional Venezuelan bread, typically made of corn.

Chicha – A traditional South American beverage, typically made of rice in Venezuela.

2 For more information on Corpozulia, you can visit their website at www.corpozulia.gov.ve. For an excellent analysis of the Wayúu struggle against coal mining and Corpozulia, see James Suggett, "Will the Bolivarian Revolution End Coal Mining in Venezuela?" *Venezuelanalysis.com*, May 29, 2008, http://www.venezuelanalysis.com/analysis/3503.

3 *Sociedad Homo et Natura* has played a significant role in supporting the indigenous movement in Venezuela, particularly the Wayúu, Barí, and Yukpa tribes. For more, visit http://nanaoaya.blogspot.com.

4 The full quote is "Yo, por ejemplo, le dije al general Martínez Mendoza en Corpozulia, donde había un proyecto allá de explotación del carbón en grandes dimensiones y entonces me trajeron unas críticas, y yo dije mire, si no hay un método que asegure el respeto a las selvas y a las montañas que tardaron millones de años en formarse por allá por la Sierra de Perijá, donde está ese carbón, entonces, si no hay un método que me demuestre de verdad verdad que no vamos a destruir la selva, ni a contaminar el ambiente en esos pueblos, si no me lo demuestran, ese carbón se queda bajo la tierra, no lo sacamos de ahí, que se quede bajo tierra, digo esto como un hecho pero que marca una línea, un concepto y que cada día debe ser más realidad, debe concretarse en nuestro modelo de construcción del socialismo…" Press Conference with Hugo Rafael Chávez Frías on May 24, 2006, in Salón Ayacucho, Palacio de Miraflores. For a clip of the press conference, visit http://www.aporrea.org/medios/n78660.html.

5 James Suggett,"Autonomy Proposed in State Legislature of Venezuelan Oil State Zulia," *Venezuelanalysis.com*, May 8, 2008, http://www.venezuelanalysis.com/news/3423. The separatist movement in Venezuela has been driven largely by Rumbo Propio, an organization created in 2005 with the stated goal of achieving independence for the state of Zulia. They are members of the International Confederation for Liberty and Regional Autonomy (CONFILAR - *Confederación Internacional por la Libertad y Autonomía Regional*). See Eva Golinger and Romain Migus, eds., *La Telaraña Imperial: Enciclopedia de Injerencia y Subversión* (Caracas: Centro Internacional Miranda, 2008), 204-207.

6 Humberto Márquez, "Barí People Left Without Land by Oil, Cattle, Coal," *IPS News*, April 11, 2008, http://www.ipsnews.net/news.

asp?idnews=41953 and James Suggett, "Venezuelan Government Accelerates Yukpa Land Demarcation but Tension Remains," *Venezuelanalysis.com*, August 29, 2008, http://www.venezuelanalysis.com/news/3760.

7　La Guajira Peninsula is a region divided between northeastern Colombia and northwestern Venezuela, which continues to be inhabited primarily by the Wayúu.

8　Pneumoconiosis is a respiratory disease caused by the inhalation of coal dust over extensive periods of time.

9　*Ley Orgánica para Pueblos y Comunidades Indígenas* (LOPCI), passed in 2006, is a law aimed at protecting and defining the indigenous rights described in the Venezuelan Constitution.

10　Article 120 of the Constitution of the Bolivarian Republic of Venezuela states, "Exploitation by the State of the natural resources in native habitats shall be carried out without harming the cultural, social and economic integrity of such habitats, and likewise subject to prior information and consultation with the native communities concerned. Profits from such exploitation by the native peoples are subject to the Constitution and the law."

11　*Ley de Minas*, Decreto N° 295 del 5 de septiembre de 1999, http://www.defiendete.org/html/de-interes/LEYES%20DE%20VENEZUELA/LEYES%20DE%20VENEZUELA%20II/LEY%20DE%20MINAS.htm.

12　To learn more about IIRSA projects in South America and grassroots responses to it, visit the BICECA Project Website at http://www.bicusa.org/en/Biceca.aspx. BICECA (Building Informed Civic Engagement for Conservation in the Andes-Amazon) is a project of the Bank Information Center.

13　The Free Trade Agreement of the Americas (FTAA) was a free trade agreement negotiated by thirty-four countries of the Americas based largely upon the North American Free Trade Agreement (NAFTA). It was never signed into agreement thanks to resistance from social movements and progressive governments including Venezuela, Brazil, Bolivia, and Argentina. For more information about the FTAA and how it was defeated, see http://www.globalexchange.org/campaigns/ftaa.

14　Arcadio Montiel currently is a member of PODEMOS, an opposition party formerly supportive of Chávez. He is a member of the Subcommission on Indigenous Law within the Permanent Commission for Indigenous Peoples within the National Assembly.

Chapter 14

1　H. Micheal Tarver and Julia C. Frederick, *The Greenwood Histories of the Modern Nations: The History of Venezuela* (Santa Barbara: Greenwood Press, 2005), 42-45.

2　Marixa Lasso, *Myths of Harmony: Race and Republicanism During the Age of Revolution, Colombia 1795-1831*, Pittsburgh: University of Pittsburgh Press, 2007, 9-15.

3 Junius P. Rodriguez, ed., *Greenwood Milestones in African American History: Encyclopedia of Slave Resistance and Rebellion*, vol. 1 (Westport: Greenwood Publishing Group, 2007), 224-225.

4 Jonathan D.Hill, ed., *History, Power, and Identity: Ethnogenesis in the Americas, 1492-1992* (Iowa City: University of Iowa Press, 1996), 180-191.

5 *Barloventeños* and *Barloventeñas* - men and women from the Barlovento region.

6 *Fundacion Afroamerica y de la Diáspora Africana* is a non-governmental organization founded by Afro-Venezuelan activist Jesús Chucho García in 1993. For more information, visit http://www.fundacionafroamerica.com.ve.

7 CONAC was in charge of managing the government's cultural programs and policies since 1975. This responsibility was taken over by the Ministry of Culture, created in 2005. CONAC was subsequently dissolved in 2007.

8 Organic Laws are laws that are rooted directly in the Constitution, so they hold greater weight in government policies and the Venezuelan courts.

9 La Unión de Mujeres Negras is a non-governmental organization created in 1989 and is currently a part of the Network of Afro-Venezuelan Organizations.

10 To read the proposals submitted by the Network of Afro-Venezuelan Organizations, see Enrique Arrieta Chourio, "Afrovenezolanidad y Reforma Constitucional Un Debate Impostergable," *Aporrea*, August 24, 2007, http://www.aporrea.org/actualidad/a40204.html.

11 For a scathing open letter to the National Assembly from Jesús Chucho Garcia in response to the reduction of their proposals to the Article 100, see Jesús Chucho Garcia, "Afro-Venezuelans: An open letter to the Venezuelan National Assembly," *Pambazuka News*, December 11, 2007, http://pambazuka.org/en/category/comment/44951.

12 La Red de Organizaciones Afrovenezolana, "Afrodescendientes Por el Sí," *Aporrea*, January 30, 2009, http://www.aporrea.org/actualidad/a71424.html.

13 La Red de Organizaciones Afrovenezolana, "La Red Afrovenezolana y La Discusion Curricular," *La Red de Organizaciones Afrovenezolana*, http://www.redafrovenezolana.com/reddiscu.htm.

14 *Defensoria del Pueblo*, also known as the Human Rights Defender or Office of the Ombudsman. The Office of the Defender of the People is one of the institutions under the Citizen Branch of Venezuela's government, created by the 1999 Constitution. It is charged with defending the human rights of Venezuelan citizens as established under the Constitution. Antonio Ramirez, "An Introduction to Venezuelan Governmental Institutions And Primary Legal Sources," *GlobaLex*, May 2006, http://www.nyulawglobal.org/globalex/venezuela.htm.

15 Humberto Márquez, "Afro-descendants Seek Visibility in Numbers," *IPS News*, June 22, 2007, http://ipsnews.net/news.asp?idnews=38278.

16 The full name is the Sub-commission on Legislation, Participation,

Guarantees, Responsibilities, and Rights of Afro-descendants (*Subcomisión de Legislación, Participación, Garantías, Deberes y Derechos de los Afrodescendientes*). It was created in 2009 and exists under the Permanent Commission for Indigenous Peoples within the National Assembly.

17 In Spanish, this is the *Dirección Nacional de Educación Intercultural Bilingüe.*

Chapter 15

1 Steve Ellner, *Venezuela's Movimiento al Socialismo: From Guerrilla Defeat to Innovative Politics* (Durham: Duke University Press, 1988), 49-50.

2 José G.G. Altuve, "Autonomía Universitaria," *Actualidade Contable FACES: Revista Ulandina de la Facultad de Ciencias Económicas y Sociales, Año 11, Numero 17, Julio-Diciembre 2008.* (Merida: Universidad de Los Andes, 2008), 5-10. www.saber.ula.ve/actualidadcontable/.

3 Steve Ellner, *Rethinking Venezuelan Politics: Class, Conflict, and the Chávez Phenomenon* (Boulder: Lynne Rienner Publishers, 2008), 178.

4 Zachary Lown, "Violence and Transformation in Venezuela's Public Universities," *Venezuelanalysis.com,* July 8, 2009, http://www.venezuelanalysis.com/analysis/4604.

5 Voting parity would make a student's vote equal to a professor's vote. Currently a professor's vote counts for forty student votes. University workers are not allowed to vote.

6 The University Council (*Consejo Universitario*) is the supreme decision-making body in the autonomous public universities. It is presided over by the Rector, two Vice Rectors, the Secretary, and eleven deans. The University Council also has representatives from the rest of the university community, which under the existing 1970 National Law on Universities includes one government representative, five faculty members, three students, and one alumni representative.

Chapter 16

1 Justin Podur, "Venezuela's Revolutionary University," *Znet,* September 22, 2004, http://www.venezuelanalysis.com/analysis/707.

2 More than twelve degrees of study are offered, including environmental studies, integral medicine, and social communication.

3 The full title of the program is *Plan Extraordinario Mariscal Antonio José de Sucre (Misión Sucre).*

4 El *Ministerio* del Poder Popular para la Educación Superior, *La Revolucion Bolivariana en La Educación Universitaria: 10 años de logros* (Compilación: Oficina de Estadística y Análisis Prospectivo, 2009).

5 Ibid.

6 Ibid.

7 Gregory Wilpert, *Changing Venezuela By Taking Power: The History and Policies of the Chávez Government* (New York: Verso Books, 2007), 128.

8   Globovisión is a private Venezuelan television network aligned with the opposition movement.

9   UNEFA – *La Universidad Nacional Experimental Politécnica de la Fuerza Armada Bolivariana* (National Experimental Polytechnic University of the Bolivarian Armed Forces) was created by President Chávez through presidential decree in 1999. As of 2009, UNEFA has sixty-one campuses located in twenty-three states. They offer eighty-three degrees including Health Sciences, Social Sciences, and Law. It claims to be the first university in Venezuela to have eliminated entrance exams.

Chapter 17

1   *Guaraira-Repano* - the mountain and national park between Caracas and the Caribbean. Formerly named, Avila Mountain, before the name was changed back to the name used by the indigenous Caracas tribe.

2   DISIP - *Dirección de los Servicios de Inteligencia y Prevención* (Office of Prevention and Intelligence Services). Venezuelan version of the US Federal Bureau of Investigation (FBI). Created in 1969, after the disbanding of the *Dirección General de Policía* (DIGEPOL - General Police Office)

3   The *Tupamaros* or the *Movimiento de Liberación Nacional* (MLN - National Liberation Movement) was a Uruguayan urban guerrilla group in the 1960s and 1970s. They became famous across Latin America for carrying out many "successful" actions, including the kidnapping of US FBI agent Dan Mitrione and the Punta Carretas prison escape. According to Coco, in Venezuela, the security forces first began to label community activists as "Tupamaros" in order to delegitimize their struggle. The 23 de Enero activists challenged the police by accepting the title and naming their organization, the Tupamaro Revolutionary Front.

4   *El hampa* - the criminals, underworld.

5   DIN - *Dirección General de Inteligencia Militar* (General Office of Military Intelligence). Created in 1974 under the reorganization plan for the Ministry of Defense from the previous year. www.dgim.mil.ve/.

6   Conversations between the 23 de Enero collectives and the Caracas Metropolitan Mayor's Office began under Mayor Alfredo Antonio Peña, but weren't solidified until 2004, under the newly elected pro-Chávez Metropolitan Mayor, Juan Barreto.

7   *Jefe civil* - civilian director from the collective who is in charge of the sector.

8   *Sambil* - a shopping mall in Eastern Caracas.

9   The concept for the commune was first proposed in Venezuela during the failed 2007 Constitutional Reform. The communes began to be implemented with the founding of the 13th of April Mission in August 2008 to promote the growth of communes. Technically speaking they are the next level of grassroots decision-making above the communal councils. Many neighboring communal councils join together to form one commune.

The communes fall under the jurisdiction of the Ministry of Communes and Social Protection (MPCyPS), which was formerly the Ministry of Communal Economy (MINEC), and before that in 2006, the Ministry of Popular Economy (MINEP). Venezuela is currently discussing the creation of a Commune Law.

Chapter 18

1 "In many cases political parties only gave representation to fellow members and true community control was hard to find when spokespersons, expected to represent hundreds of thousands of people were elected with almost no input from the community." Michael Fox, "Venezuela's Secret Grassroots Democracy," *Venezuelanalysis*, November 28, 2006. http://www.venezuelanalysis.com/analysis/2090.

2 Opposition pundits have said that only Chávez supporters can form communal councils. This is not the case. While communal councils are far more common in the poor barrios where Chávez has large support and where the resources have been traditionally scarce, they have also been formed in middle-upper class communities. Communal councils have even been used in some predominantly opposition communities in order to protect their neighborhood against Chávez programs and proposals. Michael Fox, "Venezuela's Secret Grassroots Democracy," *Venezuelanalysis*, November 28, 2006.

3 All mandated by the 2006 Communal Council Law. On November 24, 2009, the Venezuelan National Assembly approved an organic reform to the 2006 Communal Council Law, which set higher levels of community participation necessary for community assembly quorums, made the general communal council structure more inclusive and swapped the "communal banks" for "Administrative and Community Finance Units" which will no longer be treated as cooperatives, but now a branch of the communal council. Tamara Pearson, "Venezuela's Reformed Communal Council Law: When Laws Aren't Just for Lawyers and Power Is Public," *Venezuelanalysis*, December 4, 2009. "Aprobada reforma a la Ley de Consejos Comunales," *El Universal*, November 24, 2009.

4 According to the May 2008 study carried out by the Fundación Centro Gumilla (one of the most reliable independent studies on Venezuela's Communal Councils) as of March 2008, 26,143 communal councils had been formed in Venezuela, and 10,669 communal councils were in the process of forming. In July 2009, Fundacomunal President Roberto Rojas announced that 30,179 communal councils had been formed in Venezuela, with another 5,000 in the process of formation. Tamara Pearson, "Venezuela Increases Funding of Communal Councils and Comunes," Venezuelanalysis, July 23, 2009.

5 *Papita Negra* - a native potato from the Páramo region in the Andes Mountains of Venezuela's Mérida state. The Green Revolution - the export-oriented, pesticide and fertilizer-intensive style of agriculture promoted by the United States in the 1960s and 1970s. It was said that the use of pesticides and fertilizers would help producers to increase yield in order to keep up with

growing populations.

6   *Aguacil* - sheriff, constable.

7   *Lumbricultura* - worm composting.
    Tejido - fabric, cloth.

8   The Communal Councils Law was passed on April 10, 2006.

9   *Casa comunal* – community center.

10 $1 dollar = 2.15 Bs.F; 30,000 Bs.F = $13,953 dollars.

11 300,000 Bs.F = $130,953 dollars.

12 The Teresa Carreño Theater is one of Venezuela's premier theaters for symphony, concerts, operas, ballet and cultural activities. Inaugurated in 1976, with high-ticket prices, Teresa Carreño was relatively off-limits for most of Venezuela's working poor. The Chávez government has opened the doors to Venezuela's population with free or low-priced tickets. Numerous cultural and political activities and events have been held there over the last decade.

13 Marlin is a young teenage member of the community and of the women's worm composting cooperative.

14 Band-Aids - *pañitos calientes* – trivial solutions or mediocre prevention, covering up the symptoms.

15 *El Mercal* - Venezuela's state-run government subsidized food markets. The Mercal Mission was officially launched on April 22, 2003. According Venezuela Vice-Minister of Health, Dr. Julio César Alviarez, in a July 2009 speech at the United Nations, Mercal has set up 6,048 soup kitchens and 16,529 Mercal food markets throughout the country, benefiting more than half the Venezuelan population. "Viceministro Alviarez en la ONU: Venezuela alcanza los Objetivos de Desarrollo del Milenio," *Prensa Misión Permanente en la ONU,* July 9, 2009, http://www.aporrea.org/venezuelaexterior/n138358. html.

ADDITIONAL PHOTOGRAPHS

National CTU Gathering

Iraida Morocoima.

Caracas.

Historical Mural -- The Federal War & the Campesino Insurrection (Caracas).

The annual LGBT Pride March.

Ramón Virigay, and his wife, Luz Marina Tapia, FNCEZ.

FNCEZ: "Organize, Educate, and Mobilize."

FNCEZ March.

Manuel Mendoza.

Cundido Barrios.

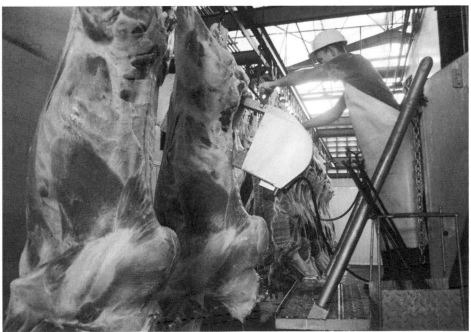

La Matanza – Industrial Slaughterhouse of Ospino.

Alfonso Olivo.

"San Carlos: Historical Witness, Cultural Site."

The Courtyard - San Carlos Barracks.

Wayúu women and children performing the traditional dance, the Yonna.

Ye'kuana Students – Indigenous Knowledge Week (Indigenous University of Venezuela).

University Entrance: "Welcome to the Indigenous University of Venezuela."

Wadajaniyu.

Students — Bolivarian School in Barlovento.

Coco – Che Guevara Collective.

Golon – Coordinadora Simón Bolívar.

Mérida.

March in Support of President Hugo Chávez (Caracas).

Organizations & Abbreviations

AD: Democratic Action Party
ANMCLA: National Association of Free and Alternative
      Community Media
BANMUJER: Banco de Desarrollo de la Mujer
BR: Bandera Roja
CEM: Center for Women's Studies
CECOSESOLA: The Cooperative Union of Social Services of
      Lara
CECOCORO: The Cooperative Union of Coro
CONATEL: National Telecommunications Commissions
CONIVE: National Indigenous Council of Venezuela
CONG: Coordination of Women's Non-Governmental
      Organizations
COPEI: Christian Democratic Party
Convenio Cuba-Venezuela: Cuban-Venezuelan Agreement
CANEZ: Ezequiel Zamora National Agrarian Coordinator
CEM: Center for Women's Studies
CIGO: Ospino Industrial Cattle Consortium
CMR: Marxist Revolutionary Current
Coordinadora Simón Bolívar: The Simón Bolívar Coordinator
CONAC: the National Council of Culture
CONATEL: The National Telecommunications Commission
CONG: Coordination of Women's Non-Governmental
      Organizations
COPEI: The Committee of Independent Electoral Political
      Organization Party
CTV: Workers Federation of Venezuela
CTU: Urban Land Committees
CUTV: The Union Worker's Federation of Venezuela

DIM: Venezuelan Military Intelligence
DISIP: Office of Prevention and Intelligence Services
FALN: Armed Forces of National Liberation
FEDECAMARAS: The Federation of Chambers and Association
    of Commerce and Production of Venezuela
FEDENAGA: National Federation of Cattle Ranchers of
    Venezuela
FEVE: The Venezuelan Confederacy of the Center of Film
    Culture
FIB: The Indigenous Federation of the State of Bolívar
FIPCA: The Industrial Meat Processing Plant of Portuguesa
FNCEZ: Ezequiel Zamora National Campesino Front
FNCSB: The Simón Bolívar National Commune Front
FRETECO: Co-managed and Occupied Factories' Worker's
    Revolutionary Front
FSBT: The Bolivarian Socialist Worker's Force
FTAA: Free Trade Agreement of the Americas
IALA "Paulo Freire": The Paulo Freire Latin American
    Agroecology Institute
IIRSA: The Initiative for the Integration of Regional
    Infrastructure in South America
INAMUJER: The National Women's Institute
INDECU: The Institute for Consumer Education and Defense
INDEPABIS: The Institute for the People's Defense in Access to
    Goods and Services
INPSASEL: National Institute for Prevention, Health and Labor
    Security
INTI: National Land Institute
INSAI: National Institute of Integral Agricultural Health
MAS: Movement Towards Socialism
MINCI: Ministry of Communication & Information
MINEC: Ministry of Communal Economy
MINEP: Ministry of Popular Economy
MIR: Leftist Revolutionary Movement
MPCyPS: Ministry of Communes and Social Protection
MPPAT: Ministry of Popular Power for Agriculture and Land
MST: Brazil's Landless Rural Worker's Movement
ORPIA: The Regional Organization of the Indigenous Peoples of
    Amazonas State
PDVSA: *Petróleos de Venezuela S.A.*

PSUV: United Socialist Party of Venezuela
PRV: Party of the Venezuelan Revolution
RCTV: Radio Caracas Televisión
RedTV: Venezuelan Broadcast Network
Red Venezolano de Medios: The Venezuelan Media Network
SASA: Agricultural Health Service
SINGETRAM: New Generation of Workers Union of Mitsubishi
   Motor Company
SUNACOOP: National Superintendent of Cooperatives
SIFA: Venezuelan Armed Forces Intelligence Service
UCV: Central University of Venezuela
ULA: University of the Andes
UNT: National Worker's Union
URD: Republican Democratic Union Party

Spanish Translations

Aguacil - sheriff, constable.

Andina – Andean.

Apureña - From the Venezuelan state of Apure (just to the South East of Barinas).

Asentamiento – Land settlement in Apure. Occupied land.

Auyama – Pumpkin.

Barrio - poor neighborhood, slum.

Bicho - literally, bug or animal.

Buhoneros - Street vendors.

Cachama - Known also as "Black Pacu." A fish predominant in the Amazon and Northern Veneuzela.

Campesinos - small farmers.

Caracazo - Spontaneous uprising in Caracas on Feb. 27, 1989, against a package of neoliberal reforms under President Carlos Andrés Pérez.

Caraqueña - A Caracas native.

Carajos - fools, jokers.

Casa comunal - community center.

Chavista - Chávez supporter.

Chavismo – Chavism.

Cimarrones - liberated slaves.

Comandante - Commander. Usually referring to President Chávez.

Compañero – Friend, companion.

Contraloría social - social comptroller or social auditing.

Cooperativista - a cooperative member.

Cuarta República - The Fourth Republic.

Cumbe - A community of escaped slaves in Venezuela.

Cuartel – barracks.

Favela - Brazilian term for barrio or slum.

Golpe Larense - Traditional music from the state of Lara.

Guaraira Repano - Mountain range & national park north of Caracas formerly called Avila mountain.

Guarimberos – counterrevolutionary rioters.

Hallacas - A Venezuelan food similar to the tamale typically eaten during the Christams season.

El hampa - The criminals, underworld.

Jefe Civil - Civil Leader.

Junta - Junta del Barrio, neighborhood council, similar to the board of directors of the community.

Lanceros - Graduates from the Vuelvan Caras Mission.

Latifundio - Large plantations.

Llanos - Venezuelan plains in Southwest region of the country.

Llanera - Person, thing or music from the Llanos, the planes of Venezuela, such as Barinas and Apure.

Lumbricultura - worm composting.

Monte y culebra - Forest and snake.

Nefasto - evil, unlucky, ill-fated.

Pana - friend (Venezuclan slang).

Pañitos calientes - Band-Aids, trivial solutions or mediocre prevention, covering up the symptoms.

Papita Negra - a native potato from the Páramo region in the Andes Mountains of Venezuela's Mérida state.

Paróquia - Parish, Venezuela uses this classification to denominate an area of land much like a small county. This is similar to the Parishes of Louisiana. In Venezuela, there are often numerous Parishes in a municipality.

Quilombos - The term for cumbes in Brazil.

Roja rojita (or *rojo rojito*) - Another name for Chavistas or Chávez supporters referring to the red colors of the PSUV party.

Sacudón - Another term for the *Caracazo*.

Tejido - fabric, cloth.

Viejitos - Old men.

Author Biographies

Carlos Martinez recently served in Venezuela as the program director for Global Exchange, where he coordinated dozens of delegations to Venezuela. His articles have been published in *Common Dreams*, *Monthly Review Zine*, and on www.venezuelanalysis. com. Carlos lived in Venezuela for two years and now resides in San Francisco, California.

Michael Fox is a journalist, a reporter, and a documentary filmmaker based in South America. He has covered Venezuela extensively as a staff writer for www.venezuelanalysis.com, and his articles have been published in *Earth Island Journal*, *The Nation*, *NACLA*, and *Yes Magazine*. He is the producer of the Venezuelanalysis radio headlines, co-founder of the internet radio program Radio Venezuela en Vivo, and co-director of the documentary *Beyond Elections: Redefining Democracy in the Americas*.

JoJo Farrell worked in Venezuela as the program director for the international human rights organization, Global Exchange. A journalist and former reporter, he teaches and lives in Brooklyn, New York.

For more information on the authors, or for additional *Venezuela Speaks!* photographs, resources and videos, visit www.venezuelaspeaks.com

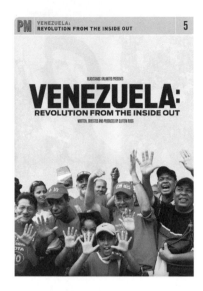

Venezuela:
Revolution from the Inside Out
by Clifton Ross
ISBN: 978-1-60486-017-7
DVD
$19.95

Venezuela: Revolution from the Inside Out is a voyage into Latin America's most exciting experiment of the new millennium, exploring the history and projects of the Bolivarian Revolution through interviews with a range of its participants, from academics to farm workers and those living in the margins of Caracas. This introduction to the "revolución bonita" ("pretty revolution") offers in-depth interviews, unforgettable images and a lively soundtrack that will open new vistas onto this hopeful human project.

As he totes his camera on bus and car trips all over Venezuela, director Clifton Ross becomes our tour guide through the Bolivarian Revolution. He sweeps us through its history and takes us to its works-in-progress on the ground. These schools, rural lending banks and cooperatives weave the fabric of Venezuela's "Socialism of the 21st Century." They show its failures and successes, its warp and woof. Through it all runs the frayed but unbreakable thread of a people in struggle.

Extras Include: *Meeting Chávez* (10 minutes) and *Message to the North American People* (12 minutes).

Featuring: Dr. Steve Ellner, Universidad de Oriente, Puerto La Cruz; José Sant Roz, Universidad Socialista del Pueblo, Mérida; Jutta Schmitt, Universidad de los Andes, Mérida; Christene DeJong, Center for Latin American Studies, University of California, Berkeley; Roger Burbach, Director of the Center for the Study of the Americas, Berkeley, CA.

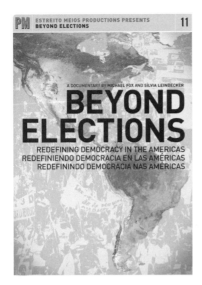

Beyond Elections: Redefining Democracy in the Americas
by Silvia Leindecker &
Michael Fox
ISBN: 760-1-3748-179-9
DVD
$19.95

What is democracy? Freedom, equality, participation? Everyone has his or her own definition. Across the world, 120 countries now have at least the minimum trappings of democracy---the freedom to vote for all citizens. But for many, this is just the beginning not the end. Following decades of US-backed dictatorships, civil wars and devastating structural adjustment policies in the South, and corporate control, electoral corruption, and fraud in the North, representative politics in the Americas is in crisis. Citizens are now choosing to redefine democracy under their own terms: local, direct, and participatory.

In 1989, the Brazilian Worker's Party altered the concept of local government when they installed participatory budgeting in Porto Alegre, allowing residents to participate directly in the allocation of city funds. Ten years later, Venezuelan President Hugo Chávez was swept into power with the promise of granting direct participation to the Venezuelan people; who have now formed tens of thousands of self-organized communal councils. In the Southern Cone, cooperative and recuperated factory numbers have grown, and across the Americas social movements and constitutional assemblies are taking authority away from the ruling elites and putting power into the hands of their members and citizens.

Featuring interviews with: Eduardo Galeano, Amy Goodman, Emir Sader, Martha Harnecker, Ward Churchill, and Leonardo Avritzer as well as cooperative and community members, elected representatives, academics, and activists from Brazil, Canada, Venezuela, Argentina, United States, Uruguay, Chile, Colombia, and more.

Beyond Elections is a journey that takes us across the Americas to attempt to answer one of the most important questions of our time: What is Democracy?

In 2006, Oaxaca, Mexico came alive with a broad and diverse movement that captivated the nation and earned the admiration of communities organizing for social justice around the world. The show of international solidarity for the people of Oaxaca was the most extensive since the Zapatista uprising in 1994. Fueled by long ignored social contradictions, what began as a teachers' strike demanding more resources for education quickly turned into a massive movement that demanded direct, participatory democracy.

Hundreds of thousands of Oaxacans raised their voices against the abuses of the state government. They participated in marches of up to 800,000 people, occupied government buildings, took over radio stations, called for statewide labor and hunger strikes, held sit-ins, reclaimed spaces for public art and created altars for assassinated activists in public spaces. In the now legendary March of Pots and Pans, two thousand women peacefully took over and operated the state television channel for three weeks. Barricades that were built all over the city to prevent the passage of paramilitaries and defend occupied public spaces, quickly became a place where neighbors got to know each other, shared ideas and developed new strategies for organizing.

Despite the fierce repression that the movement faced--with hundreds arbitrarily detained, tortured, forced into hiding, or murdered by the state and federal forces and paramilitary death squads--people were determined to make their voices heard.

"Once you learn to speak, you don't want to be quiet anymore," an indigenous community radio activist said. Accompanied by photography and political art, Teaching Rebellion is a compilation of testimonies from longtime organizers, teachers, students, housewives, religious leaders, union members, schoolchildren, indigenous community activists, artists and journalists--and many others who participated in what became the Popular Assembly of the People's of Oaxaca. This is a chance to listen directly to those invested in and affected by what quickly became one of the most important social uprisings of the 21st century.

FRIENDS OF

PM

In the year since its founding —and on a mere shoestring —PM Press has risen to the formidable challenge of publishing and distributing knowledge and entertainment for the struggles ahead. With over 40 releases in 2009, we have published an impressive and stimulating array of literature, art, music, politics, and culture. Using every available medium, we've succeeded in connecting those hungry for ideas and information to those putting them into practice.

Friends of PM allows you to directly help impact, amplify, and revitalize the discourse and actions of radical writers, filmmakers, and artists. It provides us with a stable foundation from which we can build upon our early successes and provides a much-needed subsidy for the materials that can't necessarily pay their own way. You can help make that happen—and receive every new title automatically delivered to your door once a month—by joining as a Friend of PM Press. Here are your options:

- $25 a month: Get all books and pamphlets plus 50% discount on all webstore purchases.
- $25 a month: Get all CDs and DVDs plus 50% discount on all webstore purchases.
- $40 a month: Get all PM Press releases plus 50% discount on all webstore purchases
- $100 a month: Sustainer. - Everything plus PM merchandise, free downloads, and 50% discount on all webstore purchases.

Just go to WWW.PMPRESS.ORG to sign up. Your card will be billed once a month, until you tell us to stop. Or until our efforts succeed in bringing the revolution around. Or the financial meltdown of Capital makes plastic redundant. Whichever comes first.

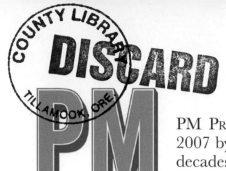

PM PRESS was founded at the end of 2007 by a small collection of folks with decades of publishing, media, and organizing experience. PM co-founder Ramsey Kanaan started AK Press as a young teenager in Scotland almost 30 years ago and, together with his fellow PM Press coconspirators, has published and distributed hundreds of books, pamphlets, CDs, and DVDs. Members of PM have founded enduring book fairs, spearheaded victorious tenant organizing campaigns, and worked closely with bookstores, academic conferences, and even rock bands to deliver political and challenging ideas to all walks of life. We're old enough to know what we're doing and young enough to know what's at stake.

We seek to create radical and stimulating fiction and nonfiction books, pamphlets, t-shirts, visual and audio materials to entertain, educate and inspire you. We aim to distribute these through every available channel with every available technology - whether that means you are seeing anarchist classics at our bookfair stalls; reading our latest vegan cookbook at the café; downloading geeky fiction e-books; or digging new music and timely videos from our website.

PM PRESS is always on the lookout for talented and skilled volunteers, artists, activists and writers to work with. If you have a great idea for a project or can contribute in some way, please get in touch.

PM PRESS
PO Box 23912
Oakland CA 94623
510-658-3906
www.pmpress.org